'In this extraordinary volume, Lawrence Friedman ta[ckles] Freud's *Papers on Technique*. No one is better equipp[ed]. Friedman has devoted his professional life to uneart[hing] unspoken intentions. He is the leading expositor o[f Freud's ideas and the] breadth and depth of thought is breathtaking. He repeatedly discovers nuances in Freud's thinking that somehow escaped detection by the rest of us. I literally found it difficult to turn off my screen and stop reading it. I lost sleep as a result, but have no regrets. It is the freshest and most absorbing book on Freud that I can remember. If you start reading it, you will return to it again and again. Do not miss it!'

–**Glen O. Gabbard, MD**, Editor, *Textbook of Psychoanalysis*

'Lawrence Friedman, one of our most incisive interrogators of psychoanalysis, describes how a treasured part of the psychoanalytic canon, Freud's *Papers on Technique*, has been misunderstood. Rather than a clear set of clinical rules, Friedman insists that it is actually a book of discovery, Freud's continuous "lab" journal of the *psychoanalytic phenomenon*. He documents how Freud's consultation room encounter was a process of empirical discovery, unfolding in unexpectedly troubling ways which led to the revolutionary understanding of the human condition.'

–**Robert Alan Glick, MD**, Professor of Clinical Psychiatry and former Director of the Columbia University Center for Psychoanalytic Training and Research

'Friedman's book offers the reader a harvest of a professional lifetime of devoted scholarship, rigorous clinical work, teaching prized around the world, and an empathic imagination possessed by only the most gifted psychoanalytic thinkers. He takes us inside Freud's mind as he is being pulled by his patients, against expectation and wish, to bring psychoanalysis into being. Dr. Friedman takes us on a thrilling ride, sharing with us the best kin of discovery – a more profound knowledge of the human condition and of our individual selves.'

–**Shelley Orgel, MD**, Past Director of the Institute for Psychoanalytic Education, NYU Medical Center

'Larry Friedman has provided the definitive reader's guide to Freud's *Papers on Technique*. He points out that these papers really constitute an integrated book that is itself a guide for the fledgling analyst. Friedman, writing with his customary personal and engaging style, tells us that as Freud gradually discovered the psychoanalytic phenomenon, he was pressed to invent psychoanalytic technique in order to avoid interfering with the development of the phenomenon. His discovery and invention occurred while psychoanalysis was evolving from its initial focus on the retrieval of repressed memories to its more mature emphasis on the integration of disavowed desires.'

–**Robert Michels, MD**, Walsh McDermott University Professor of Medicine and Psychiatry, Cornell University; Former Joint Editor-in-Chief, *The International Journal of Psychoanalysis*

# FREUD'S PAPERS ON TECHNIQUE AND CONTEMPORARY CLINICAL PRACTICE

Freud's *Papers on Technique* is usually treated as an assemblage of papers featuring a few dated rules of conduct that are either useful in some way, or merely customary, or bullying, arbitrary and presumptuous. Lawrence Friedman reveals *Papers on Technique* to be nothing of the sort. Freud's book, he argues, is nothing less than a single, consecutive, real-time, log of Freud's painful discovery of a unique mind-set that can be produced in patients by a certain stance of the analyst.

What people refer to as "the rules", such as anonymity, neutrality and abstinence, are the lessons Freud learned from painful experience when he tried to reproduce the new, free mind-set. Friedman argues that one can see Freud making this empirical discovery gradually over the sequence of papers. He argues that we cannot understand the famous images, such the analyst-as-surgeon, or mirror, without seeing how they figure in this series of experiments. Many of the arguments in the profession turn out to be unnecessary once this is grasped. Freud's book is not a book of rules but a description of what happens if one does one thing or another; the choice is the therapist's, as is the choice to use them together to elicit the analytic experience.

In the light of this understanding, Friedman discusses aspects of treatments that are guided by these principles, such as enactment, the frame, what lies beyond interpretation, the kind of tensions that are set up between analyst and patient, the question of special analytic love, the future of analytic technique, and a possible basis for defining Freudian psychoanalysis. Finally, he makes concrete suggestions for teaching the *Papers on Technique*.

*Freud's Papers on Technique and Contemporary Clinical Practice* will appeal to all psychoanalysts and psychoanalytic psychotherapists concerned about the empirical basis of their customary procedures and the future of their craft.

**Lawrence Friedman** is Clinical Professor of Psychiatry at Weill-Cornell Medical College where he is a member of the Institute for the History of Psychiatry. He is also a member of the faculty of the Institute for Psychoanalytic Education, affiliated with the New York University School of Medicine. He maintains a private practice in New York City.

# FREUD'S PAPERS ON TECHNIQUE AND CONTEMPORARY CLINICAL PRACTICE

*Lawrence Friedman*

LONDON AND NEW YORK

First published 2019
by Routledge
2 Park Square, Milton Park, Abingdon, Oxon OX14 4RN

and by Routledge
711 Third Avenue, New York, NY 10017

*Routledge is an imprint of the Taylor & Francis Group, an informa business*

© 2019 Lawrence Friedman

The right of Lawrence Friedman to be identified as author of this work has been asserted by him in accordance with sections 77 and 78 of the Copyright, Designs and Patents Act 1988.

All rights reserved. No part of this book may be reprinted or reproduced or utilised in any form or by any electronic, mechanical, or other means, now known or hereafter invented, including photocopying and recording, or in any information storage or retrieval system, without permission in writing from the publishers.

*Trademark notice*: Product or corporate names may be trademarks or registered trademarks, and are used only for identification and explanation without intent to infringe.

*British Library Cataloguing in Publication Data*
A catalogue record for this book is available from the British Library

*Library of Congress Cataloging in Publication Data*
Names: Friedman, Lawrence, 1931- author.
Title: Freud's Papers on technique and contemporary clinical practice / Lawrence Friedman.
Description: Abingdon, Oxon ; New York, NY : Routledge, 2019. | Includes bibliographical references and index.
Identifiers: LCCN 2018005965 (print) | LCCN 2018006624 (ebook) | ISBN 9781351180313 (Master) | ISBN 9781351180306 (Web PDF) | ISBN 9781351180290 (ePub) | ISBN 9781351180283 (Mobipocket/Kindle) | ISBN 9780815385745 (hardback : alk. paper) | ISBN 9780815385752 (pbk. : alk. paper)
Subjects: LCSH: Freud, Sigmund, 1856-1939. | Psychoanalysis. | Psychiatry. | Psychotherapy.
Classification: LCC BF109.F74 (ebook) | LCC BF109.F74 F75 2019 (print) | DDC 150.19/52--dc23
LC record available at https://lccn.loc.gov/2018005965

ISBN: 978-0-8153-8574-5 (hbk)
ISBN: 978-0-8153-8575-2 (pbk)
ISBN: 978-1-351-18031-3 (ebk)

Typeset in Bembo
by Taylor & Francis Books

**For Anastasia**

# CONTENTS

| | |
|---|---|
| *Personal acknowledgements* | *xi* |
| *Formal acknowledgements* | *xii* |
| Introduction | 1 |

**PART ONE**
**The text** **13**

| | | |
|---|---|---|
| 1 | Preface to Chapter One | 13 |
| | Discovering how to elicit the psychoanalytic phenomenon | 15 |
| 2 | Preface to Chapter Two | 24 |
| | A fostering kind of interest with no attached request | 28 |
| 3 | Preface to Chapter Three | 49 |
| | How to pick items out of the flow of process | 55 |

**PART TWO**
**The idea of Freudian therapy** **75**

| | | |
|---|---|---|
| 4 | What lies Beyond Interpretation, and is that the right question? | 83 |
| 5 | Is there life after enactment? | 93 |
| 6 | The delicate balance of work and illusion in psychoanalysis | 111 |

**x** Contents

7 How and why do patients become more objective? Sterba
compared with Strachey     123

8 A renaissance for Freud's *Papers on Technique*     135

## PART THREE
# The psychoanalytic phenomenon     **145**

9 Flirting with virtual reality     147

10 Ferrum, ignis, and medicina: Return to the Crucible     162

11 Is there a special psychoanalytic love?     175

12 What is psychoanalysis?     197

## PART FOUR
# Freud's own views and the future     **215**

13 One Freud or two?     217

14 The "Frame" and the future     222

15 Author interviews himself     226

*Index*     *237*

# PERSONAL ACKNOWLEDGEMENTS

I owe a huge debt of gratitude to candidates over many years who have been my partners in exploring Freud's *Papers on Technique* at the Institute for Psychoanalytic Education Affiliated with the New York University Medical School. They are all, in a way, co-authors of this book and if they look at this book, I hope they will realize that I am thinking of them and thanking them individually. I am grateful to the Institute for allowing me to program, design and teach an irregular course despite the overlap with other courses in their logical sequence.

My wife is the silent partner in this project. The word-count gives public evidence of her self-sacrificing patience, but only I know that she is an enthusiastic enabler of a writer's sporadic monomania.

The intellectual stimulation offered by my colleagues at the Institute for the History of Psychiatry at Weill-Cornell Medical School has caffeinated all my scholarly endeavors, and set at my elbow a high standard for achievement and critique, as well as morale-boosting good-fellowship. I am indebted to Dr. Jack Barchas for protecting and fostering a purely reflective "lab" within a cutting edge research Psychiatry Department.

Rebecca Lovell has my deep gratitude for her cheerful, deft and indispensable help in preparing the manuscript. Her unflappable expertise supplied needed reassurance.

# FORMAL ACKNOWLEDGEMENTS

Chapter 1 was originally published as "Freud's technique: more from experience than from theory," which appeared in the Psychoanalytic Quarterly, (2009). *Psychoanalytic Quarterly*, 78(3):913–924, 2009. Grateful acknowledgement is made to the Psychoanalytic Quarterly and John Wiley & Sons, Inc. for permission to republish.

Chapter 2 was originally published as "A reading of Freud's *Papers on Technique,*" in the Psychoanalytic Quarterly. 60:564–595, 1991. Grateful acknowledgement is made to the Quarterly and John Wiley & Sons, Inc. for permission to republish.

Chapter 3 first appeared as "The discrete and the continuous in Freud's 'Remembering, repeating and working through.'" The final, definitive version of this paper has been published in the Journal of the American Psychoanalytic Association, 62:11–34, 2014, published by SAGE Publishing, (http://online.sagepub.com) All rights reserved. Grateful permission is made to that journal for permission to republish.

Chapter 4 originally appeared in Psychoanalytic Psychology, Copyright 2002 American Psychological Association. Reproduced with permission. The official citation that should be used in referencing this material is "What lies beyond interpretation, and is that the right question?" Psychoanalytic Psychology, 19(3): 540–551. No further reproduction or distribution is permitted without written permission from the American Psychological Association.

Chapter 5 originally appeared as "Is there life after enactment? The idea of a patient's proper work." The final, definitive version of this paper has been published in the Journal of the American Psychoanalytic Association, 56: 431–453, 2008, published by SAGE Publishing (http://online.sagepub.com). All rights reserved. Grateful acknowledgement is made to that journal for permission to republish.

Chapter 6 originally appeared in the Psychoanalytic Quarterly, 76:817–833, 2007. Grateful acknowledgement is made to that journal and John Wiley & Sons, Inc.for permission to republish.

Chapter 7 originally appeared as "How and why do patients become more objective: Sterba compared with Strachey," in Psychoanalytic Quarterly, 61:1–17, 1992. Grateful acknowledgement is made to that journal and John Wiley & Sons, Inc. for permission to republish.

Chapter 8 originally appeared in Psychoanalytic Quarterly, 77: 1031–1044, 2008. Grateful acknowledgement is made to that journal and John Wiley & Sons, Inc. for permission to republish.

Chapter 9 originally appeared in Psychoanalytic Quarterly, 74:639–660, 2005. Grateful acknowledge is made to that journal and John Wiley & Sons, Inc. for permission to republish.

Chapter 10 originally appeared as "Ferrum, ignis, and medicina: Return to the crucible." The final, definitive version of this paper has been published in Journal of the American Psychoanalytic Association, 45:20–36, 1997, published by SAGE Publishing. (http://online.sag.pub.com). All rights reserved. Grateful acknowledgement is made to that journal for permission to republish.

Chapter 11. The final, definitive version of this paper has been published in the Journal of the American Psychoanalytic Association, 53: 349–375, 2005, published by SAGE Publishing. (http://online.sagepub.com) All rights reserved. Grateful acknowledgement is made to that journal for permission to republish.

Chapter 12 originally appeared in the Psychoanalytic Quarterly, 75:689–713, 2006. Grateful acknowledgement is made to that journal and John Wiley & Sons, Inc. for permission to republish.

# INTRODUCTION

This book might pass for a reader's guide to Freud's *Papers on Technique*[1] and I hope it will be used that way since any new attention to that book is worthwhile, especially in today's climate. But what I have written here is no modest, pedagogical "key to the text." Although I discuss *Papers* in detail, my purpose is both grander and simpler: I want you to share the awe I feel before Freud's little book, and to follow that awe into larger wonderings about psychoanalysis and the human condition.

A more modest hope is that you will at least hold my perspective in mind as you read and teach the book (and relate each of its parts to the book's overall thrust). At the very least I hope you are prompted to read Freud's little book again, perhaps for the first time as a continuous narrative.

## WHAT IS THIS THING CALLED *PAPERS ON TECHNIQUE*?

At the turn of the twentieth century, Sigmund Freud stumbled on a really strange phenomenon that he could induce in patients. I will call it the psychoanalytic experience, or the psychoanalytic phenomenon. It is a novel state of unusual mental freedom.

I think we have forgotten how strange that experience is. The picture of psychoanalytic treatment is widely familiar, and whatever is familiar seems natural. Furthermore, analysts at work actually have a positive obligation to regard the analytic experience as a natural thing – an uncommon thing, to be sure, but otherwise as natural as sleeping and eating. – because if it isn't natural, it might seem the result of a manipulation. Freud had his own reasons for telling us to view analysis as a normal process, and I will have more to say about that later. Even when the psychoanalytic phenomenon is recognized as an unusual creation of our culture it may seem pretty expectable on the basis of what we know about the mind. Once functions of mind are reified, as in psychoanalytic theory, a related

**2** Introduction

treatment will appear to be a logical consequence of how the mind is constructed, and therefore not particularly strange.

Thus analysts tend to think that Freud discovered mental entities (such as transference and resistance) and invented a technique to deal with them. On that account, transference was a discovery just as electricity was a discovery, and psychoanalytic technique is an invention that makes various uses of transference, much as the light bulb was invented to make use of electricity. Nothing strange about that, it would seem.

But it's not the way it happened. The relationship between discovery and invention was exactly the reverse. The map of the mind did not lead Freud to the phenomenon. The technique is not the child of the theory. On the contrary, a strange adventure drove Freud to the (reluctant) *discovery of the psychoanalytic phenomenon*, and along the way he was forced to *invent conceptual tools* (such as a new concept of transference) to grasp and manage it. There exists a record of that adventure, and the lamentable fact is that for all intents and purposes it has been lost.

Where will we find the lost record? It lies before our eyes in the pages of Freud's *Papers on Technique* (1911–1915). Does that seem pretty un-lost? Here is a book that has been sampled by every analytic practitioner and taught by every Freudian teacher through the years. Its contents have attracted countless commentaries. Its principles have been explicitly or implicitly addressed, revered or condemned, by virtually every brand of psychoanalyst. Its critics often *define* themselves by their criticism of those principles. And what I think is astonishing is that, in spite of this fabulous notoriety, the book called *Papers on Technique* remains essentially unknown ... *as a book.* [2]

By that qualification I mean to make it clear that *I am not referring to various papers on technique that were randomly collected and bound together in a book.* It would be absurd to say that any of those "papers" have been ignored. Except perhaps for the first of them ("On the Interpretation of Dreams"), substantial parts of each of these papers are probably better known to students at Freudian institutes, and at other centers at least by hearsay, than any other of Freud's writings. (After all, they present the graphic *image* of psychoanalysis.) And yet the *book* is unknown to the generality of analysts as a book.

Why make such a fuss about the book in contrast to the individual papers that comprise it? Because it is only from the sequence of papers that we can see what's going on: This book is a contemporary, real-time record of the discovery of a phenomenon of historical significance – the experience of a new degree of mental freedom.

## READING *PAPERS ON TECHNIQUE* WE WITNESS THE GRADUAL DISCOVERY OF THE PSYCHOANALYTIC PHENOMENON

The psychoanalytic phenomenon is an empirical discovery. In *Papers on Technique* we see the discovery unfold before the eyes of the first person to come upon it. We follow Freud's discovery through a process of trial and error, his dissection of its conditions, and his effort to grasp its phenomenology. Old theoretical terms are connected to each other in surprising ways. The point of it all is to pin down what elicits and what dispels this new state of unusual mental freedom.

The sequence of papers charts the evolution and interrelationship of the variables that evoke the psychoanalytic phenomenon and bequeaths to us the famous terms by which they're remembered. Freud borrows many of those terms from previous practices and from theoretical systems he was elaborating elsewhere. But in this book they are used (and modified) for a separate, almost self-contained project. The principles are often contradictory. A strained – often agonizing – process of fitting the terms to the "facts on the ground" is recorded without much concern for the grand theory of mind the terms were coined for. As was his want, Freud did the experiment with stubborn curiosity and integrity, and having gotten it over with, he went back to his real interest – theory of the mind and culture. Thus the experiment stands or falls on its own merits.

I want to make it clear that it is not an experiment in the effectiveness of treatment. (Cure is largely taken for granted and is not the variable evaluated in the experiment.) It is an experiment in the evocation of a certain state of mind; specifically, *to see what brings about that particular state and what interferes with it*. The state was called a psychoanalysis. The name meant a lot to Freud, and it is now a contested prize. But the name is irrelevant to the experiment. Basically, it is that state which is created by a genuinely non-directive therapy (if the quixotic implications of that phrase are understood as profoundly as the experiment makes possible). The content of *Papers on Technique* is not essentially a partisan or ideological matter of debate, because it is not a claim to a name; it is the discovery of a phenomenon. For purposes of the experiment it doesn't matter what you call it, or who believes in it, or whether it is superior or inferior to another phenomenon in one way or another. Nor, to begin with, does it matter whether it is useful. You can say that it wreaks havoc, or creates crippling bondage, or wastes valuable resources. You can say anything you like *about* the state, but the experiment showed what brought it about and what hindered it. In the course of the experiment, nothing is perfectly captured or perfectly understood, but the state is fairly visible. More than anything else that Freud developed, it is unaffected by new information and different perspectives. If you like, you can add other factors to your horizon – attachment, reflective functioning, dissociation, projective identification, subcortical connectomes, dialectical constructions, après coup, mirror neurons, cognitive style, temperament. The report of the old experiment just stands there pretty much unaffected. And I would add that, for reasons that will become apparent in this book, the experiment, if lost, will probably not be repeated (though as a natural science experiment, parts of it will naturally be taken up in other experiments).

## WHAT ARE SOME IMPLICATIONS OF THIS VIEW?

If *Papers on Technique* is read as a continuous recording by an empirical investigator, we should correct a number of popular beliefs. We should conclude, for example:

1. The psychoanalytic phenomenon is not an invention; it is a discovery. Freud does not select styles and put them together as a technique.

**4** Introduction

2. The technique is not deduced from a model of the mind. For instance, it has little to do with a theory of psychic energy.
3. Basic therapy principles do not express the founder's character or his preference, or his idiosyncratic judgment, or his speculation, or his habitual practice, or anyone's common-sense reasoning.
4. *Papers on Technique* is not a compilation of assorted strategic decisions.
5. *Papers on Technique* is not written primarily to caution beginners or avoid scandal.

## WHY HAS *PAPERS* BEEN MISUNDERSTOOD?

I will now suggest some reasons for the misleading beliefs.

## 1. PAPERS ON TECHNIQUE *IS READ AS A MISCELLANEOUS COLLECTION*

*Papers on Technique* is usually remembered distantly as a storehouse of miscellaneous rules and watch-words – timber for the furniture that we nonchalantly call "the frame," as though one can pick up a few pieces from *Papers* and assemble them according to taste. Some of the *Papers* (and even some passages) are so vibrant that they beg to be understood alone as mini-texts, and so compelling that they rise out of sequence and lose their relationship to their fellow *Papers*. For example, an older analyst may fondly remember an especially moving paper ("Transference-Love" is a favorite) and slip it like an encyclopedia entry into his course on the subject as a free-standing essay, unconcerned that it is part of an unsettled, equivocating dialogue that Freud had been having with himself since an earlier paper (e.g., "The dynamics of transference").

Analysts turn to their imagination for plausible reasons that someone like Freud would have compiled such a catalogue: Maybe this was a list of student errors, jotted down as they came to Freud's attention. Maybe Freud is in the analytic dressing room, trying out ways of approaching patients, fashioning smart professional postures, adding and discarding items as he settles into his practice. ("Oh, and another thing, it would be a good idea for an analyst to maintain a dignified reserve like mine.") That is a pretty impressionistic memory of *Papers*, but it must be granted that there are quite a lot of incidental observations in *Papers*. Freud certainly does not advertise the work's experimental nature. He does not say: "Here is a project; watch me undertake it." I will have more to say about that in a later chapter.

## 2. PAPERS ON TECHNIQUE *IS TAINTED BY OVERALL DISILLUSIONMENT*

And then there are the more personal reasons for the memory of a misreading of *Papers*. Analysts used to feel privy to arcane knowledge and esoteric vision. It was an intellectual priesthood, remarkably comprehensive and intellectually meticulous. Treatment terms shared in the solemnity of the whole theory, assuring practitioners that they had a solid rationale as long as they used the respected language. "Analyze the resistance; uncover the unconscious."

Moreover, the hardest rules are most venerated. It was a source of analyst's pride that they had survived a basic training so tough that they could suspend civilized reflexes without guilt. But society that rents out towers of prestige has relocated psychoanalysis to humbler quarters, and the luster of its theory has faded. Is it any wonder that the old drill-book (as it's regarded) is remembered with little love, and its rigorous dictates with some bitterness?

Analytic technique does not get a pass any more. It is left to defend itself on its own terms without the authorizing sponsorship of grand theory. Many analysts have found it hard to make the case for bare technique, unshielded by the old magisterium with its intellectual command and material reward. Many asked: Why, after all, had we been conforming? Many answered: We were doing it because it seemed especially "correct," really profound, intensely professional, disciplined and superior. In other words, for no good reason at all. Attention is called to the Master's own notorious informality in his practice – even what we might now call boundary-crossing – as evidence that *Papers* was either not meant as Gospel or was immediately superseded by Freud's further experiments (in the fashion of Ferenczi). Personally, I find it hard to understand how experienced analysts can declare without shame – as though it were self-evident – that supposedly scientific professionals should disregard the founder's reasoning and imitate his physical behavior. (I discuss this further in Chapter 13.) It seems that anything one can imagine is a good enough explanation for "what went wrong" with technique. Analytic rigidity has even been attributed to émigré insecurity, which turned a few Old World admonitions into enforceable rules so that bewildered refugee instructors might stake out a defined position in their new home, and substitute an old language of authority for their new identity as misfits.

### 3. THE LANGUAGE OF PAPERS SOMETIMES OFFENDS CURRENT SENSIBILITIES

That sort of skepticism about their own profession is relatively recent among analysts. It is an outstanding peculiarity of *Papers on Technique* that its various terms and contents, though published between 1910 and 1915, have been in play – and for the most part respected – throughout most of the Freudian Century, despite a profusion of other theoretical and technical advances, disputes, and innovations.

But today's climate has introduced an additional – and I think ironic – interference for readers, partly as a result of Freud's plain talk and urgent purpose. Freud is read nowadays through a scrim of presentism and political correctness. New readers are amazed at Freud's shameless sexism, paternalism, and assumption of professional authority. Among many new readers, an ahistorical, locked-in imagination greets all of Freud's writings. But *Papers* is especially vulnerable because of

**6** Introduction

its plain talk. (Freud would have been amazed at how much more explosive the subject of sex is a century after the psychoanalytic revolution!) When, as in this book, Freud leaves formalized theory and makes sexual references in his own voice, some readers look askance. The offense can be quite vague: I paraphrase the reception this way: "From his choice of metaphor we know what the dirty old man was thinking, even if he doesn't come out and say it." The result is that when Freud makes a point in *Papers on Technique* with a then-current colloquial witticism or a sexual metaphor, it is offensive on the face of it. Never mind that it may be, on a literal level, a piece of plain common sense, for which one scratches to find a perfect substitute. Here's an example: Freud seeks a metaphor for the impossibility of psychoanalytically eliminating just a single symptom. He compares the healing process with embryonic development. An act of insemination starts a self-governing, holistic, organic process, and cannot be directed toward partial accomplishment. Any reader will instantly understand the point: There is a voluntary beginning to analysis; it starts a natural process; thereafter the process is autonomous. It is a perfect image, partly because the analogy is organic on both sides and not entirely formal. But in my experience, today's students regularly think it is an odd and distasteful expression of Freud's infamous sexist – or even – salacious attitude. For rhetorical purposes, Freud could have contented himself with the simple abstraction, but he is trying his best in this particular book to present a durable practical *stance* for an embattled practitioner – something that will come to mind in the heat of battle; a vividly obvious image to right his balance.

Freud had painfully discovered that analysts needed to adopt an awkward and unnatural attitude if they wanted to elicit the analytic effect. He could discuss it in technical terms for the idle reader, but he recognized the absolute need to give his ground troops a common-sense way to make that odd attitude feel natural, so they can react gracefully in their "new natural-ness." To that end, the book is peppered with vignettes, contemporary jokes and vivid metaphors. Unfortunately, Freud's images are so vivid and sit so firmly in mind that their graphic memory displaces the rationale they were intended to illustrate. Readers then interpret the isolated images according to their own associations and popular imaginations of Freud (or even their imagination of Freud's associations!) (Students are surprised to discover that "the surgeon" is offered as a model of workman-like self-effacement.) Today, popular imagination of Freud's imagination, at least in *Papers on Technique*, is weighted toward shameful sexual attitudes, with a consequent blurring of substantive meaning.

## 4. SHAPE AND STYLE MISLEADINGLY SUGGEST THAT THE PAPERS IN THE BOOK ARE STAND-ALONE ESSAYS

All told, however, there can be no question about who is most responsible for the misreading of *Papers*. It is the author himself. To begin with, of course, he published the papers piece-meal before binding them in a book. By itself that's no big deal: it's the way most analytic books have come into being. What's really significant is that in their separate appearance, Freud deliberately disguised the exploratory tentativeness and uncertainty of his on-going research. He camouflaged their function as progress-reports; he made his new observations seem old hat. Even when he's repeating and retracting answers, scratching at the same itch from paper to paper, reversing himself from page to page about quandaries that can't be hidden, he quickly recovers the self-satisfied, pedagogic tone as though speaking of safely settled matters. When puzzles present themselves, he makes his self-questioning seem only the familiar rhetorical device he uses in more finished essays. He characterizes some of the papers as elementary refreshers, a sort of Cliff-notes, designed only to bring his readers up to speed. He even apologizes for publishing allegedly non-original summaries in what was supposed to be a research journal (the *Internationale Zeitschrift für Psychoanalyse*). He included tips for learners and informal confessions. He showed his usual concern for public relations and warned followers not to discredit psychoanalysis. One finds in his manner much dirt-kicking disingenuousness as though he was saying, "aw shucks, folks – this is only my quirky preference – but you might just find it congenial, so I'll throw it in." None of that sounds like on-going research.

On a more general level, Freud's well-known indifference to psychoanalysis as a treatment made it easy for readers to minimize the seriousness of this brief detour into technique. Such a reader will miss the seismic shift in the analytic view of man that takes place within the few pages of this inquiry, as Freud races toward a formula for a strange experience he had stumbled on. The race over, Freud looks elsewhere, and his overall disinterest in treatment now shakes hands with today's shyness about the very idea of "technique," to which we add popular resentment over rules, regulations, progression, evaluations and certification, with the result that Freud's exploration in the realm of technique is not seen as the major work it is.

## 5. IT IS SAID THAT FREUD DID NOT INTEND PAPERS ON TECHNIQUE TO BE PRESCRIPTIVE

Freud is often thought to have indicated that the principles in *Papers on Technique* should not be taken too seriously. In point of fact, he did not say that about the principles, but he did say it about the book. And no doubt that sort of self-erasure made it possible for surveyors to overlook it; as when, for example, the noted Freud historian Elisabeth Roudinesco (2016) skips *Papers* in her recent Freud biography to blame later, dimmer, analysts for classical formalities. Similarly, Lipton (1977) suggested that preoccupation with technique is not inherited from Freud but is a reaction to Franz Alexander's manipulative procedure. Lipton pleaded for a return to Freud's open, respectful, straightforward co-investigator relationship where both analyst and analysand are focused on the analytic goal (discovery), not the means (technical niceties). Lipton considered it a perversion of analytic treatment to try to head off every wrong turn before it happens (which is certainly one way to describe *Papers on Technique*).

**8** Introduction

Lohser and Newton (1996) draw from their impressive survey of Freud's practice a more nuanced view of Freud's range of thought and practice. Unlike Lipton, they recognize that Freud was sometimes concerned with managing the patient's experience, even though he usually assumed an equal partnership with a like-minded fellow explorer. For Lohser and Newton the Freud who treats his patient as an equal collaborator is Freud-the-scientist, the implication being that the author of *Papers on Technique* is Freud-the-neurologist or Freud-the-hypnotist. In the following chapter, I hope to convince readers that the Freud of *Papers on Technique* is, if anything, more the scientist than the Freud who "respectfully" (innocently) collaborates with his patients. When exploring with his patients, Freud is collecting reports. When writing *Papers on Technique*, Freud is examining an organism. Collaborating, he is an anthropologist; experimenting, he is a psychologist.

For a judicious and non-partisan assessment of Freud's relationship to *Papers on Technique*, I recommend Ellman (1991). In any case, there is no question that Freud came to regret writing the book. I discuss this in Chapter 13.

## 6. MANY THINK PAPERS ON TECHNIQUE WAS SUPERSEDED BY STRUCTURAL THEORY

Freud's own disinterest in *Papers on Technique* is not the greatest challenge to its lasting significance. The most substantive reason analysts have for discounting *Papers on Technique* is the subsequent establishment of the structural theory of the mind.

If analysts feel any obligation to read and teach this early work, it is often as a false start – a logical deduction from an outdated energy model of the mind – a forced conclusion from a false premise. (Chapter 1 will deal with this in more detail.) How can we take *Papers on Technique* seriously after learning about ego, superego and signal anxiety? Once we know about the mental cog-wheels that turn a patient's behaviors, how not cringe at the operatic melodrama in *Papers on Technique*, which takes at face value the whole-person clash of human desire in collision with the analyst. Compared with a psychodynamic diagram, *Papers* seems excessively Wagnerian, a throwback to Schopenhauer and Nietzsche. Those battle metaphors! That *Sturm und Drang*! Such heroic posturing! And what about those Hegelian paradoxes? Are they really paradoxes? Aren't they just early imperfections waiting for later theory to work out? It might be argued that *Papers* is the way it's bound to look to the unprepared, very first analyst, but for sophisticated modern analysts *Papers on Technique* is frankly a little embarrassing – not grown-up psychoanalysis.

More analysts nowadays understand treatment as an Enlightenment drama. Gone is the tragic analyst in *Papers on Technique* – a tormented seducer and destroyer of old longings who struggled mightily with his patient. That old analyst was whisked off stage in 1920 and returned, almost before he was missed, in the comedic role of liberator, offering patients freedom from unnecessary anxiety. The analytic couple (at least in North America) is now two civilized people working toward a common goal, their realistic egos in workmanlike embrace.

There's no question that, as theory, the later one is better. It answers more questions (which should make us happy). It's a nicer picture of psychoanalysts (which should make us wary). Unlike the earlier story of treatment, the new treatment story (with, for instance, ego-sharing between the parties) is logically deducible from its coordinate theory of the mind (the structural theory). As such, it is a valuable justification of analytic procedure. It is much more easily taught and more gratefully learned (though it will not give anyone an idea of what actual treatment is like).

And yet the new theory continues to need something from the old. Most conspicuously, the modern theory still depends on the old terms of art: Transference, resistance, defense, working through – these are still in play, more or less with the meanings given them by *Papers on Technique*. Nor is it merely a matter of terminological convenience. I think the need is deeper. The special terms developed in *Papers on Technique* are still needed for the same reason they were fashioned. They were the tools that made it possible to manage the inherent contradiction of all psychoanalytic treatment, which is to *try* for a *non-directive* treatment. (Think about it!)

Anyone practicing what is supposed to be a non-directive therapy is bound to feel compromised if he notices that he is a conjurer, casting a spell and summoning a strange experience. Better to see himself as an observer of nature than as the shadowy producer of an artificial experience. So psychoanalysts are inclined to promote Freud's terms of art to the status of observed natural entities. Practitioners look on these constructs as free-standing creatures in the jungle they are exploring. I refer to terms such as transference, resistance, working through, free-association, free-floating attention. Nowadays the analyst adds another phantom denizen of the phenomenal jungle: it is his own coordinated set of manipulations cleverly projected "out there," where it traps both himself and his patient. I wonder if the reader has recognized that I am, referring to "the frame." I will have more to say about Frame and Enactment in Chapter 14.

I do not, of course, imply that these are fictions or gratuitous attitudes. As will be seen in the following chapters, my conclusion is exactly the opposite. As ways of seeing and doing, these images and concepts are keys to the phenomenon Freud discovered. An analyst who thinks along these lines will elicit the psychoanalytic phenomenon. But they are not natural in the sense of being available for all to encounter "out there." Freud didn't bump into them. He titrated conceptions and attitudes like those until he saw which ones elicited the analytic experience and which turned it off. We do not meet them in ordinary life; they are not the ways we chunk our experience of people and interactions. Freud had to *invent concepts* to flag these perceptual and cognitive triggers. That invention, like most inventions, was facilitated by what Quine called "boot-strapping," a step-wise modification of ready-at-hand terms he had been working with before he formulated the structural theory – some of them even before the advent of psychoanalysis proper. Since these treatment terms were carefully molded in *Papers* to absorb the lessons of the new empirical experiment it is not at all surprising that they were carried forward "as-is" right alongside subsequent changes in theory of the mind – and, to some

**10** Introduction

extent, into all our treatment ideas. But they are not out there in the common world, like "animal," "spoon," "love and hate." Without that grandfathering of the old terms (resistance, etc.) – as at least a distant echo of *Papers on Technique* – there is no reason to think people would come across these "entities" all by themselves, nor the psychoanalytic phenomenon they are involved with. "Working through," "resistance," even "transference" (as meant in *Papers*) will vanish if the set-up provided by *Papers* is forgotten. But so long as those old terms are even roughly understood, they will encourage the otherwise-hard-to-describe psychoanalytic phenomenon.

Therefore, it has made sense up to now for practitioners to go on disguising their strange persona in natural images such as the surgeon or the mirror, even while the original purpose of those images is casually dismissed as out-of-date theory. But imagine that the empirical rationale in *Papers* is forgotten. And imagine that the theoretical rationale dies from theory-exhaustion. What is left? How will the clinician meet his practical needs? He can reach into *Papers on Technique*, pull out some isolated "rules," wash off their "primitive" theoretical context and use them as simple tokens of professional integrity. Until, that is, the idea of rules becomes a scandal.

Rules without roots can't stand up to a storm of criticism, especially on grounds of unscientific authoritarianism. To stand those rules upright, to make them clearly visible even for pruning or cross-fertilizing, they need to be replanted in their old context. That context is *Papers on Technique*.

## GENERAL NOTE

The following chapters were written at different times, so there is much redundancy in what follows. Despite the overlap, their differences in focus make it possible to pick out and elaborate the mind-boggling difficulties and the many separate challenges that Freud dealt with in his tiny book. I have added further redundancy by prefacing some of the chapters with general reflections on the topics. They give the reader a chance to briefly sample the gist of my exposition in somewhat more informal language. Some chapters were written for oral presentation, mindful that words to be caught on the fly profit from the simplest and most vivid locution. For that reason and for ease of written presentation, I have chosen to use the familiar third-person singular pronouns *he, his*, etc. throughout. No implications about the gender of "analyst" or "patient" are intended by this usage.

## Notes

1  Whenever the single word *Papers* appears, it should be understood as an abbreviation of *Papers on Technique*.
2  Freud published *Papers on Technique*, along with some other technical and metapsychology papers, as *Zur Technik der Psychoanalyse und zur Metapsychologie*. Vienna: Internationaler Psychoanalytischer Verlag, 1924.

## REFERENCES

Ellman, S. T. (1991). *Freud's Technical Papers: A Contemporary Perspective*. Northvale, NJ: Aronson.

Freud, S. (1911–1915). *Papers on Technique*. Standard Edition, 12. Vol. 12. Ed. James Strachey. London: Hogarth Press, 1958, pp. 91–171.

Lipton, S. (1977). An advantage of Freud's technique as shown in his analysis of the Rat Man. *International Journal of Psychoanalysis*, 58: 255–273.

Lohser, B. & Newton, P. (1996). *Unorthodox Freud: The View from the Couch*. New York, NY: Guilford Press.

Roudinesco, E. (2016). *Freud: In His Time and Ours*, trans. Catherine Porter. Cambridge, MA: Harvard University Press.

# PART ONE

# The text

## PREFACE TO CHAPTER 1

### *THE CENTRAL DISCOVERY: TRANSFERENCE ENTANGLEMENT*

*Papers on Technique* begins with an unwanted empirical discovery: I will call it transference entanglement. Not transference, mind you – that was old hat – but transference entanglement. By that I mean the way Freud's own wishes get inextricably tangled into the patient's transference. (Today we might call it enactment.) Freud is very clear that this entanglement was his paramount experience and overwhelming difficulty in the new treatment. This kind of entanglement distinguishes psychoanalysis from hypnosis since it expresses the patient's will more than the analyst's. You would expect that to be good news for Freud, who was always accused of planting his own "findings." But here, in this first attempt to grasp the analyst's unaccustomed helplessness, any familiar mechanism – even one that was usually anathema – would have been welcome. Hypnotic suggestion might impeach Freud's discoveries, but it was at least understandable and manageable. This new relationship was just baffling, and its mastery could easily seem impossible. People who natter on about the arrogance of neutrality and blank screen can have little imagination of that humbling confrontation with the Laocoön-like enactment problem – a problem we still haven't solved.

It is important to be very specific about what entangles what. Bion's rephrasing of Freud's principle is so familiar that we don't bat an eyelid when we hear someone say (usually with an ironic, forgiving smile) that we are supposed to come to a treatment hour "without memory or desire." What Freud discovered was the way transference tangled into his every wish, whether passionate or cognitive, including his scientific curiosity and wish for the material of cure. The only way to escape entanglement would seem to be to want nothing at all.

## 14 The text

Freud had discovered that he is no longer in the driver's seat. He is no longer master of the transaction, cognitively or behaviorally. He must find a way to recover his poise by thinking differently and acting adroitly. Entanglement challenges Freud's whole understanding of what transference is, since it is no longer merely a mistake or a disguise. Transference not only makes for trouble in practice; it shakes up all of Freud's guiding concepts. In its wild new incarnation, transference invades the secure notion of resistance and eats away at Freud's picture of the repressed. It changes his understanding of illness and ultimately threatens the ethical position of the analyst.

Freud's discovery of transference entanglement and his effort to extricate himself is charted in *Papers on Technique*. As he refits the old terms to their new job of helping him center himself, many theoretical dominos must be rebalanced. And it turns out that the rebalancing moves from the terms into the treatment itself: The continuous balancing of conflicting ways of seeing the patient is itself the new psychoanalytic technique.

To someone distantly remembering *Papers*, my description may seem unfamiliar and willfully hyperbolic. If he returns to the book and reads closely, he might exonerate me and pass the blame to Freud, whose rhetoric he judges to be overheated. Since *Papers* is undeniably weighted toward the experiential aspect of treatment (in contrast to the art of interpretation), the most plausible alternative to my reading might be that, in 1910–1914, Freud was in love with a mechanistic libido theory in which the discharge of energy has pride of place. What could be more natural, the argument goes, than for a hyper-intellectual like Freud to use his pet theory to explain practice and *deduce* the alleged discovery that transference is not a species of misperception but a matter of push and pull? My adversary might argue that Freud mechanically applied his mechanical (energy) theory to draw the built-in conclusion that an analyst will receive from his patient an energetic discharge (transference) which it is his job to divert and sort out. Isn't that exactly what a theory-proud person like Freud would "find," no matter *what* he actually observed? In other words, my adversary would say that Freud was entangled not with transference but with his own libido theory. On this reading, the central theme of *Papers on Technique* – perhaps the whole of it – fell out-of-date at the precise moment in the 1920s when psychic energy was kicked upstairs to a merely metaphoric status. All the dramatics that I find in *Papers on Technique* are really just personifications of an academic diagram called metapsychology. This argument is advanced to rescue the profession from enslavement to an archaic energy theory that artificially made transference central to analytic therapy. The message is: We have gone off the track. It is time to look at clinical facts with a modern eye. I will argue against this view in the following chapter.

# 1

# DISCOVERING HOW TO ELICIT THE PSYCHOANALYTIC PHENOMENON

Puzzled and perhaps a little annoyed by the persistent idea that interpreting the transference is the only way to effect analytic change, Sander M. Abend (2009) tracks the dogma back to Freud's prestructural writings on technique. Abend plainly and cogently lays out a line of thought that may have led Freud to this belief.

Having given the early ideas a really fair hearing, Abend then points to the greater sophistication of later theory and technique, and asks why, long after Freud had opened up larger vistas, he never disabused analysts of the idea that treatment progresses solely by interpreting the transference. Abend finds a clue to this riddle in the early theory of a quasi-physical libido, which Freud associated with the vivid image of catharsis. Could it be, Abend asks, that Freud was unable to pry his imagination loose from libido theory even while he was developing a subtler and more scientific theory of ego and defense? That would explain why, among the many useful approaches suggested by his later theory, only this early one won Freud's endorsement. If so, we would have to say that Freud's atavistic loyalty to libido theory discouraged analysts from employing all the tools their broadened rationale made available. Although Abend does not deny that many analysts have their own reasons for glorifying transference interpretation, I think he would be happy to leave us with the impression that the transference-only dogma is a kind of genomic parasite from Paleolithic libido theory.

I will suggest another way of reading Freud on technique that might lead to a different conclusion. We are familiar with Freud's general reluctance to give up one idea while overlaying it with a different one. But I suggest that we can learn something by turning our gaze to his specific, microscopic unwillingness to discard treatment ideas that were being updated already in *Papers on Technique* (1911–1915), even in that short interval, even before the advent of the structural theory, and even within the scope of a single paper. I will use as my example chiefly "The dynamics of transference" (1912).

**16** The text

It is impossible to read the *Papers on Technique* in sequence without realizing that this group of essays records an investigation in real time. The journey of exploration from the first paper to the last is not the kind of rhetorical fiction that Freud often uses to escort the reader through false hopes and blind alleys until, by apparent process of exclusion, he is brought to a preplanned solution. Instead, *Papers on Technique* is more like a laboratory log honestly kept without erasures, in which Freud reported serious conceptual and practical difficulties as they afflicted him and recorded his progressive efforts to cope with them. Bit by bit we see him ruminating and trying first one way and then another to get a fix on the strange treatment he had stumbled upon. Our general question, then, is why Freud published a given individual paper and the *Papers on Technique* as a whole just as they were written, rather than rewriting the whole thing (perhaps in a revised version) from the standpoint of his final understanding. At the very least, one might have expected him to footnote corrections and revisions, as he did in other updated expositions. Why didn't he do that with *Papers on Technique*?

The only possible answer, it seems to me, is that the *thing* Freud was discovering could only be described by this method of successive passes. We may imagine *Papers on Technique* to be something like those atlases of anatomy that superimpose several transparencies upon each other, layering up two-dimensional diagrams to a three-dimensional body. No one of them alone will show the thickness of the subject, and each obscures the other. Or we may compare these *Papers* with the successively displaced images on a pack of cards that display a "movie" when flipped through in rapid succession. My metaphors will not, I fear, bear close scrutiny, but they may suggest how Freud counts on us to gather into our mind the contrasting and conflicting ideas that pile up and accumulate as we tangle with the treatment phenomenon. The implication is that we must be able to think in several different ways at once, or at least in flexible alternation, as we take up our stance in psychoanalytic treatment. In the course of the book, every crucial term is both retained and radically redefined instead of being edited and replaced: *resistance, transference, memory,* and much else by implication. By defining and redefining these terms, Freud seems to be searching for their "cash value" in the consulting room, correlating their varying operational definitions and puzzling over how they relate to each other. To my mind, this strange way of apprehending analytic treatment is independently rediscovered by every learner, and I believe it is this paradoxical mind-set that, in confirmable fact, conjures into existence a specifically psychoanalytic treatment.

If *Papers on Technique* is, as I suggest, a real-time record of Freud's thinking about things he was still trying to get into focus, it follows that the way to read the book is by identifying at each recorded moment who the Freud was that was making the entry. One must first imagine the *preliminary expectation* Freud brought to a given problem, then the nature of the *practical difficulty* (and its conceptual placement) that prompted his note, and finally the resolution he provisionally reached *at that stage* of the inquiry – a resolution that may occupy as little as one paragraph. The key to the next passage or paper will then be *another difficulty* he encountered, together

The Psychoanalytic Phenomenon    **17**

with any *uneasiness left over* from the solution(s) in the preceding paragraph or paper(s). In each case, his vision of treatment is best understood as a reaction to a particular, practical problem that inspired it.

As Freud moved from hypnotic and cathartic treatments, where the term resistance had the common vernacular meaning, and began his vexed inquiry into the new, psychoanalytic treatment he had chanced upon, we see him struck by the fact (recorded in the first of the *Papers*, "The handling of dream-interpretation in psychoanalysis," 1911) that resistance could take the inconspicuous form of seemingly good-faith compliance and, moreover, it could actually *produce* something (a plethora of dreams) rather than just concealing something (memories). Most startlingly and portentously, Freud discovered to his great distress that resistance could not only fit itself into the analyst's obvious external resemblance to a parent but could also mold itself to the analyst's most personal wishes – in Freud's case, a paramount interest in dreams and pride in their interpretation. A description of this sort of resistance – such clever, whole-person, positive maneuvering, still regarded as the work of "the" resistance – pastes a new image over the previous impersonal, almost physical stickiness of unconscious memories.

As though that wasn't headache enough, Freud could not escape the thoroughly perplexing impression that this sort of thing was no occasional bump in the road. It seemed to him that his daily job had turned out to be outmaneuvering the patient's sly maneuvering – a very different and much less agreeable task than the joint effort of dislodging memories, which was what both he and his patient had initially signed on for (and which, it should be noted, remained for him the ultimate aim of psychoanalytic treatment).

This is the Freud we follow into his next lab note ("The dynamics of transference," 1912), where we virtually hear him ask: "Why ... why am I always embroiled with what the patient wants from me, when all I want is to learn about his experiences? I can understand that memories would hold themselves back. I am skilled at coaxing them out. I am famous for the kind of patience that requires. I can even understand that any diversion would be useful to a force dedicated to holding back memories. But why do these memories almost *always* conceal themselves by some sort of grabbing at *me*?" Freud seems not to have anticipated this situation, much less welcomed it as a happy confirmation of theory. He had no incentive to see a familiar rapport transformed into a duel. It was no great joy to smother (lest it give a hostage to resistance) his paramount interest in the coded secrets of humanity while patients dangled their dreams before his eyes. He was discovering that he couldn't continue in a way that had always seemed sensible. It was not clear what new sense could be found in the new doings. It was not even clear what the problem was. Freud's immediate reaction (in writing) was to assure himself that it was, in fact, no problem at all, but this reassurance was repeated suspiciously frequently. Watching Freud banging his head over and over again against this problem in page after page of *Papers on Technique*, I, for one, find it impossible to think of him as complacently fitting it neatly into a well-prepared, theory-satisfying vision.

**18** The text

In this second paper in *Papers on Technique* ("The dynamics of transference," 1912), Freud tries in several ways to assimilate the original notion of resistance and transference to the newly perceived, blunt fact that the main difficulty of treatment was the patient's wishful pressure on him. That this was an urgent and bothersome issue is shown by his repeated posing and "solving" of the problem, followed a paragraph or two later by another statement of the problem and another (or the same) declaration of victory. He is obviously not even sure how to put his question. Only midway through the paper does Freud realize that repressed material is not just an *escape* from current frustration, but also a continuous *source* of desires. Even at that point, however, he is still unwilling to identify the shape of neurotic desire with the configuration of the transference (p. 104, n1). He still insists that transference resistance is just one more ruse and distraction (though now he acknowledges that this form of the resistance has some special "advantage" [p. 104]). The exposition seems to end on that note. However, there are two paragraphs remaining in the paper (pp. 107–108). And there, in what looks like an afterthought, Freud writes as though transference and resistance are almost *synonymous*. He has suddenly gone all the way to that extreme. Yet he retracts nothing from the formulations of the body of the paper, simply saying that he is adding "another aspect" (p. 107)! And not only that: not only does this last move – a mere couple of pages long, but by far the most vehement and memorable of the paper – leave the earlier formulations inviolate; it is tacked on almost without a bridge, as though utterly unrelated to what preceded, to which, indeed, it bears no resemblance in voice or method.

What is the function of these last two appended pages that almost identify resistance with transference? Freud is telling us that it is one thing to describe interacting parts of the mind as "the" resistance using "the transference" to keep "the unconscious" from consciousness. But it is another thing ("another aspect of the same subject," p. 107) to observe what the whole *person* is visibly *doing to the analyst* as a result of the resistance ("anyone who has observed all this ... ," p. 107). What led to this postscript? We picture Freud laying down his pen after finishing pages 99 to 106, looking back and suddenly realizing that he has been downright misleading if he leaves it at that. He has not prepared future analysts for what they will *see*. They need to be alerted to – they need to be *warned about* – the *intentional*, as well as the causal, aspects of the event, for that is what they will actually experience, and it is on that level that they will be called on to react. Analysts must be ready for the interpersonal experience of resistance. So he adds pages 107–108. Freud has learned the hard way that analysts are not (merely) adjusting internal forces such as "the" resistance; they are negotiating (battling, as he sees it) with *people* who want what they want, rather than what the analyst wants. I can imagine Freud saying to the novice, "You must accept this ahead of time, so you won't be so frustrated when you get embroiled in it, as I was when – and for which reason – I was impelled to write this paper in the first place."

When we grasp the message of this addendum, we understand why it does not replace the main part of the paper. The main part consists of elaborate, redundant *explanation*, while the addendum is a short, sharp shock of *recognition*. It is a descriptive supplement, albeit a vital supplement, to the preceding impersonal speculation about "the" resistance, transference, unconscious memory, and free association, which had been laboriously worked out and apparently concluded. The main part and its addendum are two ways of perceiving the patient, and no matter how incommensurable they are, an analyst must respond to both at once.

Having registered this double vision, Freud is moved in his peroration to join the two aspects together: Every successful effort to deal with the resistance will have the effect of prying loose the patient's segregated immersion in early relationships and forcing them into open scrutiny. The resistance will fight this with transference. But that's just another way of saying that the patient fights for satisfaction. Highlighted by the analyst's interpretations, the fight over satisfaction brings the patient's segregated early relationships into contact with the rest of his world, especially with his other views of the analyst, and in that context their segregated meaning and exclusive insistence will be killed off. That is how treatment will accomplish its objective.

How much theory can we find in this concluding picture? Not much, I think. The story relies on nothing more than a rough image of fixation – the sort of fixation that almost all psychotherapists take for granted without a second thought. Libido is mentioned just once in the rousing conclusion (and there only to name what is being chased by the analyst that causes the patient to react with visible, active "passions").

That's how it seems to me on reading the *Papers on Technique*. But Abend finds the guiding spirit of libido hovering over the story, and, in truth, how could it be otherwise? When we recall how overwhelmingly important libido theory was to Freud at the time, and when we remember that analytic theory was always more important to Freud than treatment, we simply cannot gainsay Abend's point. Even if an appeal to libido as theory isn't evident in the words, in the progression or in the reasoning in Freud's technical writings, who can say it wasn't in the back of Freud's mind? What we *can* say, however, is that, up front, what was *visibly* pulling Freud forward was a set of orienting problems that all psychoanalytic therapists face all the time. Among them are questions like: What is the relationship between fantasy and memory? What does memory have to do with desire? How does fantasy – especially unconscious fantasy – get woven into current perception and striving? What is the relationship between habituated, passive perception and active, intentional recreation? How can we describe wishes as hiding but also seeking? Shall we say that the patient is handicapped or that he is too demanding?

Freud is stumbling into these problems as he discovers analytic treatment. When the patient's secret, past attachment slides into the present moment and grabs Freud by the throat, he is witnessing two aspects at once – an impersonal resistance to memory, and a patient's personal orneriness. Agitated by the liveliness of that scene, it occurs to Freud that this must be precisely where the therapeutic action is. That is, after all, a tempting inference, isn't it? Even Abend might agree that later analysts draw the same conclusion not in deference to Freud's authority, but

**20** The text

because the idea is just plain tempting. It's a neat thought, you might say. It seems to call out to the analyst.

Be that as it may, "The dynamics of transference" (1912) also retains, alongside this killing off of a relationship, the original, "impersonal" project of retrieving blocked memories by means of analyzing "the" resistance, and it retains, moreover, the explicit statement that the transference does not necessarily capture all or even the essence of the neurosis. ("[We should not be led to] conclude in general that the element selected for transference-resistance is of peculiar pathogenic importance [p. 104, n1]," which is a comment that contradicts the final pages, and will be even more dramatically contradicted – though characteristically not retracted – by the theory of the transference neurosis published just two papers later.)

It remains for the fifth of the *Papers* ("Remembering, repeating and working-through," 1914) to fuse these two attitudes together, thus squaring the circle, as it were. In this penultimate chapter of the *Papers*, Freud makes the famous, fateful, and startling démarche: He declares that memory appears as action. Here, if anywhere, we might look for the influence of libido theory. Indeed, if Abend is right, we might wonder that libido theory hadn't shouted that particular lesson in Freud's ear right at the beginning, saving him the agony of the preceding installments. But libido theory didn't speak then, and it doesn't speak now. Evidently Freud isn't talking to theory in this paper. What is guiding him, then? I believe Freud is trying to maintain the nondirective, receptive stance designed to fish memories out of dutiful associations, while in fact fielding what is closer to a full-time, personal assault on the analyst in his professional capacity. Solution: the one is the same as the other; actions are memories. *Voila!* There we have a fusion of quite different attitudes to the patient, and Freud makes no bones about – or apology for – their bundling. (See Friedman 2008.)

Considerations of space preclude detailed discussion of Freud's other writing on technique. But I would plead for a similar contextual reading of other passages that seem to be molded on libido theory. We may note in one passage, for example, that, if we take the wording seriously, Freud seems to see a convergence with – rather than a derivation from – libido theory when he writes: "I will now complete my picture of the mechanism of cure by clothing it in the formulas of the libido theory" (1916–1917, p. 154). What is he clothing in theoretical language if not what he had just discussed in terms of emotional attachment?

What about the image of the transference neurosis as a miniature neurosis, where each symptom has shrunk into an aspect of transference – the transference neurosis as a domesticated neurosis – a neurosis in captivity? But what prompted the idea? In the context of "Remembering, repeating and working-through" (1914), one might argue that this idea is an opportunistic bonus that springs to Freud's mind in the course of explaining how patients are persuaded to keep their newly indulged neuroticism confined to the couch. If you picture analysts using their authority to protect patients from acting out at home, it is easy to add that this draws everything that could be a symptom into the analytic relationship itself. It is as though Freud heard himself say, "We persuade the patient not to show off his neurosis in public; we keep it for ourselves," and was suddenly inspired to add, "Not only that! By God! We keep it *all* to ourselves! And, now, wouldn't that make it handy for *treatment?*" Ferenczi and Rank (1925) did go on to *derive* a technique from libido theory as a theory, but for our purpose what is significant is that it did not win Freud's blessing. As Abend observes, the idea of a complete and completely transposable neurosis was silently abandoned by 1937. As far as I know, it had never been implemented in Freud's practice to begin with.

All right: I'm stretching a point. The idea of a transference neurosis (in this sense of the term) has more weight than a passing thought. Even within *Papers on Technique*, it is embedded in other significant contexts; for instance, the picture of psychoanalysis as an *unfolding* rather than an operation, or the reassurance that treatment has a normal course and a natural completion. These images can be paired to images of libido discharge, to be sure. But in the first place, they can just as well be compared with the unwinding of a thread of traumatic memories, as sketched in *Studies on Hysteria* (Breuer & Freud 1895). And secondly, as noted, Freud was not overjoyed with the most direct application of libido theory to technique, advocated by Ferenczi (1920) and by Ferenczi and Rank (1925). The ties that bind transference neurosis to a concrete theory of libido (if that's what it was) were not so tight as to keep Freud from separately deriving ideas like transference neurosis and resolution of transference from the *strange phenomena he experienced* as he watched desire funnel itself into the psychoanalytic situation. It is this "translation" of desire into action that Freud pondered (or worried, as a dog might worry a bone) throughout *Papers on Technique*.

I have suggested that the problems Freud was dealing with had to do with such things as the relationships between past attachments and present desires, and the relationship of memories to demands – perennial, practical problems for any therapist. I would add one more problem that Freud did not lose sight of as easily as we do today. That is the problem of therapeutic action. Abend implies that Freud took catharsis as his model of treatment because it would enable him to say that a physical-ish libido is discharged in both cases. I suggest that, so far from satisfying himself with a favorite formula, Freud was anxiously scratching around in the sedate, new treatment to find some sort of human drama that could account for therapeutic action, some plausible treatment force that could be plainly accountable for radical change, something that could be compared to "the widening of consciousness" in hypnosis and "the transformation of symptoms and the affects" that followed catharsis (1904, p. 250). Freud had first-hand knowledge of these, and he was *hunting* for a therapeutic power of comparable magnitude in a nondirective therapy. That hunt would have been unnecessary if he had been satisfied to *deduce* it from libido theory. To the age-old question "How can talking help?", something resembling libido theory is always available as a "no-brainer" reply. But Freud did not quickly or glibly settle on what it was in this new, protracted, meandering, chatty, nondirective therapy that he could honestly recognize as so powerfully disruptive. And at the end of his search, what did he find? Was it the lightning bolt of transference interpretation? Was it the spectacular recoil from a

## 22 The text

blast of heavy libido? As easy as it would have been for an armchair libido philosopher to offer such tidy formulas, and acceptable as that would have been to analysts who are always willing to settle for verbal hocus-pocus in place of a theory of therapeutic action, it wouldn't satisfy Freud's personal, empirical perplexity. It would have been a device of theory, not a finding of fact. And in this case, Freud seems to have been more anxious to satisfy his curiosity than to crow about his theory, for the answer is presented as a throwaway line – the literary equivalent of talking to himself, sotto voce. Where, then, did Freud finally find the wrench he could identify as the therapeutically effective equivalent of catharsis? It was the self-sundering stress that patients endure when they force themselves to continue associating in the face of a powerful resistance (1914, p. 155). That, I submit, is the answer of a witness, not a theorist and certainly not a libido theorist.

It will be seen that I differ from Abend only in degree. Abend grants that the story starts with Freud's clinical experience, but he argues that it continues as blind adherence to libido theory in its most concrete form. I've drawn a different picture. We don't have Freud available to cross-examine so we will write the history in various ways. Much depends on how Freud's manner of expression strikes us. I have argued that Freud's technical writing does not much rely on abstract formulas (which may explain why those writings remain available for debate through the decades). I believe that in the *Papers* Freud is preoccupied with the most experience-near, interpersonal, almost physical aspects of the treatment situation, as it is felt by all practitioners.

In these papers, technical terms seem to me quite secondary to common-sense reasoning. A stereotype plate of loving, a sausage that spoils the dog race, a woman of elemental passion who knows only the logic of soup with dumplings for arguments, a priest succumbing to the still-persuasive, dying insurance salesman – this is the epistemological level of Freud's lesson. The rest seems to me a matter of observation and perplexity in the sweatshop of practice.

If you flick through the varying comments in *Papers on Technique*, you will find justification for many alternative treatment procedures. I think that reflects the depth and multidimensionality of the actual field of treatment, and the correspondingly fluctuating meaning of cardinal terms used to grasp it. (That seems to be what Freud means when he says that the aim of treatment can be equivalently formulated as the overcoming of resistance, the recovery of memory, and the resolution of the transference [1904, p. 253].) In any event, none of the contradictory images is deleted from the main texts. The analyst should analyze only resistance; the analyst should analyze "unserviceable" character traits. The analyst should analyze fantasies; the analyst should keep a patient's longings dangling before her as a lure. The analyst should interpret transference only when it is a resistance; the analyst should interpret the whole of the transference as embodying the whole neurosis. The analyst should float freely and not try to figure things out; the analyst should look for underlying complexes and make sure that he is in touch with the patient's daily life.

Is there any single bottom line? In particular, what is the bottom line as regards the role of transference interpretation? I conclude by neither disputing nor agreeing with Abend's preferred position on transference interpretation in psychoanalysis. Psychoanalytic treatment obviously embraces many types of inquiry and interaction. Our arguments usually hinge on which features we regard as unique to analysis and on how we weigh the trade-offs among different procedures. But I do suggest that Freud's early writings on technique and his familiar formulas keep certain primal issues before us, while his inconsistent theoretical terms and formulas spin around them like electrons orbiting their atom's nucleus.

In summary, Abend has given us a plausible account of a belief anchored in an antique, unscientific libido theory that owes its longevity to Freud's refusal to trade it in for his later, more cogent theory. For my part, I see Freud grappling with elementary practical questions that theory, whether early or late, could only embroider – questions about old patterns that play hide and seek with the analyst and tantalize him as he tries to figure out how to change unchanging natures. Those questions, I submit, are not answered by libido theory, or by its demise.

## REFERENCES

Abend, S. (2009). Freud, transference, and therapeutic action. *Psychoanalytic Quarterly*, 78: 871–892.

Breuer, J. & Freud, S. (1895). *Studies on Hysteria*. Standard Edition, 2.

Ferenczi, S. (1920/1950). The further development of an active therapy in psychoanalysis. In: *Further Contributions to the Theory and Therapy of Psycho-Analysis*. London: Hogarth, pp. *198–217*.

Ferenczi, S. & Rank, O. (1925). *The Development of Psycho-Analysis*, trans. C. Newton. New York, NY: Nervous & Mental Disease.

Freud, S. (1904). Freud's psycho-analytic procedure. Standard Edition, 7.

Freud, S. (1911–1915). *Papers on Technique*. Standard Edition, 12.

Freud, S. (1911). The handling of dream-interpretation in psycho-analysis. Standard Edition, 12.

Freud, S. (1912). The dynamics of transference. Standard Edition, 12.

Freud, S. (1914). Remembering, repeating and working-through. Standard Edition, 12.

Freud, S. (1916–1917). *Introductory Lectures on Psycho-Analysis, Part III, General Theory of the Neuroses*. Standard Edition, 16.

Friedman, L. (2008). A renaissance for Freud's *Papers on Technique. Psychoanalytic Quarterly*, 77: 1031–1044.

# PREFACE TO CHAPTER 2
## NOT WANTING ANYTHING FROM PATIENTS

In emphasizing the hard experiences Freud wrestled with in *Papers on Technique* I hope I have not left the impression that its title is deceptive, as though it is not at all a technical manual but simply and solely an account of Freud's own difficulty in practice, and his personal, one-time attempt to find a solution. Rather, as we follow Freud's uneasy handling of these problems, we see a larger figure emerging – it appears to be a dissection of psychoanalysis. And what's striking, making the lesson so peculiar, is that the outcome is not a stable formula but a *way of wrestling* with the problems. Finally, it dawns on us that *Papers on Technique* is, indeed, a technical manual because Freud's troubled *effort* to comprehend the various paradoxes – the effort itself – is also a model of psychoanalytic technique when it is duplicated under the gun in the treatment hour. The technique consists of keeping in mind these tensions, paradoxes and difficulties in the context of a particular patient. Here we have a profession so strange that a book of "do's" and "don't's," of admonitions to "look at things this way but also oppositely," qualifies as a description of its technique. In fact, that is probably the only kind of technical manual that could be written for psychoanalysis. Such idiosyncrasy says something about both the peculiar practice and the nature of the human mind. But that is a point I wish to make only by implication in this chapter.

In this chapter my aim is chiefly to portray the pages of the book as sequential markers in the discovery of the psychoanalytic phenomenon. In the previous chapter I argued that the psychoanalytic phenomenon is an empirical discovery, not an invention or a theoretical deduction. We will now follow the sequence of individual papers and see the unfolding quandaries that shed light on the new phenomenon. And we will take particular note of those strange attitudes of the analyst that elicit the phenomenon.

In the following survey of *Papers on Technique*, what stands out as the overarching theme is the fateful discovery of the appetitive nature of resistance – its

Not wanting anything from patients  25

positive aim – in contrast to its previously defined function of concealment. Mind you, Freud is not dealing here with resistance as an abstract, technical term; he is talking about what actually frustrates the analyst's purpose in the physical encounter.

The word, resistance, seems to violate the analyst's pledge of tolerance, and even the very idea of non-directive therapy. (See Friedman 1969; Schafer 1973.) But we see in *Papers on Technique* that resistance (in the form of transference) is what creates the analytic phenomenon. If you want to avoid seeming to "accuse" the patient of misbehavior, *Papers on Technique* will let you pin the label of resistance on the analyst. In Freud's little book, it is the analyst who is doing the resisting, quite apart from any countertransference. In effect, the analyst creates the psychoanalytic phenomenon by resisting the patient's bid for normal, social responses. The resistances of the analyst are what *Papers on Technique* is most famous for, and for which it is often condemned as stubborn, inhuman, and cruel.

The blunt fact of the matter is that Freud found himself in an antagonistic rather than a facilitating relationship with his patient, which would make it senseless to point to something in or about the patient that was not cooperating. (In an adversarial relationship, who is resisting whom?) And yet the singling out of resistance, as though it was an occasional, stubborn rebellion, would still be needed, not just to fill a role in theory, but for a purpose: The analyst's picture of a patient's resistance serves to stop him from sliding into the unanalytic (hypnotic) posture of a coach or a director of treatment. To avoid the hypnotist role, Freud found it necessary to go on *seeing* himself as facilitating a natural inclination (memory processing), even while learning the hard way that the patient's *natural* inclination was quite the reverse; namely, to seek satisfaction in the interaction. In order to keep the action from shaping up as a contest of wills, it was important for a non-directive therapist to assume that people have an autonomous (though resistible) natural inclination to process memories into consciousness as needed. That made the idea of a non-directive therapy imaginable: The analyst can retain a non-directive stance if he can imagine a natural process that parallels his own direction when a way is cleared for it. But in this non-directive treatment, clearing a way for it isn't as easy to picture as it was in the memory-retrieval model. If resistance is a matter of seeking as well as hiding, an analyst must also be prepared to fend off the pressure to respond non-analytically. One must find a way to transfer to the patient the analyst's own paradox. How can a patient be induced to look dispassionately at what he is passionately involved in? What would incline him to split his sensorium, and even his will?

Unlike many later analysts, Freud is here unwilling to fudge the issue by simply naming a mental "function" that intervenes as a *deus ex machina* to serve the analyst's purpose (such as an observing ego). For Freud to be confident that he was not acting like a hypnotist, he would have to locate a genuine *motive* inside the patient for deflecting his own effort. (Freud's identification of the patient's incentive, incorporated in the original notion of "working through," is discussed in Chapter Three.)

**26** The text

A larger question is posed by the new "normalizing" view of transference and resistance. Freud acknowledged in *Papers* that patients are simply behaving naturally in reaction to the analytic situation. The question of how *natural* behavior can provoke change in a non-directive therapy will henceforth bedevil psychoanalysis. The therapeutic action of psychoanalysis includes a force entirely new to the great tradition of ancient and honorable talking cures listed in Jerome Frank's (1961) famous common factors of efficacy. (And see Friedman 1975.)

Having found that patients use the analyst's special interests for purposes of resistance, Freud gradually comes to realize that what patients naturally aim for is a relationship with him, and *that* is what's resisting the treatment (Friedman 1988, pp. 14–37). We might say that Freud discovered that the psychoanalytic phenomenon is what happens when a patient can no longer "manipulate" the analyst, (i.e., act on him the way people normally communicate). In the psychoanalytic phenomenon, both parties can see the unconscious come to life, watch resistance and transference overlap in a new light, and appreciate the unconscious as something more dramatically personal than an archive of traumatic incidents. But, as Freud reported in his first paper (see Chapter One), this psychoanalytic phenomenon depends on the analyst being able to suspend his wishes, so as to immunize himself against "manipulation." Freud therefore accepts whatever the patient is doing as *memories*, not doings. Accordingly, instead of just fending off bids for a social relationship he will instead think of what comes to his attention as free, naturally occurring offerings set out by the patient for both parties to work on with the aim of broadening the field of consciousness. The elusive nature of psychoanalytic treatment becomes tangible in the particular twist Freud gives the old technical terms so they will bolster his grip on the paradoxical elements of the new psychoanalytic phenomenon. The terms are given new duties and their meanings shift accordingly. They include memory, resistance, transference, the unconscious, the relation of past to future, the analyst's behavior, discipline and attention, the plan and rationale of analytic treatment. There is no fanfare, but it is not a small revolution.

What finally emerges is a strange scene: We have a therapist exerting personal influence while thinking he is merely witnessing his patient. We see an active analyst who feels himself to be passive. We watch a therapist begin by opposing his patient, and end by inching toward seduction. Finally, in working out these problems, Freud squarely faces up to the ethical precariousness of such a profession, and commiserates with his students to whom, in conclusion, he tacitly offers his comradely commiseration.

## REFERENCES

Frank, J. (1961/1963). *Persuasion and Healing: A Comparative Study of Psychotherapy*. 2nd ed. Baltimore, MD: The Johns Hopkins Press.

Friedman, L. (1969). The therapeutic alliance. *International Journal of Psychoanalysis*, 50: 139–153.

Friedman, L. (1975). Elements of the therapeutic situation: The psychology of the beginning encounter. In: *American Handbook of Psychiatry*. 2nd ed., Vol. 5. Eds D. X. Freedman & J. E. Dyrud. New York, NY: Basic Books, pp. 95–113.

Friedman, L. (1988). *The Anatomy of Psychotherapy*. Hillsdale, NJ: Analytic Books.

Schafer, R. (1973). The idea of resistance. *International Journal of Psychoanalysis*, 54: 259–285

# 2

# A FOSTERING KIND OF INTEREST WITH NO ATTACHED REQUEST

Neither his own later theorizing nor subsequent generations of psychoanalytic practice have elbowed Freud's early *Papers on Technique* (1911–1915) into obsolescence. Rich in detailed wisdom, spoken in that irresistibly congenial voice, this work is probably our most succinct definition of the psychoanalytic profession. But it is also puzzling in many ways.

Before it appeared, Freud defaulted again and again on his promise of imminent publication and discarded several initial compilations, as though an unspoken problem held him back (Gay 1988). What he finally wrote does not look like a technical handbook. In some ways it resembles a postural armature for analysts rather than a treatise on technique, although, as we shall see, that appearance is deceptive.

One thing is certain: if this work is a technical manual, it is a most peculiar one. It does not apply a settled theory to the aims of treatment. On the contrary, as we follow the discussion we become aware that a major theory shift is underway, assimilating an old treatment paradigm to a new one. Before our very eyes a scheme for retrieving memories is gradually overlayered with a plan for integrating wishes.

## TWO ASPECTS OF TRANSFERENCE

For the moment I will skip over the first and least ambitious paper in the series, "The handling of dream-interpretation in psycho-analysis" (1911). The second paper, "The dynamics of transference" (1912a) is the strangest, and its strangeness sets the stage for the work as a whole. It begins with the insistence that no matter how indistinguishable transference is from real love, "the part [it] plays in the treatment can only be explained if we enter into its relations with resistance" (p. 104); but the paper ends with the declaration that the phenomena of transference "do us the inestimable service of making the patient's hidden and forgotten erotic impulses immediate and manifest. For when all is said and done, it is impossible to destroy anyone *in absentia* or *in effigie"* (p. 108).

Between the first assertion that even if it is love, transference is chiefly important to treatment as resistance, and the second assertion that because it is love, it gives treatment access to its object, Freud leaves a record in this one short essay of persistent vacillation between his two treatment paradigms. I will suggest a reason why he did not simply switch from one paradigm to the other, erasing the first before publication.

## THE OLD THEORY: STUDIES ON HYSTERIA

The old treatment paradigm is a version of the grandfather model proposed in Studies on Hysteria (Breuer & Freud 1893–1895). In that work Freud suggested that the hysterical mind contains partially isolated complexes of repressed patho-genic memories and ideas, encapsulated in concentric layers of related memories and ideas which are so arranged that the more accessible to consciousness are the more deceptive. The treating physician and the patient are both engaged in freeing up the underlying memories so that the sequestered memories may rejoin the natural march of ideas into consciousness, come into contact with each other, and "discharge" themselves.

It happened that Freud's patients sometimes developed romantic feelings for him as they worked to free up their memories. Faithful to his model, Freud believed that those romantic feelings were just like all the other deceptive associations among the nexus of ideas marching toward consciousness, except that these "transference" associations had slipped out of their intrapsychic network and attached themselves by mistake to the person of the analyst. Freud wrote that the romantic feelings disappeared as soon as they were directed to their proper associative links. At that time Freud used the term, transference, in a simple, literal sense. Transference was simply an occasional, unimportant, and neutral slip. (This seems to be the meaning of transference that connects most directly with its prepsychoanalytic meaning. See Kravis 1992.)

A little more experience must have quickly taught Freud that transference is neither occasional nor accidental and that, far from being easily redirected, its power is almost beyond belief. By 1915 he will warn beginning analysts that the tasks of interpreting and dealing with reproductions of the repressed are as nothing compared with the difficulties encountered in managing the transference, which are "the only really serious difficulties he has to meet" (1915, p. 159).

## THE MISSION OF PAPERS ON TECHNIQUE

What *Studies on Hysteria* had to say about transference could not withstand the test of even a short span of time. No honest practitioner could enjoy such complacency about transference for very long. But in addition to supplying an education in difficulty, the passage of time also brought an increasingly sophisticated account of

**30** The text

mental functioning. In the interval between Studies on Hysteria and *Papers on Technique* Freud's thinking gave a wish-oriented tilt to a theory that, in the earlier work, had been tilting toward ideas. We might suppose that Freud would want to update his concept of transference and all the rest of treatment theory.

Which of these factors generated *Papers on Technique?* Was Freud trying to square his account with the hard facts of experience? Or did he revise the description of treatment used in Studies on Hysteria because it was based on an obsolete, idea-processing model of the mind, now upstaged by his new model which emphasized lurking wishes (Interpretation of Dreams, 1900) and enduring attachments and desires (Three Essays on the Theory of Sexuality, 1905b)?

We naturally assume that Freud would be concerned about the mismatch between his old, ventilating rationale of treatment and his new, appetitive theory of the mind. We suppose that he would feel obliged to map the new picture of the mind onto the rationale of treatment when he next wrote about that subject. We expect *Papers on Technique* to be a systematic tidying-up of treatment theory; we are prepared for a theoretical next step. Expecting that, we find ourselves in confusion. The great puzzle of *Papers on Technique* is that Freud refuses to use that work for the systematic purpose we expect.

*Papers on Technique* shows us a changing theory but – against all expectation – it turns out not to be a programmed revision. I suggest that Freud's alterations in *Papers on Technique* were inspired by practice difficulties: he revises theory only in order to help with problems of practice and only insofar as the revision helps to solve those problems, and no further. Systematizing for its own sake is avoided. We must ask why.

In answer to this question a disappointingly trivial possibility suggests itself: Students of Freud cannot escape the impression that he found treatment the least interesting aspect of psychoanalysis. We can speculate about why that was so. Most likely the challenge of treatment was overshadowed by his larger ambition to be a conquistador – the discoverer of a new world of mind. And some part of his indifference may have been the result of his native wisdom that let him understand treatment too easily and too "instinctively," making it seem unworthy of serious effort and pride: Freud appears to have become an "old" therapist all too soon.

Whatever the reason, Freud's relative indifference to treatment theory requires us to consider the possibility that he thought it unnecessary to formally revise his 1895 picture of treatment because he knew that the hammer of common, clinical hardship would do a good enough job of pounding out the old views to fit the new, appetitive theory of the mind. Some weight must be given to this possibility because in the years between Studies on Hysteria and *Papers on Technique* Freud was experiencing the direct impact of his patients' strivings and becoming viscerally aware that he was not just witnessing their memories. For instance, in an 1897 letter to Fliess, Freud identified resistance as a distinct (and distinctly unattractive) subpersonality representing "the child's former character, the degenerate character," which is marked by that frustrated, infantile "longing" which, if unrepressed, would have rendered the patient a "so-called degenerative [case]" (Masson

1985, p. 274). Of course, these words must have been shaped by the theory he was working on (the theory of sexuality), but Freud's tune in this passage conveys an experience of unwelcome pressure. And if we are deaf to the tune, we can find it set to words in Freud's statement that the patient who was initially "such a good, noble human being becomes mean, untruthful, or obstinate, a malingerer ..." (p. 274). Freud would know that even if he did not revise his theory, analysts would soon enough learn that there was more to resistance than silence.

Was Freud, then, content to let the common-sense experience of the encounter bring treatment theory up to date? That is an unlikely explanation for his non-chalance. Although he might well have assumed that any prolonged experience with patients would independently correct the overly sanguine teachings of Studies on Hysteria, one would have expected Freud to be so proud of how specifically his new theory of wishes predicted the actual details of what he was discovering in practice, that only a significant restraining motive could keep him from publicly showing the fit and utility of his new ideas, as he did privately in a letter to Fliess in December 1895 (Masson 1985), where he wrote:

> A hysterical attack is not a discharge but an action; and it retains the original characteristic of every action – of being a means to the reproduction of plea-sure ... aimed at another person – but mostly at the prehistoric, unforgettable other person who is never equaled by anyone later.
>
> *(pp. 212–213, original emphasis)*

And five months later, again to Fliess,

> A second important piece of insight tells me that the psychic structures which, in hysteria, are affected by repression are not in reality memories – since no one indulges in memory activity without a motive – but impulses that derive from primal scenes.
>
> *(p. 239, original emphasis)*

A few weeks later he wrote that "symptoms ... are the fulfillment of a wish" (p. 251, original emphasis).

The 1897 letter to Fliess (cited above, p. 568), which shows Freud's personal, atti-tudinal reaction to resistance, also emphasizes the impressive therapeutic leverage he obtained from his new theory of the mind. The new theory allowed him to revisualize resistance both as sexual ("longing") and as the person's actual (infantile) personality – not a stubbornness related to sex but sex and personality themselves. Freud had dis-covered that the secret to clinical success with resistance is to acknowledge its appetitive nature – its positive desires – and not to regard it as a shutting down.

Thus, while Freud was preparing The Interpretation of Dreams, he was also rethinking patients in treatment. And his students who read his new libido theory went on to explore its implications for treatment. We see that direct effect in the work of Ferenczi and Rank (1924) and Sachs (1925).

32　The text

But even after 15 years of rethinking treatment in terms of his new theory of the mind, Freud did not undertake to formally and publicly revise it in his *Papers on Technique*. Specifically, he did not promptly paste an up-to-date, appetitive theory of treatment over the old, ideational one found in Studies on Hysteria. For example, he did not publicly announce what he had privately written to Fliess, that both theory and practice show that resistance is not a maneuver but an infantile personality. In *Papers on Technique*, Freud is not a theoretician reworking old concepts for the sake of consistency; he is a clinician who has met trouble and, like all clinicians in such circumstances, is calling on both old and new theory for all the help he can get. What trouble had he encountered?

## "THE DYNAMICS OF TRANSFERENCE"

The problem presents itself to Freud chiefly in the phenomenon of transference. As he works on the problem his conception of transference changes. In Studies on Hysteria, he had described transference as an insignificant mistake. By 1912, writing "The dynamics of transference," he has to grant that transference is no more mistaken than any other love. My point is that the revision occurs in the course of trying to solve a problem. It is of secondary importance to Freud in this work that the revision is demanded by his new theory of wish and love. What concerns him is that, in practice, transference love cannot be handled by the analyst as though it were an error. His beginning problem in these papers is an uncomfortable piece of empirical knowledge: Freud had discovered that a treatment designed to aid memory finds itself mainly tied up in difficulties of love. One finds that the transference is the guts of treatment trouble. That is a portentous discovery because, as it happens, what one makes out of the fact will decide one's model of treatment.

Faced with the brute fact that transference is intimately connected to trouble in treatment, Freud calls on theory to explain why that should be so. In "The dynamics of transference" he applies libido theory and scrutinizes the result: Libido, besides being frustrated by the circumstances of the patient's life, fundamentally resists new attachments ("The libido ... had always been under the influence of the attraction of ... unconscious complexes ... and it entered on a regressive course because the attraction of reality had diminished" [1912a, p. 103]). Freud reasons that, whenever analysis threatens to disrupt the patient's infantile scene, the hidden libido is transferred to any "suitable" (resembling) features of the analyst as a last-ditch "compromise between [the demands of resistance] and those of the work of investigation" (p. 103). In other words, under pressure of novelty, conservative forces use compromise formation to hold onto earlier aims. Perhaps this is analogous to the way a dream finds a day residue to express a repressed content.

Such a situation would seem to have three aspects: if the hidden libido which was attached to archaic objects becomes associated with the current image of the analyst, we might expect that (1) its archaic meaning will be masked, (2) its aim will be (obscurely) fulfilled, and (3) the patient's attitude toward the analyst will be changed. But as yet Freud is not equally interested in all of these consequences.

More than halfway through "The dynamics of transference" he still seems to be working with his earliest model of treatment, according to which disguised ideas and memories spontaneously file into consciousness when the patient's affection for the doctor neutralizes their blockage. Because he is thinking in terms of the memory-retrieval paradigm, Freud makes no comment about the implication that transference is (1) a disguise and (2) a covert satisfaction; he probably takes it for granted that all ideas are more or less disguised, and that satisfactions come and go with memories. What is important for treatment, according to the memory-retrieval paradigm, is that memories and ideas should keep marching into consciousness where they can be deciphered. And that is why Freud's only interest at this point is the third implication – that the transference compromise hinders cooperation with the analyst. In other words, what is important to Freud is that the transferred libido affects the patient's attitude toward the analyst in a way that stops him from reporting ideas and memories.

In writing this, I have deliberately oversimplified Freud's earliest views. He was always aware that he needed more from his patients than their memories. But during the reign of the memory-retrieval paradigm, the rest of the patient's work was referred to parenthetically. We will see his attitude change drastically within the space of two pages of "The dynamics of transference," but his change of attitude will not lead him to reject the older paradigm.

That is because, even though his new libido-theoretical formula – the formula that transference is a compromise between the work of investigation and the purpose of resistance – gives Freud potential access to almost every view of transference that will later be developed, the way he uses this formula at any given moment naturally depends on what at the moment he takes to be "the work of investigation." According to the memory-retrieval paradigm, which is what he is using in the first half of "The dynamics of transference," the work of investigation consists of letting ideas and memories rise into consciousness. So Freud at this point naturally thought of the transference compromise as a "stoppage" (specifically, a stoppage that exploits a resemblance between the analyst and old imagoes).

Again, this is oversimplifying Freud's view. What he actually writes is, "transference is carried out; it produces the next association, and announces itself by indications of a resistance – by a stoppage, for instance" (1912a, p. 103). "For instance" implies that resistance can show itself in other ways than by stoppage. But my oversimplification is also Freud's momentary oversimplification, as witness his next question: "How does it come about that transference is so admirably suited to be a means of resistance?" (p. 104). That this question remains outstanding shows that Freud is still thinking of resistance simply as stoppage; otherwise he would have considered the question answered. After all, he had just stated that transference disguises its source and (partly) expresses an infantile wish, and that would be explanation enough of how transference is so admirably suited to be a resistance if "resistance" has the broad meaning that it eventually acquired. But Freud knew he had left a question unanswered since he was thinking of resistance as a stoppage of thoughts, and he had not explained why transference regularly stops thoughts. All

**34** The text

he had done was to report that a thought about the analyst is followed by a stoppage.

Not only is Freud right in considering the question unanswered, it turns out that it is unanswerable on theoretical grounds. As a bare formula for intrapsychic equilibrium in general, transference cannot account for such a particular behavior as a refusal to talk. Only an affect would be specific enough to even roughly suggest a predictable behavior, and for that reason Freud says, "The answer to the question which has been repeated so often in these pages is not to be reached by further reflection but by what we discover when we examine individual transference-resistances occurring during treatment" (p. 105). What he finds in the consulting room is, in effect, that some transferences are marked by antagonism and some by unconscious, erotic conflict – and Freud seems to want to rely on common sense to explain why these make a patient uncooperative.

Common sense agrees that an angry patient is likely to refuse the analyst's request. But common sense does not tell us that repressed, erotic impulses regularly silence a patient. Freud's forays lead him only deeper into the woods. Repressed erotic impulses will not automatically show themselves in any single action, such as silence, and Freud knew it.

That is not to say that Freud was wrong in suggesting that patients may use repressed, erotic impulses to produce stoppage. In a sense, this hypothesis anticipates the one he will later use in the theory of signal anxiety. The hypothesis is that the patient employs a possibly irrelevant (1912a. p. 104, n.) sample of repressed, erotic attachment to warn himself away from a dangerous exposure of his major libidinal investments. And on a purely observational level every therapist has seen patients deploy troubled sexuality to halt free development of other awareness.

But what is important for our purpose, and even more important to Freud in "The dynamics of transference," is that, as stated, his theory simply is not true. As stated, the theory is that repressed erotic impulses are peculiarly suited to stop the patient's remembering and reporting. But repressed erotic impulses are no more useful for stopping reports than they are for starting them or continuing them. In 1911 it is reported that Freud told a meeting of The Vienna Psychoanalytic Society, "The transference which otherwise – so long as it is in the unconscious – serves the healing process, becomes conscious to [a fleeing patient] in order that she may be able to stay away" (Nunberg & Federn 1974, p. 204, italics added). And in "Remembering, repeating and working-through" (1914) he indicates that during the phase when transferences become "hostile or unduly intense and therefore in need of repression, remembering at once gives way to acting out" (p. 151, italics added), implying that transference tends to convey such sensitive information that it becomes the matter protected rather than a way of protecting the matter. Furthermore, by repeating his thematic question, Freud has already indicated that the inclusion of repressed desires in the transferential compromise formation does not explain why it results so regularly in stoppage. Finally, it stands to reason that if repressed, erotic impulses can be counted on by themselves to bring reporting to a halt, the patient would not need to invoke any resistance. The resistance would

A Fostering Interest **35**

simply be those repressed erotic impulses that the analyst is seeking, a conclusion very close to the one Freud reaches at the end of the essay.

It looks as though this attempt to explain the connection between transference and stoppage had reached a dead-end. And I suspect that Freud knew it, since he suddenly shifts his attention from the phenomenon of stoppage (so central in the memory-retrieval model) to the stormy, self-righteous, demandingness of a patient under the influence of transference resistance, whom he describes as

> flung out of his real relation to the doctor ... at liberty ... to disregard the fundamental rule of psycho-analysis ... [forgetting] the intentions with which he started the treatment [and regarding] with indifference logical arguments and conclusions which only a short time before had made a great impression on him ....
>
> *(1912a, p. 107)*

The patient is acting as adversary in a "struggle between the doctor and the patient, between intellect and instinctual life, between understanding and seeking to act ... . It is on that field," Freud writes, "that the victory must be won ..." (p. 108). With this dramatic picture, the paper concludes fast and powerfully, shaking completely out of the reader's mind the whole preceding discussion of stoppage and leaving only the famous, vivid, digressive afterthought: "[I]t is impossible to destroy anyone *in absentia* or *in effigie*" (p. 108).

It might be objected that the paper had been building to this conclusion; that the original topic was not stoppage but resistance, which "announces itself by a stoppage, for instance" (p. 103). It might be argued that in his peroration Freud was simply turning to another, even more important, "instance" of the effect of resistance, for example, "acting in." It is important to decide whether that is the right way to read "The dynamics of transference," because reading it that way teaches a very different lesson than the one I shall propose.

## WHAT IS THE RELATIONSHIP BETWEEN THE END OF "THE DYNAMICS OF TRANSFERENCE" AND ITS BEGINNING?

Freud introduces this last section of the paper by writing "[W]e must turn our attention to another aspect of the same subject" (1912a, p. 107). After painting his vivid picture of transference-resistance, he declares that anyone who has observed it will "look for an explanation of his impression in other factors besides those that have already been adduced [i.e., besides its usefulness in stopping free association]" (p. 107). We might call this "other aspect" of transference its positive side. This aspect is not the absence of an action (stoppage, silence), but a florid action itself, a passionate demand. It is this demand that makes the patient's unconscious impulses "contemporaneous and real" (p. 108) and gives the analyst something more than an effigy to deal with. Transference may be the perfect resistance insofar as it brings reporting to a halt, but it is also the necessary (and troublesome) vehicle conveying unconscious material into the field of analytic operation.

Now, if Freud is here winding up his original explanations of the relationship of transference to resistance, why would he call this last consideration "another side" of the issue? Isn't the patient's passionate demand just what it means for the libido to attach itself to the analyst in a disguising and obstructive fashion – the definition of transference-resistance already given? Rather than "another side," the "contemporaneous and real" passion of transference seems to be just a more graphic elaboration of this formula. In fact, we have noted above that in his earlier letter (1897) to Fliess (Masson 1985) Freud had painted this picture not as "another side" of the issue, but as a definition of resistance!

Suppose that Freud simply wanted at last to gather up the other two implications of libido theory – that transference not only alters the patient's attitude and interferes with his cooperativeness, but also disguises repressed wishes and partially fulfills them. Suppose Freud had noted that those aspects, though largely irrelevant to a memory-retrieval theory of treatment, point to another theory of treatment more consistent with The Interpretation of Dreams and Three Essays on the Theory of Sexuality. Suppose, in other words, that theoretical completeness had inspired "The dynamics of transference," and his intention was to revise his account of treatment and transference so that it would conform with those landmark books. If that had been the case, he could have solved the puzzles of transference and resistance without all the backing and filling we find in this paper. All he needed to do was bring what he wrote on the last page to the beginning of the essay:

> The doctor tries to compel [the patient] to fit these emotional impulses into the nexus of the treatment and of his life-history, to submit them to intellectual consideration and to understand them in the light of their psychical value.
>
> *(1912a, p. 108)*

From that description of what the doctor is trying to do it would have been instantly clear that the doctor can be thwarted in many ways. Putting that definition at the beginning of his paper, Freud could have advised us right away not to visualize resistance narrowly as stoppage but broadly as a refusal to fit emotional impulses into the nexus of the treatment and life-history, or a refusal to submit them to intellectual consideration, or to understand them in the light of their psychical value, a refusal that is neatly embodied in transference. Indeed, after all is said, the paper leaves us with no doubt that the conservativeness of a patient (his resistance) lies not in his refusing a procedure but in his avoiding a necessary attitude. In effect, Freud succeeds in tracking down non-cooperation from its spoor in non-productivity to its lair in non-integration. And yet despite that net accomplishment, most of the paper labors to connect transference and stoppage. In short, this paper resists being read as a systematic effort to catalogue the meanings of transference.

I believe that the only way to understand the structural consistency of "The dynamics of transference" is to take Freud seriously when he says that in discussing passionate transference wishes, he is turning away from the resistance significance of transference (which he is still thinking of as stoppage) and turning toward another aspect of transference which he thinks of as a type of behavior – a treatment "difficulty" that accompanies resistance. In other words, whatever Freud's purpose is in *Papers on Technique*, it is a purpose that is served more specifically by the memory-retrieval paradigm and its definition of resistance than by theoretical consistency, which would simply call for a different definition of resistance.

Our task is to discover that purpose. When we know Freud's purpose, we will know why he declined to build a new theory of resistance and a new theory of treatment entirely out of the effigy-killing material contained in the final two pages of "The dynamics of transference," and I think we learn some other useful lessons in the process.

## WHAT WAS FREUD'S SITUATION AT THE TIME?

Freud's situation should help us decipher his purpose, and here I will venture my own imaginings: Freud began his design of psychoanalytic treatment with a search for memories, but painful experience finally made him doubt that patients were pounding on him so relentlessly just in order not to remember something. A theoretician at his desk might stubbornly stick to that doctrine, but, as Freud indicates (1912a, p. 107), no one on the scene could believe it.

I imagine Freud to have been pondering the fact that treatment, as it is experienced in real life, cannot be visualized as clearing the way for a spontaneous welling up of memories. It is not memories that well up; it is wishful efforts. (Transference is always obtruding itself.) The analyst's job is not to facilitate a natural surfacing of memories; he does not free memories. His struggle is to persuade the patient to remember – a persuasion that is just part of a larger effort to engage the patient in a reflective activity. In this struggle what opposes the analyst is the patient's preference for a non-reflective action (the fulfillment of unintegrated wishes). Strictly speaking, then, although it is not something that Freud spelled out, what "resistance" resists is the analyst, not the emergence of memories (cf., Gill 1982). The analyst's persuasion is not exercised on behalf of the patient's frustrated, natural process. The analyst is not, in this first instance, an ally. (Needless to say, the later development of ego theory and split-ego hypotheses will complicate the formula [cf. Friedman 1992], but I think dynamic understanding of how and why the analytic enterprise is taken over by the patient has progressed since 1912 more in words than in ideas.)

By itself, this discovery would logically have led Freud to renounce the ideas we find in the main body of "The dynamics of transference," redefine resistance as the patient's natural disinclination to be lured away from infantile wishes, and dispel the mystery of why transference is such a perfect resistance by simply pointing out that transference is the perseverative reach for a compartmentalized childhood goal, inherently opposed to contemplation, synthesis, and re-contextualization.

Because the theory does not move in this logical fashion, we should look for a practical incentive that would motivate Freud to cling to his earlier view – the

**38** The text

view that resistance is a force opposing a natural inclination to remember, and that transference is the chief resistance because it is the best incentive for not remembering, tacking on as a mere addendum the discovery that the desires embodied in transference are important to treatment in their own right, and that resistance is a wish to act, and not just to be left alone.

## DIVIDED CONSCIOUSNESS: A GOOD REASON TO KEEP THE OLD MEMORY-RETRIEVAL MODEL

I believe that, compared with the newer model of attitude-induction, the memory-retrieval model has an important advantage that persuaded Freud to preserve it together with its narrow view of resistance. The advantage can be described in several ways: (1) The memory-retrieval model allows the analyst to see himself as relatively passive and therefore objective, since his main action is blocking a blocker (resistance).[1] (2) According to the memory-retrieval model, the analyst is on the side of a natural process, not the inventor and manipulator of an artificial process. (3) For that reason the analyst can fit himself into the traditional role of the physician who accepts help from a limited, natural rapport in order to foster normally occurring healing processes. In contrast, the analyst of the new model does not deal with normally emerging memories but deliberately encourages the unusual elaboration of profound wishes and enlarges and sustains the patient's personal attachment, something that would be considered unethical by other physicians. (Freud faces that fact frankly in the last of the *Papers on Technique*, "Observations on transference-love" [1915].) (4) The fundamental rule, which is the linchpin of Freud's technique, was invented for the memory-retrieval model, and the memory-retrieval model gives the fundamental rule its simple reasonableness, allowing it to be assigned and accepted as a rule. (5) The belief that resistance-free memories appear spontaneously at the defile of consciousness is a useful tool even as a myth. Like a Buddhist mandala – a diagram that guides the viewer into an altered state of consciousness – the picture of thoughts and memories parading in front of one's grandstand is a schematism that the patient can use to divide his consciousness. He can parade and watch at the same time. The myth was already effective in the first cases of Studies on Hysteria (Breuer & Freud 1893–1895). Breuer's patient, Anna O., invented an elaborate version of the myth for her own use.

These advantages converge on that last consideration, which I believe is the decisive one. Ever since its inception psychoanalytic treatment has been characterized by the division of consciousness. I believe that in order to promote the division of consciousness, Freud found it useful to keep defining resistance as a blockage of naturally emerging memories and memory-related ideas, even though he had discovered that what he was dealing with had the character of demand rather than the quality of memory and forgetting..[2]

Studies on Hysteria had provided an image of a naturally rising order of memories, and that remained an invaluable prop for the analyst who has to coach his patient in the difficult act of reflecting on purposes while speaking without purpose. It would be hard to describe, define, advise, or accept this basic analytic procedure if one lost touch with the early memory-retrieval model.

In other words, the memory-retrieval model is an image of disinterested reporting. I suggest that the reason so much of "The dynamics of transference" is devoted to the memory-retrieval paradigm is that its mission is to prevent the impressive phenomenon of passionate transference from overwhelming the image of – the confidence in – the demand for – disinterested reporting.

If this hypothesis is correct, one might imagine Freud's thoughts to have progressed in the following way as he moved through the argument presented in "The dynamics of transference": "I see that transference always lies behind treatment difficulty. I think it's an excuse for the difficulty. Yes, I'm sure it's an excuse, but why do patients keep using that particular excuse? I guess it's a good excuse because it is a small, vivid sample of their genuine reason for noncooperation. But patients seem too frantically dedicated to that excuse for it to be merely an example of what they're afraid of. Actually, I have to admit that transference is not an excuse at all: it is a basic demand which is honestly opposed to our effort, and because it is honest, we must encourage it. But let's still say that it's also an excuse, because then we can counter the transference demand with our own demand in the form of the fundamental rule, persuade the patient (just as we used to) that our demand is actually his wish (i.e., we only want his ideas to follow their normal course), and thereby transform the transference into an excuse for holding himself up."[3]

## THE IMPLICIT, NEW THEORY OF TREATMENT

As the argument in *Papers on Technique* proceeds, a new goal of treatment appears. The new goal is derived from the merger of two theoretical models. In the first model – the world of Studies on Hysteria – treatment is memory-retrieval. It is a hunt for forgotten events and unintegrated memories, pursued in partnership with a patient who, though he may be discouraged by the pain and difficulty of the search, obtrudes no other enduring purpose. The new model of treatment that Freud is superimposing in these papers is a hunt for inflexible wishes, undertaken against the will of a patient who is motivated in other directions. The patient wants something else from the analyst than a cure, and his other wish is not just to be left alone. The patient is not simply torn between discovery and concealment. The analyst is not the only persuader in the room.

## ADJUSTMENTS REQUIRED BY THE NEW THEORY

The new hybrid model affects all aspects of treatment, and *Papers on Technique* follows out its influence. To be sure, the work includes many useful, miscellaneous suggestions. But there is an observable continuity: In one crucial area after another, Freud is finding a way to think in terms of the earlier theory of treatment

**40** The text

(ventilating memories) while heading toward the new treatment goal (the integrating of freshly enlivened wishes). Thus he is required to redefine repressed memory in terms of persisting desires. And then, as we have seen, he must redefine resistance so that it suggests revelation. Next he has to touch up the picture of psychoanalytic integration so that it portrays enactment without losing its family resemblance to remembering.

## FIRST PAPER: "THE HANDLING OF DREAM-INTERPRETATION IN PSYCHO-ANALYSIS"

The central message of "The handling of dream-interpretation in psycho-analysis" (1911) is that the analyst cannot afford to make dreams dear to himself any more than he can afford to make himself hostage to other withholdable or distracting material. We also find practical arguments for not dwelling overmuch on dreams, such as the danger that prolonged dream analysis might displace fresher material. But the familiar theme shared with the rest of *Papers on Technique* is the need for disciplined heedlessness on the part of both patient and analyst, the obligation to maintain a not-caring attitude, the avoidance of goal-directed attention, and the stifling in the analyst of any wish that the patient might satisfy other than obedience to the fundamental rule.

## THIRD and FOURTH PAPERS: "RECOMMENDATIONS TO PHYSICIANS PRACTISING PSYCHO-ANALYSIS" AND "ON BEGINNING THE TREATMENT"

The commitment to passive receptivity and the forswearing of goals and ambitions by both patient and analyst is discussed further in "Recommendations to physicians practising psycho-analysis" (1912b) and "On beginning the treatment" (1913). These two papers describe how the patient is encouraged by the fundamental rule to abandon wishful action and discover the peculiar skill of experiencing passionate interests dispassionately. (We might compare the data obtained in this way with memories recollected in tranquility.)

## FIFTH PAPER: "REMEMBERING, REPEATING AND WORKING-THROUGH"

The following paper, "Remembering, repeating and working-through" (1914), describes a very different kind of experience, parallel to the first but with memories recollected in anything but tranquility. In this paper we are told that strivings may be considered memories, represented as a compulsion to repeat, and moreover that striving is indeed the way that memories are most likely to appear in treatment. "As long as the patient is in treatment he cannot escape from the compulsion to repeat ..." (p. 150). In this paper, even the old stoppage is considered to be a memory in the form of repetition (p. 150). ("He is silent and declares that nothing occurs to him. This, of course, is merely a repetition of a homosexual attitude which comes to the fore as a resistance against remembering anything" [p. 150].) But the memory paradigm remains a necessary orienting paradigm in treatment even if it does not describe what actually happens.

> For [the physician], remembering in the old manner – reproduction in the psychical field – is the aim to which he adheres, even though he knows that such an aim cannot be achieved in the new technique.
>
> *(p. 153)*

Not only does this paper revise the meaning of memories, making them seem more like wishes, it effectively strips individual memories of their role as separate agents. That is, the revision does not simply reassign individual memories to individual wishes. Wishes, having amplified the meaning of memories, now present themselves as aspects of a striving person, or part of the person's personality, or part of his neurosis. Memory is now seen as a facet of a general structure of idea and wish.[4]

## THE IMPLICIT, NEW THEORY OF RESISTANCE

The healing movement in treatment used to be the march of memories and related ideas into consciousness, and, accordingly, resistance was pictured as the force that stopped that movement (Freud 1904, p. 251). The new theory holds that the natural flow is not toward memory per se but toward unmodified enactment. (I overstate the case for the moment to highlight the shift in theory.) What now, according to this theory, is the resisting force that must be overcome? Logically, it would be the force of the unconscious wishes themselves. Implicit in the new theory is the doctrine that the resistance is the wishes themselves in their unintegrated form. Or perhaps it would be better to say that it is the tendency of the wishes to express themselves without integrative modification, or that resistance is a bad attitude in respect to recontextualization, or even that resistance is the patient as he is. (In view of the fact that this implication is never explicitly published, we are surprised to see how explicit Freud had already made it in 1897, in the letter to Fliess cited on p. 568 above.)

## THE NEW THEORY OF CURATIVE WORK

Since for all practical purposes resistance now means something different than it did in the old theory, the work needed to overcome it must also be viewed differently. As we have noted, the analyst's job is no longer to clear the way for upwardly pressing memories. Rather, the analyst is required to encourage a divided awareness in the patient, separating active aspirations from passive observation. The effort toward the double awareness is called working through.

> One must allow the patient time to become more conversant with the resistance that is unknown to him, to work through it, to overcome it, by

**42**  The text

continuing, in defiance of it, the analytic work according to the fundamental rule of analysis. Only when the resistance is at its height can the analyst, working in common with his patient, discover the repressed instinctual impulses which are feeding the resistance …

(1914, p. 155 and p. 155, n.). (Pace Strachey, I use Freud's revision of the first sentence. I discuss Strachey's refusal to accept this in Chapter 3.)

Just as wishes replace memories in the new theory of treatment, the act of working through replaces the act of remembering: instead of recovering memories simpliciter, treatment cultivates current wishes and finds memories that fit them. (Freud wrote that working through in psychoanalysis performs the function that catharsis performs in hypnosis.)

## NEW PROBLEMS OF PASSIVITY AND THE NEW FUNCTION OF THE FUNDAMENTAL RULE

Working through is simply adherence to the fundamental rule insofar as it operates against resistance. So it is not surprising that the implicit change in the meaning of resistance gives a new significance to the fundamental rule. Let us examine that change now.

The defining characteristic of the fundamental rule is disciplined passivity, actively utilized. As a step toward the active uncovering and identification of memories, the fundamental rule requires, first, a quietistic passivity in both analyst and patient. The passivity required of the patient is explicit in the rule. That of the analyst is implicit: In effect, the analyst suppresses all other wishes save that the patient follow the fundamental rule. He asks no love gratifications. He suspends his wish to conquer knowledge frontiers (there is also a heuristic principle in that, of course). He does not try to impress the patient or inspire him. He does not seek confirmation of his kindness in being empathic. (He is like a surgeon doing his job in a humble, matter-of-fact fashion, aspiring to no role that could be denied him.) He asks only one thing: that the patient follow the fundamental rule. One notes that it is only through the fundamental rule that the patient can please the analyst.

Since the fundamental rule originated in the earlier memory-retrieval model, it carried with it the notion of a built-in order of recall. The fundamental rule was tailored to suit a supposedly predetermined march of memories, which both patient and analyst could witness passively in line with their mutual, active purpose of reconstruction.

In the new model the rule has taken on a different quality. As regards activity, there is no simply stateable objective that both parties can strive for. Thus it would no longer make sense for the analyst to put his hand on the patient's head. (If he were employing suggestion, what would he suggest would happen? More puzzling still, what would he want to happen?) What can the patient and analyst be trying for when they are no longer searching for memories? For practical purposes, the process has become the goal, and that is harder to define and to pursue.

As the goal becomes less definable, passivity becomes more problematic.

## THE PARADOX OF THE ANALYST'S PASSIVITY

The analyst's passivity becomes problematic because his activity is no longer limited to preserving the patient's own initial wish (to discover the pathogenic memory). Now the analyst must inspire a new, overt, personal longing that the patient never anticipated when he started treatment. And, probably of greater concern to Freud, the analyst now must also put himself in opposition to what he has invited – in some ways opposing an appeal by the patient that is expressive and not just obstructive – whereas in the past the analyst only opposed what he regarded as interference.

In these circumstances, it would seem that no theoretical handling can make the psychoanalyst's passivity comfortably straightforward. But his model of treatment will determine just how painful it must be. It is less painful when the analyst can refer to Freud's early model. *Papers on Technique* takes advantage of that fact. It recommends that analysts adopt a non-interfering style of attention. In line with that recommendation most of the instructions in *Papers on Technique* are negative: don't do this and don't do that. A reader can easily overlook the active, goal-directed behavior that Freud is also suggesting. For instance, it turns out that free-floating attention and suspension of formulations are recommended for only part of the analytic field. Quite a different approach is recommended in dealing with resistance. Resistance is handled more deliberately both by the analyst and (in the course of working through) by the patient.

How does Freud reconcile these two attitudes toward impulse? By appealing to the memory-retrieval model. A rule that respects the natural order of memory-thoughts reassures the analyst that he is being appropriately passive even when he is actively policing the right-of-way needed by the patient's independent thought processes. The analyst's interventions are initiated only to facilitate the natural progression of the patient's own memories. Stoppage is a logical and mutually accepted signal for the analyst to cease musing and start thinking on behalf of his patient in an active, practical way.

As long as Freud can borrow from the memory-retrieval model the idea that resistance is stoppage, the paradox can be overlooked: the analyst is active only when the patient offers nothing to attend to in a passive way. If the analyst were to give up the memory-retrieval model and see himself principally as a seducer and controller of the patient's active wishes, it would be hard for him to recover the balance between passive contemplation and active provocation. These implications become apparent in *Papers on Technique*, and as we read it, we understand better why Freud wanted to retain the memory-retrieval model.

Thus, we can see the usefulness of the double model as we observe how the concept of working through sharpens the paradox: On the one hand, impulses responsible for the patient's productions are non-judgmentally allowed to emerge; on the other hand, the same impulses, when responsible for resistance, are not simply allowed to emerge but are immediately inspected, deciphered, and judged.

One must allow the patient time to become more conversant with this resistance ... Only when the resistance is at its height can the analyst, working in common with his patient, discover the repressed instinctual impulses which are feeding the resistance ...

*(1914, p. 155)*

## PARADOXES OF THE PATIENT'S PASSIVITY

As for the patient's passivity, that also is newly paradoxical because transference is no longer an associative error that he can simply watch. The patient no longer has an unequivocal assignment.

In the days when obeying the fundamental rule meant entertaining memories and ideas, the patient could detach himself from the resistance by attaching himself to the analyst (who is memory's ally). The analyst could be relied on to overcome the resistance and let memory speak its piece. But in the new theory (where resistance is almost a synonym for impulse) the fundamental rule requires the patient to sustain a connection with the resistance as well as with the analyst's viewpoint. The impulses must come to life and be owned by him. Now attachment to the analyst plays on both sides of the net: love for the analyst (1) induces desire, (2) focuses it on the analyst, (3) commits the patient to his demand (so that he can experience it consciously), and (4) persuades him to disown his demand (so that he can contemplate it).

The fundamental rule now means that, for love of the analyst, the patient must express his desire while distancing himself enough to relinquish efforts at satisfaction. As we have noted, a corresponding change occurs in the analyst's free-floating attention: it is no longer a simple receiver of surfacing memories; it is also the analyst's suppression within himself of any wish that the patient might use to settle transference longings.

## THE NEW VIEW OF THE PATIENT'S ATTENTION

The conclusion of "The dynamics of transference" was that the patient has to experience his wishes alive in order for them to be changed (i.e., in order for them to be integrated with the rest of life). Implicit in that paper, and explicit in the later paper, "Observations on transference-love" (1915), is the principle that treatment requires a simultaneous conscious activation of repressed wishes and a cool contemplation of their significance, so that they are experienced both as wishes and as objective features of the conflicted self. The patient must feel both "I want ..." and "it is a (troubling) feature of my mind and my life that I (conflictedly) want ...". Correlatively, the patient must feel, "The analyst has and won't give me ...," and "I carry with me an unsatisfiable wish for ..." The fundamental rule compels these pairs to go together. Their going together is called working through.

This new model is familiar to all analysts. It is the combination of involvement and distancing that grossly identifies the analytic project. *Papers on Technique* teaches how to achieve a dual consciousness. Seen that way, the work reveals itself as a technical manual after all, and not a secretive shell game, always saying what not to do but never saying what to do.[5]

## THE FINAL PAPER, "OBSERVATIONS ON TRANSFERENCE-LOVE," AND THE ANALYST'S NEW POSITION

The suggestion that transference is a libidinal revival was left dangling at the end of "The dynamics of transference." Now, in "Observations on transference-love" (1915), the final paper of the series, we see Freud pick up the theme again and work out the details. At last the animating function of the transference is fully acknowledged. But the special significance of the paper does not lie in a theoretical exegesis that could as well have been written at the beginning of *Papers on Technique*. What Freud accomplishes in this paper is something subtler and riskier, and something that could only be done properly at the conclusion of the work. In effect, "Observations on Transference-Love" is a study of the analyst's new role and perilous new responsibility, and for that reason it is appropriately reserved as a capstone for all of the paradoxical considerations of the preceding papers. In particular, this paper is designed to prevent the analyst from taking up any facile position in regard to the transference.

> I shall state it as a fundamental principle that the patient's need and longing should be allowed to persist in her, in order that they may serve as forces impelling her to do work and to make changes, and that we must beware of appeasing those forces by means of surrogates.
>
> *(p. 165)*

> It is, therefore, just as disastrous for the analysis if the patient's craving for love is gratified as if it is suppressed. The course the analyst must pursue is neither of these; it is one for which there is no model in real life.
>
> *(p. 166)*

> The lay public ... will doubtless seize upon this discussion of transference-love as another opportunity for directing the attention of the world to the serious danger of this therapeutic method. The psycho-analyst knows that he is working with highly explosive forces and that he needs to proceed with as much caution and conscientiousness as a chemist.
>
> *(p. 170)*

According to the old theory, the analyst could claim to be championing the patient's effort to recover memories. He could think of his manipulativeness as strengthening one side of the patient's internal battle. In that theory the fundamental rule was merely a formalization of memory's intrinsic nature. In the new theory, by contrast, the fundamental rule reflects not the patient's (memory's) wish,

**46** The text

but the analyst's professional identity: indeed, the power of the fundamental rule lies in the fact that the analyst's advocacy of the rule is his only self-disclosure and his single communicated wish. In the new theory the analyst actually seduces the patient's wishes and, by being a seducer with only the fundamental rule as a desire, requires the patient to frustrate himself to please the analyst. The analyst is now responsible both for luring the patient's wishes and for luring the patient to betray them. To please him the patient must partially forgo even the reach for satisfaction.

Later, Freud will make this a natural function of the observing ego (see Schafer, 1990). Subsequent literature will refer to split egos and therapeutic alliances, etc. The analyst will again be able to imagine himself as strengthening a natural inclination of the patient. The onus that falls on the analyst as a consequence of the new theory of treatment will then be obscured. But in 1915 the onus is still clear. And it is the burden (in both senses of that word) of "Observations on transference-love." No wonder that Freud was proudest of this courageous paper.

## CONCLUSION

Speech is naturally provocative and manipulative (see Austin 1962). But "working through" requires the analysand to speak non-manipulatively about his manipulative intentions. He is supposed to report his wishes without letting them compose his report. If the wishes authored his report, the report would disguise the wishes in ways that implemented their thrust. Nonmanipulative reporting is an asymptotic goal to which the patient can bring a certain kind of effort, a resolution to forgo the manipulative power of communication under intense pressure to manipulate. The inevitable failure of the effort is called "resistance."

The effort to associate freely requires one to identify with one's striving and also with a self that could dispense with that striving. Obviously, this double-track experience is both a cause and a result of living beyond one's momentary means. Larger possibilities are already available to anybody who can perform such strange gymnastics, and exercise will surely stretch those possibilities further.

Freud's *Papers on Technique* are instructions for dividing attention this way. His formula was discovered by painful trials with a treatment originally tailored to an earlier rationale. The cardinal features of that earlier treatment (free association; the reconstruction from memories, etc.) proved to be so vital to the new treatment, and so difficult to write a prescription for, that their original rationale (clearing away of blocked memories) remained a useful adjunct even after the grand treatment strategy had outgrown it.

Freud had a way of cornering experience into demonstrating usable structure within the seemingly ineffable powers of mind, and nowhere is his dissection more revealing than in the conceptualizing of psychoanalytic treatment. The odds could not have been very great that these early descriptions of the intangibles of treatment would survive almost a century of stressful testing. Watching Freud use theory to meet and match the practical problems of treating people, one wonders why psychoanalysts feel the need to fall back monotonously (and therefore unconvincingly) on Freud's abandonment of the seduction hypothesis to make a case for the empirical nature of psychoanalysis.

## Notes

1 In describing transference interpretation, Freud may have recalled his struggles to convince critics that his interpretations of verbal associations were not arbitrary. In the Postscript to the report on Dora (1905a) he had written that handling transference is "by far the hardest part of the whole task. It is easy to learn how to interpret dreams, to extract from the patient's associations his unconscious thoughts and memories, and to practice similar explanatory arts: for these the patient himself will always supply the text: Transference is the one thing the presence of which has to be detected almost without assistance and with only the slightest clues to go upon, while at the same time the risk of making arbitrary inferences has to be avoided" (p. 116). Freud may have regarded inferences from behavior as less publicly demonstrable than those made from verbal associations, and that may have contributed to his reluctance to abandon the memory-retrieval model.
2 What he had discovered was that memories are a means of dealing with desire; in the new paradigm we suffer not from memories but from wants, which are modified during treatment by the act of remembering.
3 Thus one consequence of the double-track model of attention (wishing and reporting) is to make it possible to view behavior (communication) as both an evasion and a demand. And that is characteristic of psychoanalysis.
4 Many analysts (e.g., Ferenczi & Rank 1924; Sachs 1925) will, in a one-for-one fashion, replace the hunt for concealed memories with the effort to dislodge hidden libido from concealed actions. It is a simplification that Freud will object to precisely because it neglects the double-track of consciousness (see Grubrich-Simitis 1986).
5 Discussing Freud's determination to make reference to an objective reality notwithstanding his recognition of the transferential nature of perception, McLaughlin (1981) writes: "Freud had to make the distinction between two realities in order to create the unique circumstances of the analytic situation, without which there would be no analytic process. Freud's operational set was that within the analytic situation the patient would experience the transferences as real; yet the analyst (and eventually the patient) would consider them objectively as nonreal anachronisms. This artifice provided an enormously facilitating and constraining therapeutic dialectic for the analyst and patient. It was indeed a stroke of genius to hit upon a mode that allowed freedom and protection for both parties in a real-unreal intimacy, a simultaneity of close hovering and distancing from, of seeking of likeness and difference, of cursive merging and discursive objectifying" (p. 643).

## REFERENCES

Austin, J. L. (1965/1962). *How To Do Things with Words*. 2nd ed. Cambridge, MA: Harvard University Press.

Breuer, J. & Freud, S. (1893–1895). *Studies on Hysteria*. Standard Edition, 2.

Ferenczi, S. & Rank, O. (1924). *The Development of Psycho-Analysis*. New York, NY: Nervous and Mental Disease Publishing Company. Published in English in 1925.

Freud, S. (1900). *The Interpretation of Dreams*. Standard Edition, 4/5.

Freud, S. (1904). Freud's psycho-analytic procedure. Standard Edition, 7.

Freud, S. (1911–1915). *Papers on Technique*. Standard Edition, 12.

Freud, S. (1911). The handling of dream-interpretation in psycho-analysis. Standard Edition, 12.

Freud, S. (1905a). Fragment of an analysis of a case of hysteria. Standard Edition, 7.

Freud, S. (1905b). *Three Essays on the Theory of Sexuality*. Standard Edition, 7.

Freud, S. (1912a). The dynamics of transference. Standard Edition 12.

Freud, S. (1912b). Recommendations to physicians practising psycho-analysis. Standard Edition, 12.

Freud, S. (1913). On beginning the treatment. (Further recommendations on the technique of psycho-analysis I.) Standard Edition, 12.

Freud, S. (1914). Remembering, repeating and working-through. (Further recommendations on the technique of psycho-analysis II.) Standard Edition, 12.

Freud, S. (1915). Observations on transference-love. (Further recommendations on the technique of psycho-analysis III.) Standard Edition, 12.

Friedman, L. (1992). How and why do patients become more objective? Sterba compared with Strachey. *Psychoanalytic Quarterly*, 61: 1–17.

Gay, P. (1988). *Freud: A Life for Our Time*. New York, NY: Norton.

Gill, M. M. (1982). *Analysis of Transference, Vol. 1. Theory and Technique*. Psychological Issues Monograph 53. New York, NY: International Universities Press.

Grubrich-Simitis, I. (1986). Six letters of Sigmund Freud and Sandor Ferenczi on the interrelationship of psychoanalytic theory and technique. *International Journal Psychoanalysis*, 13: 259–277.

Kravis, N. M. (1992). The 'prehistory' of the idea of transference. *International Review of Psycho-Analysis*, 19: 9–22.

Masson, J. M. (trans. and Ed.). (1985). *The Complete Letters of Sigmund Freud and Wilhelm Fliess, 1887–1904*. Cambridge, MA and London: Harvard University Press.

McLaughlin, J. T. (1981). Transference, psychic reality, and countertransference. *Psychoanalytic Quarterly*, 50: 639–664.

Nunberg, H. & Federn, E. (Eds.). (1974). *Minutes of the Vienna Psychoanalytic Society Vol. 3 1910–1911*. New York, NY: International Universities Press.

Sachs, H. (1925). Metapsychological points of view in technique and theory. *International Journal of Psychoanalysis*, 6: 5–12.

Schafer, R. (1990). The "resistance" and Freud's countertransference. Presented to a Panel on Freud's *Papers on Technique* at the Meeting of the American Psychoanalytic Association, December 5.

# PREFACE TO CHAPTER 3

## WORKING THROUGH IS THE PATIENT'S PRIVATE EXPERIENCE

*Papers on Technique* mainly lists the analyst behaviors that produce the psychoanalytic phenomenon. How those behaviors work is a different question.

An experienced analyst puts the matter aside, secure in his familiar routine. But has there ever been a novice (trainee or patient) who does not ask himself "How can non-directive talking change a person?"

Freud was the real green beginner. He did have an old plan for an old treatment, but none for the new one, and like all beginners he was doubtful about how "mere" talking can cure. Yet nothing compelled him to confess a doubt about mechanism in a book on technique, which describes mainly what induces, and what inhibits, the psychoanalytic *experience*. Why did he bother to add the eternal puzzle of therapeutic action to his many other quandaries? The *occasion* is clear enough: Students asked what they should do when a perfectly conducted treatment didn't seem to be working. Everything was in order: The analyst's correct speech had convinced the patient of the analyst's truths. It had been assumed that the truth will make one free, yet nothing happened. Where had the machinery failed? The answer required some reference to a theory of therapeutic action.

But that is not the only reason Freud took up the question. He seems to have been privately uneasy about the problem. The need for time and patience would not have surprised him, viewing mankind as he did. But a *gap in his understanding* of what's at work – that's a different matter. That's the sort of thing that would nag at Freud until he could answer to his own common sense how such a quiet, passive procedure as the new non-directive psychoanalysis could wreak such a drastic change in person's lives.

In "Remembering, repeating and working-through," Freud reported that the pain of treatment held the answer to the riddle of therapeutic action. What brought change was trying to free-associate against (what feels like) self-interest. Freud gave this unpleasant-but-productive predicament a proper name, "working

**50  The text**

through," and he promoted it from a few lines at the tail-end of the paper up into its very title.

The profession always hugs Freud's terms to its bosom, and it did so dutifully with the term, "working through." As so often with *Papers on Technique*, what it hugged was the word, not the concept. Working through is usually understood as perseverance, and sometimes as a synonym for everything in analysis. Many later analysts wondered what all the fuss was about, especially after the term entered everyday language. It was, after all, the answer to a student's (practical) question, and readers seem to have thought that a grand-fatherly "there, there: you're doing O.K." was all that what was needed, and therefore all that was given.

One might have expected analysts to be a little puzzled that a whole paper and a technical term were used where "Have Patience!" would do. And why would ordinary patience be placed in the paper's title on a par with the truly revolutionary proclamation of inter-translatability between remembering and repeating? Slow and Steady Wins the Race? Rome Wasn't Built in a Day? These as a technical breakthrough? But that is how many or most readers accepted the contribution of the working through concept. Largely overlooked was Freud's brief indication that it was also Freud's *sotto voce* answer to his own nagging g question.

The reason *Freud's* "working through" deserved a place in the title was that it embodied his long-sought treatment rationale: It was the Hard Task that answered to the Hard Question. Freud is relieved to see it. The solution comes as a terse comment at the end of his paper – just a throw-away line because it concerned a private quest and private relief. He whispers the answer: Therapeutic action is the emotional *torque* of working against – rather than with – one's vital interest. Working through is the *experience* in the free-associative treatment of a sort of self-betrayal. Yes, that's the sort of thing that could have a revolutionary power comparable to the old blast of catharsis – the standard of undeniable therapeutic power. Freud would soon walk away from all these technical matters, but he couldn't leave until he had *seen* the locus of therapeutic action with common-sense eyes.

That claim of mine will be disputed. I will be reminded that Freud famously dismissed the "action" question by saying that the only unanswered question is why therapy *doesn't* work. And indeed the later structural theory may well have finally put the puzzle of therapeutic action to sleep with a formula stating, for example, that the superego is modified to reduce anxiety, which allows the ego to gather forbidden material into its control. Or, for example, that the observing ego is "assisted" by the analyst to see that ancient fears are unrealistic. (Or, finally, as the old Freud seemed to suspect, that there often *is* no therapeutic action.)

The fact is that Freud could have used that sort of formula even before elaborating theories of superego, signal anxiety, etc. But at the time of *Papers on Technique* Freud craved a "real" explanation. Here he is not trying to make an observed phenomenon mesh with a prepared theory, or simply describe it in current jargon. Freud's special mind-set in this particular project is probably farther from that sort of smoothing-out activity than anything else he recorded since the early days of his psychoanalytic work. It seems to me that *Papers on Technique* is unique in Freud's published writing, in that it records the actual discovery of the analytic phenomenon *in statu nascendi*.

These pages bear witness to the intensely personal, non-theoretical impact on Freud of the psychoanalytic phenomenon as it surprised him in his early practice. We are given a "you-are-there" view of Freud as he came upon the analytic experience (and as it came upon him) with distressing force. Anyone who doubts that should look again at the dramatic confession tacked on to "The dynamics of transference," which says, in effect, "What I have written so academically does not begin to convey the havoc a transference can wreak." It was to master this and other unwanted features of the analytic experience that Freud set out in *Papers on Technique* to grasp the raw power of the psychoanalytic phenomenon. His visualization of working through made it comprehensible to him. In *Papers on Technique* we see the natural scientist, the biological field worker, the zoological observer, and not just the supremely conquering theoretician. We should not try to assimilate the book to Freud's other writings. If *Papers on Technique* had been recognized as the immediate record of Freud's troubled search for understanding, later analysts might not have beaten the bushes searching for that new, specialized procedure, called "working through," until the phrase became a kind of lullaby for analysts and a cliché for the laity. They might have realized that working through is not a technique; it was the answer to a question – a very worrying question – about therapeutic action. It is not something the analyst does to – or with – his patient. It is an uncomfortable aspect of the patient's private *feeling* in the treatment related to self-confrontation. Its special discomfort is its power. (I believe, however, that there was a more profound reason that Freud's definition of working through was blotted out as soon as it was printed. I shall take that up in Part II of this Preface below.)

From *Papers on Technique* we can see that Freud was intensely interested in the psychoanalytic phenomenon *at the time he was discovering it*. That interest did not last. Except for those years, Freud was much less interested in the analytic phenomenon, *per se* than in what he could discover *through* it – and that is an understatement. Simply put, *Papers on Technique* is not a typical work of Sigmund Freud, and it is a mistake to line it up with other comments about therapy. Even the memory of a time of puzzlement and discovery seems to have faded from his mind and was replaced by the "face" appearance of *Papers on Technique* as a manual of elementary instruction and admonition. (I will return to that in Chapter 13.) But no matter how complacent Freud became about therapeutic action in later years, one need only read the pages of *Papers* in sequence to see that he was working very hard at that time on the crucial difficulties of the "action" question, sometimes vividly and sometimes *en passant*, but steadily until he had done his proper job. Then, apparently, he felt he could leave it – forever, as it turned out.

**I**

Freud's answer brought him into troubling territory. He was locating the action of psychoanalysis in a patient's private experience. That is where working through

**52 The text**

happens, according to *Papers on Technique*. The analyst's words did not mold the patient's thought; they alerted his attention. The source of the resistance was learned by the patient, and it was "learned by acquaintance," as philosophers would say. The patient's fidelity to free association had confronted him with a newly conscious experience of contradictory vital interests. He would personally feel the pressing value (i.e., what's at stake) of *not* speaking freely, and he would feel it at the very moment that he nevertheless continues to speak freely. In other words, he feels his strong *reason* for staying the old way as he gives it up for a conflicting purpose. He consciously recognizes its incompatibility with the rest of his equilibrium by experiencing the loss as it gives itself up for negotiation. Working through amounts to working against interest (as interest is presently constituted). Working through allows what *feels* like an unwise move to happen anyway. It is the hard climb – the essential unpleasantness – the forced expansion of awareness, that makes treatment work.

That may be a shaking experience for the patient, but it also poses an unwelcome problem for analysts. The problem is the difference in "species" between the *analyst's public, orienting words* and the *patient's private experience*. It is the famously indeterminate relationship between the conveyance of a common meaning and the living subjectivity that emerges. With this universal question hanging over us, Freud had located the therapeutic action squarely in the patient's newly vivid private experience of the *source* (personal gain) of his resistance. Exposing the source drains its usefulness, and the patient scratches himself on its warnings as he works his way through it, but that painful experience opens it to negotiation with the conflicting motives for change (or to be loyal to his pledge of free association).

When it comes to speech, the built-in uncertainty about what, exactly, gets launched (its real meaning) and who controls the reception (what is heard) is not comfortable for a therapist. It is, of course, the normal and inevitable problem of conversation. But in ordinary speech we can rely on a core of shared, standard meanings, and that is usually all we care about. But psychoanalysts are mostly interested in individual nuance and associative reverberations. So it was not welcome to hear from Freud that the sources of resistance are sequestered in the patient's head.

An ironic example of the difference between the public meaning of speech and how it's received is Strachey's response to Freud's instruction. In translating the crucial passage of Freud's written instruction concerning working through, Strachey "heard" Freud to mean exactly the reverse of his expressed intention. (Here the twist was visible and declared by Strachey.) As a consequence of Strachey's "better" understanding of Freud's public words, the concept of working through became something else than Freud designated – anything and everything else – sometimes even a reiteration *by the analyst* (!) of well worn interpretations!

Since Strachey conscientiously admits his disobedience to Freud's written instruction, it would not have had such a profound effect, were it not that analytic readers were themselves as adverse to Freud's meaning as Strachey, and for the same reason. The crucial, experiential, self-analyzing function of working through was hard for analysts to accept because, though *influenced* by the analyst's speech it was *ungoverned* by his articulation. I suggest that analysts regard this final, private read-out of meaning, unmonitored by the analyst, as a slippery slope that could undermine the analyst's confidence as a responsible therapist no matter how earnestly he tracked subsequent associations. At any rate, analysts resolutely shut out the plain meaning of this brief passage.

## II

Freud's discovery of the psychoanalytic phenomenon carries him back and forth between such perplexities. Paradox runs through *Papers on Technique* like a stretched-out Buddhist *koan*. It begins to seem that a set of paradoxical attitudes in both parties is what produces the psychoanalytic phenomenon.

A startling discovery begins Freud's journal. (See Chapter 1.) It turns out that if the patient catches wind of any personal interest of Freud's, he automatically throws anchor there, and the analytic journey will not launch. If Freud was longing for something – even something as useful as a dream – an analytic phenomenon would not appear. It makes sense, doesn't it? Unless his patient realized that Freud couldn't be pleased or displeased, the essential non-directiveness of the treatment would be compromised. Instead we would have the ordinary social phenomenon of mutual adjustment, compromise and impression management. A close and concerned involvement with someone who doesn't want *anything* from you is not an experience you will find anywhere but in a psychoanalysis. It is the fulcrum of therapy. It is the stairway to the psychoanalytic phenomenon. (And, of course, it is an impossible ideal.)

But what have we here? A therapy without a purpose? A purpose unknown to the therapist? Wasn't Freud hopeful – at least hopeful that his patient would eventually become more familiar with himself? Could that wish possibly be concealed, and wouldn't it be deadly if the healing motive was concealed? Wasn't Freud obliged to monitor progress and its road-blocks? And wouldn't he need to bring along measures, indices, of some sort to monitor that? Freud's balanced free-floating receptivity against a focused act of spotting "resistances." Can that still be called a non-directive therapy?

Such waffling is characteristic of the psychoanalytic method. The waffling is not vacuous because special concepts orient the analyst to specific alternating or double foci – the famous "rules," or ideals that flag certain types of awareness that might be blurred by other types of awareness and warn him not to move too far in either direction. Some of these contradictions are very basic to the human condition, and some so general that they preoccupy philosophy of mind. An example is the problem of the One and the Many. That phrase always sounds portentous and eerie. But if you give it even a moment's thought you recognize it as a simple description of the human mind. It is one of those awful philosophical problems that's mixed in with the meat and potatoes of psychotherapy practice. Worse still, that problem is hardly separate from problems of change and permanence, atoms and flow, etc.,

**54** The text

etc. We leave most of these to philosophers if we choose, but some of them we cannot dodge, especially when we are doing research. Freud was doing research, and he had to tangle with the problem of deciding what is an *item* to think about in the offering from the couch.

There's a sense that Freud is starting from scratch in *Papers*, and the empiricist's methodological problems hit him hard and fast. He must decide what are items to think about, and whether the analyst's speech is still an item when it falls into the river of the patient's thought. Working through and items to think about are both on the laboratory bench in this short paper. And yet some people think this is a primer for the children!

# 3

# HOW TO PICK ITEMS OUT OF THE FLOW OF PROCESS

Tell me where is Fancy bred,
Or in the heart, or in the head?

*– The Merchant of Venice*

Although it is a bit irregular to begin a formal essay with a declaration of personal feelings, I have learned that readers need to know my motive in order to catch the drift of my argument. Without such a declaration they are likely to imagine a grander critique than I intend, and even some sort of partisan campaign. Here, then, is how the chapter came about.

I have had the experience of trying unsuccessfully to convince colleagues that they are misreading Freud's comments on working through in his *Papers on Technique* (1911–1915). Since my reading seemed to me fairly plain, I was puzzled by why it was so hard to make my point. I asked myself what might be the good reasons for the "resistance." I thought I found the answer in the inherent difficulty of imagining at once both discrete units and continuous process, as Freud was demanding of analysts. That double vision is something that long ago had fascinated me in Freud's theory (Friedman 1988). But there was a problem with that answer. The same cinching together of units and continua was evident in an earlier part of the same paper, and analysts never balked at that. Why was the one instance accepted by all, whereas the other has been steadfastly ignored by many? Then I noticed that the two instances differ as to which member of the treatment couple was presenting a continuum, and which one was transmitting discrete units. It seemed that analysts can comfortably picture themselves fielding unitary messages that emerge from the continuum of the patient's activity, and yet find it uncongenial to imagine their own discretely crafted responses dissolving into a river of the patient's continuous experience. Overall, I thought, analysts were wrestling

# 56 The text

here with a fundamental philosophical problem, and I thought it would be reassuring to recognize that the difficulty is ancient and honorable, and a conundrum for all thinking beings.

Thus, I am not campaigning for or against any practice or theory. In a certain sense, my goal is to sympathize with a common misreading. Further, I wish to make it clear that this is not a chapter on technique; it is a chapter about a paper on technique. I don't know how to avoid the paradox I am pointing to. I am trying to answer a question about the community's reception of an idea and dwell a little on the nature of the problem as it is written about in this one text. I add some comments on the psychoanalytic literature and the philosophical background, in order to "naturalize" the conceptual difficulty, but I make no effort to trace the history of the problem in either discipline.

## THE CONTEXT OF THE TEXT

Readers might find it hard to join me if they are familiar with the Working Through paper only as a free-standing essay like the bulk of Freud's work. My discussion of two passages in "Remembering, repeating and working-through" is based on a particular reading of the whole book in which they appear, Freud's *Papers on Technique* (1911–1915). I believe that this slight and early-conceived book is often misunderstood because analysts, when not actually discounting it as theoretically unfinished, often read into it what we all know to be Freud's general outlook, and ask not what Freud says in a particular passage but what he must have meant in view of what everybody knows to be his general model of the mind and treatment goal. I have argued (Friedman 1991a, 2008, 2009) that the technique book is not an application of theory. It stands alone among Freud's works as a chronicle of successive efforts to wrestle with the raw experiences that led him to adopt the principles of psychoanalytic technique, in the process layering sometimes divergent conclusions one on top of the other without retraction, each understood only by grasping a specific difficulty he was wrestling with at that moment in his practice.[1]

## FIRST EXAMPLE OF THE MERGER OF DISCRETE ITEMS AND A CONTINUOUS PROCESS

> We must still be grateful to the old hypnotic technique for having brought before us single psychical processes of analysis in an isolated or schematic form. Only this could have given us the courage ourselves to create more complicated situations in the analytic treatment and to keep them clear before us.
>
> *(Freud 1914a, p. 148)*

This is a remarkable confession by Freud. Does he really mean it? "Only this could have given us the courage… ." The need for courage testifies to the dizzying dilemmas, practical and cognitive, that Freud was struggling to master in the *Papers on Technique.* But by the same token, the passage is also a tribute to *a certain kind of preliminary thinking* that one needs in order to get a purchase on those difficulties.

We can be sure that it is not a confession of cognitive weakness. Excessive modesty and fearfulness were not notable characteristics of Freud. Although it is mostly the editorial "we" and "us" (i.e., himself) that he speaks for, one suspects that he regards himself as the best of Everyman on this journey, summoning his followers along the path (the sort of thinking) that leads to the summit. And if one still suspected that Freud was confessing his personal need for a simple-minded myth to reassure him on his way to a tougher truth, that suspicion would vanish on noting that the new, complex truth *includes* the preparatory simplification, for in the passage that leads up to what might seem a sentimental farewell to the early model, he has actually promised it lifetime employment. The old terms will remain in place forever: "The aim of these different techniques has, of course, remained the same. Descriptively speaking, it is to fill in gaps in memory; dynamically speaking, it is to overcome resistances due to repression" (pp. 147–148).

What, then, is that simpler kind of thinking that allowed Freud to venture into the forbiddingly complex scene of the analytic encounter? It is the kind of thinking that finds "single psychical processes of analysis in an isolated or schematic fashion." The operative words are "single," "isolated," and "schematic." That's the old way. And what, by contrast, is the complexity that continues to need those single, isolated, and schematic elements as a counterpoint? It is the progressively layered "takes" on the phenomenon of analytic treatment that make up the *Papers on Technique.* As Freud's thinking develops in the pages of that book, the plot thickens: transference is a prime example. Transference morphs from the simple slippage in *Studies on Hysteria* (Breuer & Freud 1893–1895) into a general human function. And yet it is not just a general human function, because in treatment it has certain peculiar features – or perhaps it doesn't. Analytic love is as realistic as any love but yet somehow more devious and intense. That's a typical, self-contradictory complexity in the new model. Complexity is rife in the new notion of memory. Here memories are retrievable episodes, but yet memories are often not anecdotal, not naturally segregated, not articulated, not calling up the past, often not thoughts (just connections), frequently not incidents (but habits and character), sometimes not even actual (but just virtual). Complexity now afflicts the analyst's attention: it is *unfocused*, floating attention, but yet a laserlike *focus* on resistance. Most fateful, perhaps, is the new complexity Freud faces up to in the analytic relationship: Who is on whose side in this project; is it or isn't it a battle? These are just a few of the many examples of complexity in *Papers on Technique.*

If we position ourselves alongside Freud in 1914 and look with him at what he is facing as he writes his report, we can easily sympathize with his astonishment that he had been able to master so much complexity. We may even wonder whether he had come upon character analysis earlier than supposed and lacked only the nosology. The true shift is that now he is not looking at a symptom (such as a stifled memory) or an avenue for its removal (like abreaction). He is seeing – or rather experiencing (and sometimes fighting) – a whole person. And that person is

## 58 The text

behaving this way and that from moment to moment, all the while claiming something personal that Freud had not originally been hired to provide. Freud could thread his way through that formidable scene only with the courage provided by a manageable earlier vision of simple parts (specific memories) and process (conscious recollection).

Analysts still find that view daunting and must, like Freud, project parts and processes into their experience of a patient's organic wholeness, conceptually freezing his slippery, variable behavior into some kind of mental portrait. Like all human beings, but more urgently because of their heavy obligation, analysts have an insatiable need for stencils to mark out simple units from the continuum in front of them. Nothing is more characteristic of the analytic literature than the drive to name things. A new term, a vivid image, a portable phrase – these are what we all hunger for and count as progress.

Such is the heritage of the many doubled visions prescribed by Freud throughout *Papers on Technique*. In imagining and conducting treatment, we must in general think two ways at once – as though looking at discrete objects "inside" the patient, and also as though confronted with a whole organism that exhibits itself in a somewhat unpredictable process.

What I want to call attention to at this point is that, although these paradoxes were so formidable that Freud needed the aid of a simple memory-retrieval model to lure him into the complex treatment event, the final, tangled vision was effortlessly adopted by generations of practicing psychoanalysts, as were many other impossible paradoxes in Freud's recipe for producing an analytic process. Daunting though it is to perceive memories and behavior as actually the same thing, analysts received the injunction almost without noticing its paradoxical nature. They observed behaviors, and they translated them into memories as a matter of course, and although much more went on in treatments, they felt this aspect to be perfectly natural. In practice, at least, the double vision was routine. (When this stance is criticized lately, it is more for being unrealistically pretentious than for being paradoxical.) Theorists, as we know, recognized that the whole-person aspect of the model (and therefore its process aspect) needed some further work, a job that was undertaken by the misleadingly named "ego psychologists." (One thinks of Hartmann [1951], Waelder [1930], and Schur [1966].)

I now ask the reader to contrast this smooth reception of a hybrid vision of discrete units and continuous process with the profession's very different reading of the last pages of the same 1914 paper, where a similar challenge is presented.

## SECOND EXAMPLE OF THE MERGER OF DISCRETE ITEMS AND CONTINOUS PROCESS

> I have often been asked to advise upon cases in which the doctor complained that he had pointed out his resistance to the patient and that nevertheless no change had set in; indeed, the resistance had become all the stronger, and the whole situation was more obscure than ever. The treatment seemed to make no headway. The gloomy

foreboding always proved mistaken. The treatment was as a rule progressing most satisfactorily. The analyst had merely forgotten that giving the resistance a name could not result in its immediate cessation. One must allow the patient time to become more conversant with this resistance with which he has now become acquainted, to work through it, to overcome it, by continuing, in defiance of it, the analytic work according to the fundamental rule of analysis. Only when the resistance is at its height can the analyst, working in common with his patient, discover the repressed instinctual impulses which are feeding the resistance; and it is this kind of experience which convinces the patient of the existence and power of such impulses.

*(Freud 1914a, p. 156)*

Here Freud tells us that all the analyst need (or can) do is to prime the patient's attention with words, and then follow the patient's reported experience. Only the patient is in a position to notice and therefore feel acutely his *good reason* (his passionate incentive) for fudging his honesty. He meets that counterinterest for the first time as it squeezes him against his pledge of honesty and makes brutally clear what he's giving up by being honest. Freud is neatly describing a process with two stages: One (objective) is the naming of an obstacle, presumably the behavioral evidence of interference with the process. The other (subjective) is the patient's discovery of the personal interest that is at risk, which is the specific, personal *meaning* of the phrase, "the resistance" (i.e., the *reason* for noncompliance). That discovery is made as the patient works stalwartly right through the sacrifice toward the fulfillment of analytic openness. Note that the term *working through* is expressly coined to refer to an action on a *resistance*, because the "through" depicts a rough trip under assault from a countervailing barrage. One can work *on* many things but, as the term is used here, there is nothing one can work *through* other than a resistance. The term is invented to give that activity both a name and a picture.

It is worth asking why the plain meaning of this passage is regularly ignored in favor of any and all associations that an analyst may have to the English words, "working" and "through." Admittedly, the terms and metaphors of *Papers on Technique* have all suffered wear and tear as guild passwords while their meaning has been assimilated to that of everyday speech. And how could it be otherwise? Having entered the general language, these terms and images can claim whatever meaning is bestowed on them by common usage, just like any other term in a natural language. Thus one frequently hears, "On personal reflection, I think *it* means this ..." instead of "I think *Freud* meant that ... ." And even when marking it specifically as Freud's invention, some analysts may start from its widespread meaning and try to imagine why the Freud they imagine *would be likely* to use such a word, rather than looking at why he *did* use it. (The metaphor of the "surgeon" in *Papers* a good example.)

But even allowing that to be the common fate of so many terms from *Papers on Technique,* in the case of "working through" the degree of resistance to Freud's actual expression is striking. Indeed, the tradition of misreading starts with the translator. An analyst who consults the main text of the *Standard Edition* will not be

**60** The text

reading what Freud wanted him to read. There is nothing covert in Strachey's choice. His footnote (Freud 1914a, p. 155) describes and defends his act of overruling Freud.

Strachey thinks Freud wanted to say that the analyst acquaints the patient with a resistance by giving it a name. That would seem to be the implication of Freud's original versions, written before 1922. Strachey acknowledges that Freud changed this wording in a second edition (published in that year) of what I presume to be the *Sammlung kleiner Schriften zur Neurosenlehre* (1918) – the only form of the paper that went through two editions. From then on, Strachey tells us, Freud's preferred expression (which Strachey rejects as senseless) is what we find on p. 118 of the *Gesammelte Schriften* (1925) and p. 118 of *Zur Technik der Psychoanalyse und zur Metapsychologie* (1924). In these later versions, Freud changed "nun bekannten Widerstand" (the resistance with which [the patient] is now acquainted) to "unbekannten Widerstand" (the resistance with which [the patient] is not [yet] acqainted). So Freud finally wanted the sentence to read "Man muss dem Kranken die Zeit lassen, sich in den ihm unbekannten Widerstand zu vertiefen ... [The patient must be allowed time to immerse himself in the resistance that is unknown to him ...]" (1925, p. 118). That seemed plainly senseless to Strachey, who wondered how Freud could say that the patient is unacquainted with the resistance after it has already been named. Unable to account for Freud's revision, and thinking to rescue him from self-contradiction, Strachey refused the new wording and substituted the one that Freud had erased.[2]

It is an unusual lapse for Strachey. Common sense says that there is absolutely no way an author can make his meaning clearer than by going to the trouble of altering an expression for a new edition. When he does that, he is saying as emphatically as possible, "I'm afraid I made you think XYZ in my first edition, and I now want to be sure you do *not* get that impression." If a word can be read in two ways the author might let the reader fend for himself, but he would not let it rest if a substantive issue was at stake. Therefore, if an author goes to the trouble of changing his wording, it behooves the translator to try to fathom what that issue is. It wouldn't have taken much thought, either, in this case. Obviously, Freud was going out of his way to emphasize that referring to something is not the same as being acquainted with it. One thinks of Bertrand Russell's distinction (1940) between knowledge of fact, which can be learned second-hand, and knowledge by acquaintance, which cannot.[3]

Strachey can also be excused for tripping on the ambiguity of the term *resistance*. Suppose one said (just for fun), "The resistance that motivates the resistance is part of the patient's resistance." The layman would laugh but every analyst would know what was meant. In one sense, "the resistance" is an omnibus term referring to the collection of conservative forces that oppose treatment. In another sense, "resistance" is an operational term for a move in a direction opposite to the analyst's aim. In a third sense, "the resistance" refers to the highly specific, personal state inside the individual's mind that accounts for those other two. It might be said that knowledge of the existence of a resistance in the first of the meanings is

The patient's private experience **61**

beyond observation; it's an a priori, theoretical *premise* of treatment, almost the justification for undertaking treatment. In its second meaning, the analyst knows there's a resistance from his *observation* of blockage in the flow, and from that he can *infer* a resistance in the third sense that underlies it. But he would not have knowledge of resistance in that third sense (knowledge by acquaintance), since he cannot personally meet the patient's internal event. Only the patient can be *acquainted* with resistance in the third sense.[4]

Freud is telling us that the patient, in order to work through the named resistance, must contribute something the analyst doesn't initially have and can't give him. The analyst can only point the way to the living experience of conflict. As already mentioned, it is a two-stage process, the first part of which is the analyst's (directing attention), and the second part – the working through part – requires the patient's struggle. As the patient becomes aware of his counter*motive* he can let the analyst know more about the particularity of the resistance, beyond the visible consequence of it that the analyst had spotted. We can see why Freud thought that the naive analysts in this passage who complained to him about the ineffectiveness of their interpretation were counting on suggestion rather than psychoanalysis to do the work. In contrast, Freud depicts the analytic mechanism of cure as the blunt, personal, conscious experience of – indeed, the forced "acquaintance" with – internal conflict: "it is this kind of experience ... which convinces the patient of the existence and power of such impulses... . From a theoretical point of view one may correlate it with the 'abreacting' of the quotas of affect strangulated by repression ..." (pp. 155–156).[5]

Strachey's mistranslation is a harbinger of the many arbitrary meanings later attributed to the term. As against them, and at the cost of repetition, let me summarize my reading of the concept in this paper: Working through does not mean working out an issue. Nor does it mean ironing out a resistance. It means working in the teeth of the resistance. The patient must continue to carry out his analytic duty in the face of the resistance. Then he will have the something else that is needed besides the analyst's interpretation. What would that be? He will experience the impulse that is the source of the resistance. Only the patient can feel that impulse; the analyst can only name it, and then hear about it from his patient. What is the feeling the patient will have? I think it is obvious when you consider what a resistance actually *is*: The patient will feel the interests that would ordinarily turn him away from declaring themselves. Reading a thermometer is not the same as making the acquaintance of burning heat. Fidelity to the fundamental rule requires a patient to work through his resistance as one would walk through fire, and thereby feel the heat. The patient will feel both sides of a conflict at once; he will explicitly experience the incompatibility of conflicted interests. Working through a resistance, the patient will be working against half of himself, and he will not escape conscious awareness of what it is inside him that the "against" is against. Freud's reply to the inexperienced analyst is that a patient does not endure that experience no matter how plausibly informed, as long as he is acquainted only with his presented and presentable self.

## FROM INFORMATION TO EXPERIENCE

Instead of this meaning, why has so much of the usage reduced the term *working through* to one or another tediously banal homily? Bear in mind that, along with two other terms, *working through* is in the very *title* of this paper. The purpose of the paper is to transform the psychoanalytic meaning of remembering and repeating and make them the famous pillars of psychoanalytic thinking. But what of the title's third element? Should Freud have called the paper "Remembering, repeating and repeating?" Ask yourself how likely it is that Freud would dedicate one of his few *papers on technique* partly to the profound principle that analytic treatment takes a while. Or that once isn't enough for an interpretation. Or that patients should work hard. Or that treatment should be complete. Could any serious writer fill a full page with such an instruction? Why not six words? How was it possible for analysts to picture as an exercise in plodding patience what Freud found comparable to a cathartic explosion? Analysts must have some strong incentive to turn away from the gist of Freud's discussion of working through, and it is that *incentive* for misreading (not the misreading itself) that I am concerned with here. (As I will note below, there are within the Freudian tradition exceptions to this avoidance, notably Ellman [1991], Schafer [1992], though somewhat hesitantly, and Loewald [1960] in his grand scheme. But it seems to me that these have not influenced the general discussion of working through among Freudian analysts.)

I suggest that the two passages from Freud's 1914 paper present analysts the same underlying problem (discrete items vs. the continuum of life), but the form of the problem in the first excerpt is easily handled (how to think of a patient's continuous action as discrete memories), while that in the second (how to make discrete, repeatable interpretations inform a patient's ongoing experience) seems almost untouchable. I will look at the common problem, and then ask why they are so differently received.

## THE UNDERLYING PROBLEM: ISLANDS IN THE STREAM

Analysts want to be able to target their attention and speech to specific items so they can know what they're doing and do what is best. An amorphous flow of experience threatens to undermine their control and their objectivity. (The flow literally takes the object out of objectivity.) And yet what their patient offers them as behavior is not a text but a seamless flow of action. At first they looked at words and associations, which seemed tidy enough, but in *Papers on Technique* the material had come to embrace, in addition to not talking, talking too much, symptomatic gestures, the direction and misdirection of the patient's yearning, and, as Freud finally noted (1914a, pp. 155–156), everything about the patient that is related to his troubles.

That's at the level of practice. On the level of theory, the corresponding problem is how to squeeze together knowledge of fact and knowledge by acquaintance. Knowledge of fact can easily be captured in words and concepts. It grasps something delimited – something with borders – something nameable. It uses adjectives that can be "downloaded" into various times and places. A fact can come out of the analyst's head, so to speak, and go into the patient's head. Knowledge by acquaintance, by contrast, is gained by a unique, private experience over a stretch of time, and shares with time the quality of flow. Declarative memory is associated with the first; the second has more to do with recognition, and its description is somewhat arbitrary. I need hardly add that these are rough classifications: there is no knowledge by acquaintance that isn't permeated by a myriad of unworded background descriptions and vice versa. In other words, there is no theory-free knowledge, and no purely abstract theory. Theory is always absorbed, and gets part of its meaning, from a background of the familiar world, while, from sense perception on up to thinking, the "blooming, buzzing confusion" of the familiar world is being unceasingly coded into theoretical concepts.

## WHY IS FREUD'S CONCEPT OF WORKING THROUGH UNWELCOME?

Difficult as it is to think of description and acquaintance together, that difficulty did not keep analysts from accepting Freud's demand that they think of memory as both reportable units (discrete memories) and a continuous flow of life and behavior. But when, analogously, they were asked to equate their categorized target – an observed resistance – with the patient's flow of live experience (his inner struggle), analysts on the whole turned a deaf ear. They preferred to hear a simple encouragement to keep on urging their interpretations. Why was the tension between description and experience so much harder to accept when *making interpretations* than when *grasping phenomena*?

Freud gives us a clue in our first citation. His original confidence came from the memory-retrieval model of treatment. There the analyst is free to follow along with the unarticulated flow of process, waiting for defined memories to emerge from the *patient* of his own accord. Without that picture to start with, Freud would have been as helpless as any other untrained beginner to parse the continuous display in front of him. When he learned that things were not that simple, Freud saw that the helpful, articulated map of memories could be accommodated to the new complexity by layering it translucently over the picture of patient's action. The resulting equivalence allowed the analyst to spot discrete memories emerging, encoded, from the patient's action. By this equation, the analyst still imagines himself "fielding" discrete information thrown out by the patient. In the notion of working through, however, the translation from a continuum to discrete units goes the other way. Freud is asking the analyst to recognize that *his own* discrete message (his interpretation of "a" resistance) is tossed into the patient's unarticulated experience, with which it must find a way to blend. The kind of "resistance" that an analyst is able to capture in a common description is just a *clue* to an intensely *individual need*, which is the resistance in its personal specificity.

**64** The text

Both memory-equated-to-action and interpretation-tied-to-working-through are examples of the many paradoxes that characterize *Papers on Technique*. To be sure, Freud does not present them as paradoxes. Instead he persists in referring to "the" resistance as though it were a barricade, a *thing* – something that can be captured in a word, just as he insisted that behavior is *really* remembering. But right from the first of the *Papers*, the expressive nature of resistance was becoming more and more prominent, starting with the discovery that patients are not just *hiding* their wishes but *acting* on them. (One could say that the *Papers*, as a unified project, is a treatise on the positive aspect of resistance, in all the senses of "positive.") In Freud's depiction of working through, the resistance-as-named is just a tag – a describable, public trace of the patient's private visceral experience of wishes that are frustrated by cooperating with the analyst. Those wishes (including wishes for protection) constitute the real-time, intimately personal cost of free association.

So now we can see why the relatively simple and common-sense conception of working through in *Papers* was nevertheless difficult to digest: On the one hand, there's the individual gut reality of a resistance inside a suffering patient. On the other hand, there's an articulated interpretation, a description so generalizable that it can be duplicated here and there, now and then, sometimes identically in hundreds of copies of a professional journal. How could such a contrast be welcome to analysts? Does an analyst really want to brood on how those two things manage to get together? On what common ground can they meet? Why even pose the bewildering question of how a detachable, generalizable, repeatable description can match up with an ongoing flow of subjective experience in time? Would it help our work in any way to start groping for subtle threads that tie the patient's inner flux to our fixed words? Is it wise to open the door to doubts about whether there is any specific connection at all between the analyst's interpretations and their intended target? It might make us think that it's all just the impact of one person on another. This is no longer a matter of contemplation; it hits the analyst where it hurts. Unlike Freud's double vision of the patient's action as being also his memory, this idea seems to insert a lot of intervening processes and variables between the analyst's words and his impact. It does not merely superimpose one *vision* on another; it raises doubts about the analyst's own *action* – his act of interpreting. It was one thing, as described in the first passage, for the analyst to tolerate a lot of continuous and variable living by the patient, since it's draped over the patient's own neat, well-articulated memories. It's a different story if we're required to picture the patient's unique, continuous, amorphous processes dissolving the analyst's neat, defined capsules of fact. And it poses a question: If patient's action is regularly translated into words by the analyst, are the analyst's words likewise received by the patient as actions? And does that mean that the analyst's interventions are not capsules of fact but mere gestures toward a patient's subjective experience, both of them being continuous processes with blurred outlines that only the patient can experience? Of course, Freud wasn't picturing such an extreme situation. But his explicit and all-too-plausible two-stage formula of "working though" is unsettling enough, and analysts would naturally feel safer

The patient's private experience **65**

fusing it into a single compound made up of the analyst's verbal gesture and the patient's phenomenological experience, thus collapsing inner fact, public name, and process function into one term: The Resistance. By treating resistance as a single unit (and ignoring Freud's distinction in the passage we have examined), analysts could, like Strachey, suppose that both parties became acquainted with the resistance in the act of naming it. In other words, it was more practical to think of the process of the patient's mind as being already frozen into units. When Glover (1931) found reason to doubt the automatic identity of interpretations-made and interpretations-received, he had the saving grace to treat divergence as an exception rather than the rule, but analysts probably realized that he was opening a can of worms. To this day, the question of what is actually produced in the patient's mind as a result of an analyst's intervention (and the concomitant question of what the interpreting analyst's action actually is) is an unaskable question for some classical analysts. (For others, it can be mooted by talking about "bypassing" the ego, or by relying on the unconscious telephone metaphor.)

What, after all, *is* the nature of communication, analytic or otherwise? What, exactly, happens when you say something to somebody about himself? My conclusion is that practicing analysts have good reason to steer clear of this speculation. Start down that path and paralysis threatens (like the famous centipede's crippling self-reflection). There are enough problems to contend with in practice without such distractions. A practitioner may be well-advised to turn away from that and tend to business – refuse Freud's emendation and restore his first wording. Even if Freud didn't want to let us off the hook, he had inadvertently made it possible by allowing readers of his original misphrasing to comfortably assume that the patient has become acquainted with a resistance upon hearing the analyst's interpretation. It's not that analysts require simplicity; after all, they ceaselessly and nimbly negotiate the intricate commerce between the patient's action and its meaning. But practical dangers lie in wait with Freud's concept of working through for a practitioner who wants to know what he has done to his patient.

What are the alternatives? As a very rough working model, we may prefer to think that the living experience in the depths of the patient has the same generalizable form as the analyst's generalizable description. We might wish to imagine that the patient's experience of the resistance already includes his own interpretation, as though the patient had been talking to himself without paying attention until he hears the analyst whisper the very words in his ear that he has heard inside himself. We suppose that when the patient hears his analyst's interpretation, provided that it is correct, the *sotto voce* resistance recognizes its fortissimo echo and swims up to meet its twin. That may sound strange, but Freudian analysts, with the usual exception of Loewald (1960), have generally learned to live with it (jettisoning topographic gradations in the process). It is a cruder model, to be sure, but not necessarily incorrect. It is, in fact, the way we manage all conversation. And if we choose the model, we can disregard Freud's 1922 revision: If the analyst's interpretation reminds the patient of his own unrehearsed interpretation, and if the resistance is a thing that analyst and patient can look at together, we can say that

**66** The text

the interpretation has acquainted the patient with his resistance, and all that's left is to repeat it frequently in various contexts, that is, to "work it through" in the sense that Freud rejected and posterity accepted. What we lose in that option is what Freud wanted to add in this paper, which is a reminder that, besides being a name for a common obstacle, "the resistance" also names a highly individual motivation (something fed by an individual's personal "impulses"). And in practice we can correct for the error by following the advice of Schlesinger (2013) to focus on ensuing associations, and of Faimberg (1996) to "listen to the patient's listening."

## THE PROBLEM: THE HARD-TO-THINK-ABOUT CONTINUUM

Analysts have largely assimilated Freud's paradoxes into their peculiar workaday life with no need to engage in philosophical hairsplitting. But in recent years vexatious philosophical problems have buzzed into their consulting rooms. The reader will think of the mind-body problem, the question of the analyst's authority, worries about the analyst's subjectivity, and problems of free will. These are, like all philosophical problems, interwoven with one another. But the form of the problem that Freud's 1914 paper encountered overshadows them in scope and urgency. Analysts have always been aware of the tension between articulated thought, with its relatively neat definitions, and unarticulated experience that lacks a clear outline. They are aware of it because they characteristically deal in *units* of interpretations, and yet they hope to induce a transformative *process*; they engage in a cloud of relationship, but they deliver specific, propositional information. It can be argued that genuine theories of therapeutic action are rare because psychoanalysts don't want an image of transition (the *process* of change) to compromise their freedom to identify a variety of specific *forms* in the patient. Without forms to take a bead on and relate to one another in a variety of ways, an analyst might drown with his patient in the surge of shapeless process. He would prefer to stand lifeguard on the shore. Process represents change, which is therapeutic action, but it is objects that allow the multiple perspectives that bring about the change. (I have elaborated this elsewhere [Friedman 2007].) Loewald (1960) was a master synthesizer of parts and process, so he was able to present a theory of therapeutic action by juggling continuities and states, process and structures (see Friedman 1991b), but the hostile early reception he received shows just how threatening that project is for the working psychoanalyst.

## HOW DOES THE THEORIST WORK ON THIS PROBLEM?

As Ricoeur (1965) demonstrated, Freud constructed a theory that allowed for both psychic "things" (e.g., structures) and organismic process (e.g., drives, libido). Although in many ways these views are mutually exclusive, Freud recognized that both of them must figure in any true-to-life portrait of the mind. Thus Freud (1937) implied in his final paper that a mental "thing" (the ego) that figures so conspicuously in his model is not to be taken as more real than the process of the mind as a whole.

The patient's private experience **67**

Nevertheless, it remains a challenge to us all, as is apparent in the resistance to Freud's corrected notion of working through. It is difficult to embrace in a single vision two disparate realities: There is the "thing" aspect of reality – items, units, foci of attention. And there is the "stream" aspect – the continuum, the unified flow of time and life, the passage rather than the stations. The problem lies in the heteronomy of such things as borders and field, the discrete and the continuous, definitions and objects, gradations and stages, parts and whole, structures and process, and (ultimately) change and identity.

The so-called ego psychologists (a better name would be holistic psychoanalysts), such as Kris (1950), Hartmann (1951), Rapaport (1960), Gill (1963), and Schur (1966), were in effect working on the contrast of the mental continuum with its definable contents. It should not be forgotten that Freud already carved a place for this kind of thinking by inserting a transformative category called "sublimation" into his theory of parts. Loewald (1960) saw that sublimation was no bit-player, and he moved it to center stage (see Friedman 1982). Kohut's "area of progressive neutralization" (1971) is another example. More recently, Donnel Stern (1997) has written about relatively amorphous, unformulated experience flowing into some-what unpredictable explicit outcomes that are themselves open to various for-mulations. Wilma Bucci (2002) describes the transformation of unarticulated into articulated meanings. Bion (1962) added a "metabolic" process to Kleinian units. Fonagy et al. (2002) and others focus attention on a process of mentalization and reflective functioning that precipitates definable units out of continua of awareness. These new trends join older ones: George Herbert Mead (1934) referred to an unarticulated source of initiative that gets its definition from external and inter-nalized social coding (see also Bergson 1912; Bruner 1990.) These theorists join an existential-phenomenological tradition (see Merleau-Ponty 1962; D.N. Stern 2010). Gendlin (1962) typically used the gerund "experiencing" to escape from what he regarded as artificially static items of experience that analysts talk about. Loewald (1960) did the same thing for Freudian theory, putting the entire spatially visualized psychic apparatus into motion.

In the past, many Freudian analysts shunned the process outlook because it did not seem to afford them a foothold for careful treading. We know how to respond to something only if we're able to determine that it is "a" something, and that it is the sort of something we can call up a response to. Freudian analysts wince when they hear talk about "ways of being with another" because they recognize that it opens the door to noncategorized (and therefore unmonitored) provocations and unprescribable responses. Partly for that reason, Freud wanted his followers to con-tinue to think in terms of retrievable memories even while turning attention to living processes. For many readers of "Remembering, repeating and working-through," the first injunction overshadowed the second.

In our two quotations we have seen Freud enjoin analysts to look for repeatable memories (that have some generality), on the one hand, and continuous behavior (which is an immediate happening), on the other, as two sides of the same coin. Interpretations connect abstract knowledge to transient experience. And interpretations

**68** The text

are just a small sample of the tacit formulations inside the analyst's head. For we must remember that in its broadest sense theory is simply a formalization of the working hypotheses everyone frames about everyone we deal with. And the analyst has an additional mandate: It isn't sufficient for him to recognize the person on his couch; he must also have many ways of thinking about him since he is not just dealing with his patient but trying to stay free of automatic "role responsiveness."

Newer theory, old philosophy, and recent research are struggling to complete Freud's task on a theoretical level. Some theorists clear the deck by simply abandoning discrete items of mind (see Friedman 1988). If an analyst leans strongly in that direction, he may despise talk of intrapsychic "objects" as being artificial distortions of the real, live human being. ("Life is green; theory gray, etc.") Existentialist psychologists voice that complaint. Much of the animus against "ego psychology" arises from those who prefer process. (They do not realize that the "ego psychologists," too, were engaged in restoring the organismic, process significance of the Freudian parts [see Friedman 1989].) Since people ordinarily recognize mental "objects" only in a casual, untheorized, taken-for-granted way ("He has no shame"), extremely detailed, conscientious efforts to explicitly work out the relationship between parts and process, aspects and flow, may look like obsessional scholasticism. Any effort to abstract "standard," constant parts from the unique flow of life is sometimes condemned as arrogant prejudice, disrespectful of individuality, and a grandiose pretense of expertise in the face of untameable novelty. (See Friedman [2002] on abstraction and [1999] on realists and nominalists.)

In turn, those who match their theory more poetically to the flood of life are sometimes deemed gullible and sentimental. We hear the complaint that a process theory cannot be considered psychoanalysis because it is not "conflict psychology." Of course that begs the question, but what it expresses is the fact that conflict is a way of isolating elements. Psychoanalysis defines elements by opposing them to each other. Without conflict, we might have only an impoverished description of a patient's general anguish. If parts are ruled out as artificial inventions of a prejudiced observer, it is hard to carve clinical phenomena into shapes.[6]

## IT IS A PROBLEM FOR ALL KINDS OF THINKING

The history of this problem suggests that truth straddles the fence, and we must be able to think both ways. And there is nothing special to psychoanalytic thinking about the problem of lifting something unchanging out of the flow of time. (For a discussion of abstraction, see Friedman 2002.) One recognizes the antiquity of the problem. The river of Heraclitus that you can't step into twice is just the most familiar image of it. The entire history of philosophy can be seen as a study of this problem. Lifting something out of the flow of time is just what thinking does, and science does it with a vengeance (Meyerson 1908). What is special to the study of the mind is a certain desperation. In other domains, thing-making can use spatial

The patient's private experience **69**

location to orient definitions. Physical things transition in time, but they reassuringly stay within spatial envelopes. Things of the mind are different. Internal mental things do not occupy a given space at a given time, and so we cannot quite settle on them as things, even though we nominalize them as things when we talk about them (Bergson 1912). And we tend to picture them in spatial terms even though we don't take the picture literally. The only way Freud could dissect the mind was to lay it out on a spatial table. He never lost sight of the metaphoric nature of his maneuver, but Loewald (1960) was pilloried for ever-so-gently reminding analysts that the structural theory was a spatialized metaphor for something of a different sort. It must surely be one of the attractions that neuroscience holds for psychoanalysts that it provides spatial equivalents for mental things.

It would be an error to dismiss arguments about these difficulties as quibbling about language or indulging the narcissism of small differences. Taken to extremes, the polarity of concreteness vs. abstraction moves people to contrasting views of life and, perforce, professional practice. I have hinted at this above, but anyone who cares to tangle with the same issue writ large in philosophy or intellectual history may glimpse what is at stake in the balance between discrete thought and continuous experience by revisiting the 1928 face-off between Martin Heidegger and Ernst Cassirer in Davos, Switzerland (M. Friedman 2000; Gordon 2010).

## *THE MORAL OF THE STORY*

As in most philosophical issues, the Zeitgeist (fashion) rules. But there is some room for individual choice. Analysts will, for characterological reasons, lean to one side or the other of these philosophical problems. The polarities cannot be avoided in practice any more than they can be settled in philosophy. There is something here to discomfort everyone. The power of Freud's theory is that it lives awkwardly with both sides of the controversy, but no more awkwardly than necessary. One might say that Freud's theory of the mind is the paradigm of a theory that accepts the disharmony of the continuous and the discrete (Ricoeur 1965; Friedman 1988). It is therefore positioned to orient a practitioner who must deal with both worlds at once.

## Notes

1 *Papers on Technique* does not pull together scattered contributions bearing on the subject; it is a consecutive series of installments written between 1911 and 1915 that chart in real time the progressive discovery of the ingredients of psychoanalytic treatment. The series of papers, supplemented by six other technique papers, was ultimately published along with metapsychology papers as a book, *Zur Technik der Psychoanalyse und zur Metapsychologie* (Freud 1924). Although the tone of the *Papers* is didactic and deceptively settled, each one of the series is just the report of that moment – one stage of an ongoing investigation that takes its leave from suggestion, catharsis, and dream interpretation, and journeys onward to psychoanalysis proper. Although Freud uses an exploratory question-and-answer style that elsewhere serves as a teaching device for expounding already achieved conclusions, in *Papers* this is not a rhetorical artifice, and its progression reveals it

**70** The text

as Freud's conversation with himself. The book is best understood by reading the individual papers consecutively as though they were a file of undoctored laboratory notes, recording the attitudes and behaviors that were found to turn on or turn off the new psychoanalytic phenomenon. The overall discovery required a progressive working out of puzzles and challenges presented by patients' behaviors. Most of the discoveries were learned from untoward consequences of analyst actions that would thenceforth be regarded as errors. Freud conveyed this experimental data in the form of warnings of the sort "If you do such-and-such, you will experience the following difficulties." The ways Freud works out the dilemmas constitute psychoanalytic technique. The "mistakes" are mostly natural behaviors of any therapist. That fact reveals the unique character of psychoanalysis and explains a peculiarity of *Papers* that has misled many commentators: It is assumed that, no matter what it's called, a list of warnings about mistakes cannot be a primary text on technique. But this *is* the primary text on technique, and it does proceed very largely – though not exclusively – by saying what not to do, and then providing a way of thinking that makes that discipline feel reasonable. As Freud works out the reasonableness of the odd interaction, the nature of the analytic interaction and the analytic process gradually comes into view. His solutions are conveyed in reproducible images, pithy phrases, and colorful metaphors for analysts to use as reminders of how to evoke an analytic process and avoid scuttling it. (Unfortunately, these terms and metaphors are often more memorable than their original meanings.) Two of the hallmarks of psychoanalytic technique are apparent here: its inhibition of natural response, and its paradoxical ideals. Freud published this progressive series of papers together as a book, the unmodified early solutions sitting side-by-side with later revisions, leaving the impression that an analyst must replace his social responses with several difficult and contradictory attitudes, and Freud sometimes says as much (see Friedman 1991a, 2008, 2009). It is sometimes necessary to look behind Freud's rhetoric. If instead of being read as a record of Freud's own mistakes, *Papers on Technique* is read as random corrections of miscellaneous howlers perpetrated by stupid or unethical students, reining them in with rigid rules to match their dull wit (as Freud did indeed sometimes suggest), a unique insight into the discovery and rationale of psychoanalytic treatment will be lost. To counteract this, educators should make use of Ellman's astute, paragraph-by-paragraph commentary to *Papers* (1991), which is ingeniously accompanied by a point-for-point comparison with some contemporary theorists. Ellman's reading is very close to my own, though he retains a bit more of what generations have layered over the original meaning of working through.

2  Strachey's misunderstanding of Freud's message goes beyond a single word. In this paragraph, Freud first says that the analyst apprises the patient of the resistance. Freud's verb is *mitteilt*. Further down, Freud writes that the analyst should realize that it isn't sufficient to name the resistance (the verb is *benennen*). In other words, the analyst has *apprised* the patient of the resistance by *naming* it. Then, in effect, Freud wants to say in the second edition that this activity of the analyst (*mitteilen* by *benennen*, or apprising by naming), while alerting the patient to the resistance, leaves the resistance still unknown, or unfamiliar (the adjective is *unbekannt*). The patient will yet need the actual experience of the drive that feeds the resistance, and only then, presumably, will he have become acquainted with it. Instead of following the logic of this passage, Strachey first promotes *mitteilt* to *acquainted*, and then ignores the further specification that it is mere naming. That specification should have sent him back to retranslate *mitteilt*, but he lets it stand as *acquainted*, which, then, renders senseless Freud's substitution of *unknown* for *known* a few lines below. In short, it is Strachey's own mistake that forces him to "correct" Freud. In contrast, Riviere, in her translation (Freud 1914b), gets it exactly right.

3  Some people associate "acquaint" mainly with the word "acquaintance," as in "He's not really a friend – just an acquaintance." But, as the *Oxford English Dictionary* indicates, being acquainted specifies empirical knowledge, not superficiality.

4  Actually, this distinction precisely reflects one of the changes undergone by the concept of resistance in the course of these papers. Originally "resistance" designated a phenomenon that the analyst did know by (bitter) acquaintance. He could feel it in his muscles

(so to speak) as it pulled against him when he tried to drag traumatic memories out of repression. Had Freud retained that original sense of resistance from pre-psychoanalytic treatment, Schafer's criticism of the term (1992) would be well founded: "resistance" would simply reflect Freud's countertransference. But Schafer's criticism is not valid against the radically changed concept in the mature psychoanalysis established by Freud in 1914. Indeed, Freud's new meaning is exactly opposite to the one Schafer criticized, since it is designed to bolster the analyst's *patience* while he lets the analysand be the one who feels the struggle. It is a testimonial to the strength of the age-old misunderstanding that even a fair and empathic reader like Schafer finds the "pressuring sense" of the term in his close reading of this paper, and can allow only one point at which a "slight but significant revision of wording ... [is] the beginning of his transition to the modern understanding of the idea" (p. 225). It is not a slight revision of wording; it is the sense of the whole paper – indeed of the whole book. Schafer's "modern meaning" is the express meaning for which the term *working through* was devised.

5 Freud seems to have been straining his eyes to spot an organic, shape-shifting power within the seemingly ideational or intellectual new treatment he had discovered. I have the impression that he could not mollify his own skepticism until he identified an engine within the new treatment equivalent to the old blast of hypnotic catharsis so obviously commensurate with its claimed effect. He knew that discovery was his main interest, not treatment, and it would be all too easy for him to gloss over the question of healing. At the end of this paper, almost as an aside to himself, Freud adds (with a sigh?) that he has at last found that sort of force in the concept of "working through" (p. 156). How far he would have been from being able to check off the missing explosive factor if "working through" merely meant patiently wearing down a resistance by repeated interpretations! In passing, one may observe that Freud's biologism is not confined to a hypothetical and presumably discredited energy hypothesis but extends to the commonsense experience of push and torment and the stubborn strength of motivation. "Working through" is better thought of as "suffering through" than as diligent repetition.

6 Brenner attempted to circumvent that difficulty by allowing all psychic phenomena to be simultaneously flexible and formed: "compromise formation" (see Friedman 2011). But if this formula were carried to its logical conclusion and all determinate parts, all structures and levels of awareness, were erased, the mind would be a featureless continuum. About such a mind all we could say is that everything about it expresses everything else about it. (In reality, most process theories smuggle defined entities back into the mind in the form of enduring dramas called fantasies.)

## REFERENCES

Bergson, H. (1912). *Matter and Memory*, trans. N. M. Paul & W. S. Palmer. New York, NY: Cosimo, 2007.

Bion, W. (1962). The psycho-analytic study of thinking. *International Journal of Psycho-analysis*, 43: 306–310.

Breuer, J. & Freud, S. (1893–1895). *Studies on Hysteria*. Standard Edition, 2.

Bruner, J. (1990). *Acts of Meaning*. Cambridge, MA: Harvard University Press.

Bucci, W. (2002). From subsymbolic to symbolic and back: Therapeutic impact of the referential process. In: *Symbolization and Desymbolization: Essays in Honor of Norbert Freedman*, ed. R. Lasky. New York, NY: Other Press, pp. 50–74.

Ellman, S. T. (1991). *Freud's Technique Papers: A Contemporary Perspective*. Northvale, NJ: Aronson.

Faimberg, H. (1996). Listening to listening. *International Journal of Psychoanalysis*, 77: 667–677.

Fonagy, P., Gergeley, G., Jurist, L. & Target, M. (2002). *Affect Regulation, Mentalization, and the Development of the Self*. New York, NY: Other Press.

**72** The text

Freud, S. (1911–1915). *Papers on Technique*. Standard Edition, 12: 91–171.

Freud, S. (1914a). Remembering, repeating and working-through. Standard Edition, 6: 147–156.

Freud, S. (1914b). Further recommendations in the technique of psychoanalysis: Recollection, repetition and working through. *Collected Papers*, 2: 366–376.

Freud, S. (1918). Erinnern, Wiederholen und Durcharbeiten. In: *Sammlung kleiner Schriften zur Neurosenlehre 4*: 441–452. Leipzig & Vienna: H. Heller.

Freud, S. (1922). Erinnern, Wiederholen und Durcharbeiten. In: *Sammlung kleiner Schriften zur Neurosenlehre 4*: 441–452. 2nd ed. Vienna: Internationaler Psychoanalytischer Verlag.

Freud, S. (1924). Erinnern, Wiederholen und Durcharbeiten. In: *Zur Technik der Psychoanalyse und zur Metapsychologie*. Vienna: Internationaler Psychoanalytischer Verlag, pp. 109–119.

Freud, S. (1925). Erinnern, Wiederholen und Durcharbeiten. In: *Gesammelte Schriften 6*:109–119. Vienna: Internationaler Psychoanalytischer Verlag.

Freud, S. (1937). Analysis terminable and interminable. Standard Edition, 23: 216–253.

Friedman, L. (1982). Sublimation. In: *Introducing Psychoanalytic Theory*, ed. S. L. Gilman. New York, NY: Bruner/Mazel, pp. 68–76.

Friedman, L. (1988). *The Anatomy of Psychotherapy*. Hillsdale, NJ: Analytic Press.

Friedman, L. (1989). Hartmann's ego psychology and the problem of adaptation. *Psychoanalytic Quarterly*, 58: 526–550.

Friedman, L. (1991a). A reading of Freud's *Papers on Technique*. *Psychoanalytic Quarterly*, 60: 564–595.

Friedman, L. (1991b). On the therapeutic action of Loewald's theory. In: *The Work of Hans Loewald: An Introduction and Commentary*, ed. G. I. Fogel. Northvale, NJ: Aronson, pp. 91–104.

Friedman, L. (1999). Why is reality a troubling concept? *Journal of the American Psychoanalytic Association*, 47: 401–425.

Friedman, L. (2002). Symbolizing as abstraction: Its role in psychoanalytic treatment. In: *Symbolization and Desymbolization: Essays in Honor of Norbert Freedman*, ed. R. Lasky. New York, NY: Other Press, pp. 204–230.

Friedman, L. (2007). Who needs theory of therapeutic action? *Psychoanalytic Quarterly*, 76 (Suppl.): 1635–1662.

Friedman, L. (2008). A renaissance for Freud's *Papers on Technique*. *Psychoanalytic Quarterly*, 77: 1031–1044.

Friedman, L. (2009). Freud's technique: More from experience than theory. *Psychoanalytic Quarterly*, 78: 913–924.

Friedman, L. (2011). Charles Brenner: A practitioner's theorist. *Journal of the American Psychoanalytic Association*, 59: 679–700.

Friedman, M. (2000). *A Parting of the Ways: Carnap, Cassirer, and Heidegger*. Chicago, IL: Open Court.

Gendlin, E. T. (1962). *Experiencing and the Creation of Meaning: A Philosophical and Psychological Approach to the Subjective*. New York, NY: Macmillan.

Gill, M. M. (1963). *Topography and Systems in Psychoanalytic Theory*. Psychological Issues Monograph 10. New York, NY: International Universities Press.

Glover, E. (1931). The therapeutic effect of inexact interpretation: A contribution to the theory of suggestion. *International Journal of Psychoanalysis*, 12: 397–411.

Gordon, P. E. (2010). *Continental Divide: Heidegger, Cassirer, Davos*. Cambridge, MA: Harvard University Press.

Hartmann, H. (1951/1964). Technical implications of ego psychology. In: *Essays on Ego Psychology: Selected Problems in Psychoanalytic Theory*. New York, NY: International Universities Press, pp. 142–154.

Kohut, H. (1971). *The Analysis of the Self: A Systematic Approach to the Psychoanalytic Treatment of Narcissistic Personality Disorder*. New York, NY: International Universities Press.

Kris, E. (1950/1975). On preconscious mental processes. In: *Selected Papers of Ernst Kris*, ed. L. M. Newman. New Haven, CT: Yale University Press, pp. 217–236.

Loewald, H. W. (1960). On the therapeutic action of psychoanalysis. *International Journal of Psychoanalysis*, 41: 16–33.

Mead, G. H. (1934). *Mind, Self, and Society from the Standpoint of a Social Behaviorist*, ed. C. W. Morris. Chicago, IL: University of Chicago Press.

Merleau-Ponty, M. (1962/1989). *The Phenomenology of Perception*, trans. C. Smith. London: Routledge.

Meyerson, E. (1908/1930). *Identity and Reality*, trans. K. Loewenberg. London: Allen & Unwin.

Rapaport, D. (1960). *The Structure of Psychoanalytic Theory: A Systematizing Attempt*. Psychological Issues Monograph 6. New York, NY: International Universities Press.

Ricoeur, P. (1965/1970). *Freud and Philosophy: An Essay on Interpretation*, trans. D. Savage. New Haven, CT: Yale University Press.

Russell, B. (1940). *An Inquiry into Meaning and Truth*. London: Allen & Unwin.

Schafer, R. (1992). Resistance: The wrong story? In: *Retelling a Life: Narration and Dialogue in Psychoanalysis*. New York, NY: Basic Books, pp. 219–247.

Schlesinger, H. J. (2013). *The Texture of Treatment: On the Matter of Psychoanalytic Technique*. Hillsdale, NJ: Analytic Press.

Schur, M. (1966). *The Id and the Regulatory Principles of Functioning*. New York, NY: International Universities Press.

Stern, D. B. (1997). *Unformulated Experience: From Dissociation to Imagination in Psychoanalysis*. Hillsdale, NJ: Analytic Press.

Stern, D. N. (2010). *Forms of Vitality: Exploring Dynamic Experience in Psychology, the Arts, Psychotherapy, and Development*. Oxford: Oxford University Press.

Waelder, R. (1930/1976). The principle of multiple function: Observations on over-determination. In: *Psychoanalysis: Observation, Theory, Application. Selected Papers of Robert Waelder*, ed. S. Guttman. New York, NY: International Universities Press, pp. 68–83.

# PART TWO

# The idea of Freudian therapy

## INTRODUCTION TO PART TWO

In the previous chapters I argued that, despite its misleading title, *Papers on Technique* is a consecutively developed book with a beginning, middle, and end, and that as such it has been buried. Yet the book's ghost haunts psychoanalytic controversy. Ectoplasmic fragments appear here and there, randomly selected, dimly recalled, and arbitrarily re-defined. The shade of the book is weirdly hard to bury; the various sects and schools of analysis tend to identify themselves by where they stand on terms from that book. Indeed, we might almost define psychoanalysis as, "a thought-collective that argues about terms from Freud's *Papers on Technique*."

But although the arguments continue in its *terms*, the *subject* of the book – the central idea of Freudian therapy – is lost. Those famous terms were actually mere pointers to Freud's *observations*. They all converge on the underlying phenomenon Freud discovered. That subject can only be gleaned by following the progression of experiments in the consecutive pages of Freud's monograph. And the phenomenon Freud had sighted provides the *rationale* for the treatment. Without the glue of the central idea, debaters swat at debris; terms, metaphors and images buzz around, colliding with each other and with every practitioner's wish and fancy. Past-pointing arguments make difficult technical decisions unresolvable and reduce discussion to jousting postures.

In the following chapters, I will discuss some technical problems in terms of Freud's discovery in *Papers on Technique*. For example, in Chapter 4 I look at the understandable dismay felt by analysts when they ask themselves: "Can the entire value of this long, intense, personal relationship really be equated to the interpretive *sentences* I pronounced from time to time?!" Their answer, of course, is: of course not. Many seem to think a personal relationship contradicts the presumably austere spirit of *Papers on Technique*, as though one's psychoanalytic credentials will be challenged if anything but an impersonal interpretation slips out to their patient.

**76** The idea of Freudian therapy

In point of fact, Freud insisted that an affectionate relationship was a necessary ingredient in the treatment process, though it is true that the goal of treatment is to minimize that factor. And it is also true that psychoanalysis has from the start anxiously patrolled its irregular border with hypnosis and frowned on terms and images that blurred that boundary. But the original warning in *Papers on Technique* that analysts should avoid non-interpretive aims (as when they cultivate dream reports) did not arise from fear of influencing patients, but on the contrary from the experience of *losing* influence altogether; by giving a hostage to the patient and thereby forfeiting the power of free association upon which analytic treatment depends. I sometimes have the impression that readers who are trying to grasp Freud's idea will try out every conceivable speculation about his character and outlook before they will look to see what he wrote on the page. A case in point is his caution about self-disclosure. They may think "it's just like Freud" to insist on a "one-person psychology" by putting a mirror between himself and his partner. In fact, Freud started out wanting to share his interest in dreams. It comes as a shock when patients "play" him, by drowning him in dreams. The evidence is that, whatever one finds in *Papers*, Freud was personally never willing to give up a feeling of companionship with patients in a shared joy of discovery. (See Lohser and Newton [1996].)

It's easy for us today, using hand-me-down terms, to fool ourselves that formal definitions somehow map naturally onto clinical phenomenology like a shifting GPS map onto the road we're driving. But Freud couldn't satisfy himself so easily with mere terminological answers to real life problems. (He couldn't just say: "It's the resistance, stupid.") So he spent page after page in *Papers* trying to figure out the enigma of patients' non-cooperation. The puzzle held him up in his report, from paper to paper, as he tried to work out the paradox. Unlike the cooperative patients of his pre-psychoanalytic practice, *it became apparent that analysands were not basically on his side in the battle.* Radical freedom is not wanted, and patients (not just "the" resistance) will make use of the analyst's manifest interest to select attitudes and guide attention. Even the analyst's subtlest disclosure deflects free association to the service of resistance. Freud wrestles with this problem, and out of that wrestling comes a deeper and tougher understanding of what resistance *is*. For instance, resistance is often far more charming than a mere stubborn refusal to cooperate, as it was originally pictured. One of the reasons that interpretation is the preferred mode of communication is that it keeps the analyst from being beguiled by the lures of conversation. The analyst's usual reason for keeping his communication spare ("interpretation only") is to avoid nudging patients in a favored direction, thus using suggestion rather than insight. But in fact, the traditional "all-business" style protects the *analyst* from being reflexively "hypnotized" by the patient's "cooperation" just as much as it protects the patient from being cultivated by the analyst's private preferences.

I urge readers of *Papers on Technique* to leave their familiar clichés at the door and look at the big picture inside: What he will see happening there is the transformation of a guided therapy not unlike many other talking treatments into something else – not just a different treatment, but a new kind of human experience. It is an experience that appears if and only if an analyst makes an effort to faithfully attend to patients with a minimum of the mutual seduction, persuasion, and intimidation that ordinarily accompany human interaction. Freud discovered (he didn't *hypothesize* it) that the trick is to minimize the analyst's *wanting*. That is a difficult task if ever there was one! Hence an ideal image of aspiration is needed to show the analyst how to set his compass. And from *Papers on Technique* the profession developed "interpretation only" as such an ideal image. (I will have more to say about ideals in Part Four.)

Some time ago, analysts were shaken by Franz Alexander's procedure, vaguely understood as healing patients by acting like an improved parent. They feared it would encourage Pygmalion fantasies That furor has died down. Nowadays analysts' fear of their huge hypnotic power is more likely to draw snickers from the cognoscenti. Today the shoe is on the other foot. It is the patient who has the upper hand. The contemporary critic of interpretation laughs at the analyst's desperate hope that his interpretive discipline will protect him from being seduced into an enactment by the *patient's* vitality.

There has always been a temptation to attribute a pristine objectivity to psychoanalytic interpretations. But today's animadversion against the worship of interpretation does more than cut it down to size. It is part of a new skepticism about the analyst's ability to control anything at all, including his thought, his action, and the separation between thought and action. At its extreme, the challenge is not just that treatment depends on "something beyond interpretation"; the challenge is that *everything* is beyond interpretation, since there is no such thing as a deliberate, objectively focused act in the first place, or even a realistic view of what one has just said. It is pointed out that we are always fitting into the other person's meaning-schemas without knowing it, by adjusting our own meaning to his.

Of course, ideals being what they are, there is plenty to be skeptical about in this ideal – the ideal of a completely informational, non-tendentious interpretation uninfluenced by the analyst's personal feelings. Common sense says that no interpersonal act (even a fist to the jaw) is without interpretive meaning, and no interpersonal ascription ("this is what you are like") is innocent of personal attitude and propagandistic intent. Kenneth Burke (1965/1954, p. 37) said, "we interest somebody by appealing to his interests." What is speech, after all, but the civilized way we act on each other? Trying to make speech even just a little bit less of a personal action is already very difficult and painful for both parties. It's a sacrifice for the both analyst and patients, who scan for the other's interests as contextual guides for their actions, responses, and understandings (and even simply to specify their meaning). We naturally *want* to be "confined" by our sense of situation and partner, in order that what we do (whether sympathetically or antagonistically) will be "appropriately" geared to our wants and theirs. Therefore, an analyst who wants to grant his patient the largest degree of freedom will need some *unnatural* image that he can hold before himself and try to approximate. One such image is the ideal interpretation. (Another is free-floating attention.) Freud's experiment in *Papers* showed what happened to patient's response (in his case, their dream reports) when he moved too far from that neutral image: The scale then tilted from free thought

**78**  The idea of Freudian therapy

to an ordinary social interaction around the terms at hand, which in Freud's case happened to be pleasing him by gratifying his fascination with dreams.

A therapist can use the image of an (unattainable) objective interpretation to measure how far he has intruded himself, and then base his behavior and his understanding of what ensued by factoring in the personal bias he had disclosed. What will ultimately make the difference to the patient is not so much the analyst's collective words, as the way they have directed the patient's attention. We may note that this is a relative matter. Freud did not stop exhibiting special interest (sometimes even delight) in his patients' dreams. He observed the overall theme of self-effacement only to the extent of somewhat *moderating* his inquiry. (Those who object that a patient will always detect the analyst's special interests should be reminded that there is a world of difference between saying: "I would not want you to tailor yourself to the intense interest in X that you see me trying to hide from you," and saying (sub rosa) "Please gratify the intense interest in X that I am calling to your attention.") What is important is the central *idea* of freedom from interpersonal pressure. We want to be able to say to a patient: "You will find in the psychoanalytic relationship the only situation where somebody is intensely interested in you without wanting anything from you" – or (more realistically phrased) "this is the only place where you will find someone who obviously thinks that you deserve such a one-way devotion, even if he/she fails to supply it in various ways." It is not a saintly pose (and certainly not a parent–child relationship): It is, as everyone finds out soon enough, a harsh practice. Nobody wants it, on either side of the couch (although patients may implicitly come to appreciate its value). The keystone of the analytic edifice has a Delphic inscription: "You cannot please or displease me. Nothing is more favored here than anything else." No displeasure is welcome, but no special favor is cruel. And that is why exaggerated images must be posted in front of analysts to preserve the ideal as a target. As always, it is not the rules but the rationale that makes the difference. Here the rationale is the patient's freedom: And the images and concepts are there to preserve the rationale, not to sanitize the consulting room. (See Freud's comments about ethics and transference love.)

## *WHAT IS LEFT STANDING AFTER CRITIQUE OF INTERPRETATION?*

If you were to poll analysts on how much of treatment lies "beyond interpretation," you would find a wide range of responses, with fewer today at the puristic end. But in circles that consider themselves Freudian you would not see that difference mirrored in an equally wide variety of techniques, or even great contrasts in analytic discipline. And that is noteworthy, since without fealty to selfless interpretation as the ultimate tool, Freudian analysts might well have scratched for a way of freeing the patient's insights from the analyst's personal interests. What is the new image of self-effacement that restrains the analyst's normal sociability? What ideal image guides him in the absence of the old faith in the ideal interpretation? To serve the purpose, it would have to be more realistic than its predecessor, more practical and less oracular than interpretation. (And wouldn't it be nice if it was humble?)

## ENACTMENT AND FRAME

How about enactment theory? It seems to fit the bill. There is no unlovable austerity in it, no arcane complexity. On its face, it is a common-sense notion: companionate, free-standing, realistic, and ready for use without a lot of explication. (It is almost visible.) Enactment theory, and its premise, the Frame, have a modest ring, especially since they embrace the analyst's countertransference as well as the patient's transference. And, if that isn't enough to recommend it, it doesn't even smack of *technique!*

So it might seem that we can dispense with *Papers on Technique* if we talk instead about enactments and how to handle them. Then we could free ourselves from uncertain (interpretive) authority, and move freely and honestly, while nevertheless observing the limits that reaffirm our special, Freudian discipline and self-effacement.[1]

Enactment concepts are easier to use than to theorize (which is one reason for their popularity). Strictly speaking, the concept of enactment migrates into the territory of (micro) sociology (the study of a small tribe with two members). That is how it differs from a traditional analysis of transference and countertransference. Once our subject is the sociological fact of a *shared*, lived-out drama, the joint configuration will replace its individual components as our basic, first-order fact. The tiny collective will now be our individual, so to speak.

I believe there is some conceptual fudging at work in these intersubjective theories, and I will state my bias now. There have always been efforts to blend descriptions of social action and private experience, and today there are whole schools of thought that even postulate the existence of a joint mind (an image I find a little creepy). But I believe groups and individuals are different slices of the universe, carved at different levels of abstraction, and interrelated by separate rules of causation with different reference to time and memory. An enactment is a drama of two persons, witnessed, as by an empathic observer, just as it would be on the stage, where it could be re-enacted with a different cast. We can say that an analytic office is a place were two people enact a psychoanalysis. In fact, all parties *should* take up that perspective from time to time, because that perspective is always present in both party's minds, and, like all patterns, usually hidden. But it is equally important to remember that, in the land of enactment, saying "here is an enactment" is exactly the same as saying "these two people are interacting," neither more nor less. To speak of enactment shifts our eyes from the mutually influenced experiences of two people to the single (abstract) form of one shared drama, observed by an imaginary outsider (often one's critical peers), and observed by each party separately. These are three (!) different observations. Since there is some form to every social interaction – indeed to every action – it is impossible to contrast enactment with something social that is not an enactment. And if we believe in the unconscious, we cannot sequester unseen and unintended enactments as the focus of our interest, since they would be echoing and reverberating on myriad levels all the time.

**80** The idea of Freudian therapy

UNLESS … unless … unless we allow ourselves to abstract from the interaction an aspect where individual expression breaks free from interaction, and tailors itself to autochthonous ends. That brings us back again in the land of impossible ideal images. We have had to relinquish some of the common-sense, nail-and-peg solidity of the Frame, and the "gotcha" quality of enactment. In clinical reality, enactment and frame are used the same way that other Freudian ideals are used: We all know there is a *sliding scale* stretching from blatant collusion to an *ideal* independence that is *not* an enactment and is never actually reached. For practical purposes, if a pattern (1) of previous concern (2) looks and feels sufficiently similar to a pattern of interaction with the analyst, and (3) has passed unobserved, most will consider it an enactment. And it just doesn't matter that framing it as an enactment is another enactment within another drama, or even that we know we're chasing a will-o'-the wisp. It's a matter of more-or-less, and of what's useful, as measured against an unreachable ideal of not-an-enactment, i.e., the ideal of personal autonomy. We haven't really left *Papers on Technique*.

Enactment is implicitly a way of referring to a *departure* from the peculiar (partial) asociality that was described in *Papers on Technique*.

What about "the frame?" Asked what would be not-an-enactment, many enactment-spotters will reach for the inevitable, last-ditch end-run around *Papers on Technique* and say: "Not-an-enactment" is what stays inside "the frame." But this frame is not, for example, the sociological frame of Goffman (1974/1986), which provides a mutually agreed-upon context of understanding. An analytic frame is the exact opposite. It is something that (ideally) excludes *all* fixed contextual frames of the sociologists. That's what free association means. The analytic frame encloses and protects the anomic wilderness on the couch from the outside, structured society.

*Papers on Technique* might reasonably have been entitled: "How to [try to] Avoid Enactments." (cf. Freud's dictum that there is no model for the analytic relationship in real life.)

I must apologize now for my archness. Spotting enactments is a move toward "normalizing" the analyst's self-image, which is a good thing, and it fogs over the stark sinews of technique, as must happen at work. But when it comes to the *understanding of* what was going on in a particular hour, and what the analytic project is all about, the regular use of less troubling terms that secretly derive from *Papers on Technique* is self-defeating.

Enactment has no meaning in any other context even though it feels free and sufficient unto itself. If you think enactments should be studied, that is reason enough to treasure *Papers on Technique*, for that is the book that defines enactment in the only way it can be defined; that is, by saying what a non-enactment would be. It gives an operational definition of the non-enactment phenomenon in terms of what promotes or dissolves it. Most of those who think in terms of enactments are depending on Freud's book whether they know it or not.

In fact, enactment as a theoretical concept is quite useful in bluntly provoking the elusive question that lurks in the center of the psychoanalytic project: What (theoretically, and in general) is expected or demanded of the patient? Freud did

Introduction **81**

not hesitate to acknowledge the difficulty of the question and he required an answer for his own peace of mind, even at that early time, and even in such a brief span of work as *Papers*. (Later, when his interest in the question had faded, he would abbreviate his answer and simply refer to the need for an "unaltered" ego.) What is "the good patient" (to use Henry Smith's term)? What sort of companion is the analyst reaching for or presupposing? Many analysts have been self-serving and unrealistic in their expectations of cooperation. (See Friedman [1969].) Their program often assumes that patients will act against interest, insofar as "interest" means an organismic inner reckoning. Patients are expected to stubbornly "work" at undermining an illusion that their analyst is stubbornly creating for them (an illusion about the nature of the relationship). Why would anyone agree to something that flies in the face of desire? It is, of course, the old question of therapeutic action that bedevils any non-directive treatment, but especially a circular theory of motive and belief. What do you present to someone to change the way he experiences what you present to him? Psychoanalysis is better suited to explain why patients don't change than why they do. Freud troubled himself with this question in *Papers*, and his brief answer is found partly in his account of the patient's attachment, and partly in his concept of working through, neither of which is popular now.

This motivational conundrum is not a frivolous theoretical jig-saw puzzle. It reflects the great haunt of analytic therapy: the precarious cultivation of a dangerous illusion of the analyst's permanent attachment. It is the major dramatic configuration that stands out in Freud's initial exploration of the novel psychoanalytic experience. Some theories offered as replacements for *Papers* may owe their popularity to a more comfortable portrayal of the treatment scene than the moral and emotional no-man's land that Freud stared at without blinking. On the other hand, it may be that Freud's willingness to confront the strain head-on in *Papers* is the reason that "Transference-Love" is the one paper teachers are likely to retrieve from *Papers on Technique*. Chapters 8 through 10 will discuss this further.

## Note

1 This usefulness supposes that enactment has been purged of the moralism that attends the phrase, "acting out," which used to flash a watch-tower torch on unwanted behavior. That connotation is now confined to everyday speech, where it doesn't pretend to be other than a synonym for misbehavior or outright delinquency.

## REFERENCES

Burke, K. (1965/1954). *Permanence and Change: An Anatomy of Purpose*. 2nd ed. Indianapolis, IN: Bobbs-Merrill.

Friedman, L. (1969). The therapeutic alliance. *International Journal of Psycho-Analysis*, 50: 139–153.

Goffman, E. (1974/1986). *Frame Analysis: An Essay on the Organization of Experience*. Boston, MA: Northeastern University Press.

Lohser, B. & Newton, P. M. (1996). *Unorthodox Freud: The View from the Couch*. New York, NY: Guilford Press.

# 4

# WHAT LIES BEYOND INTERPRETATION, AND IS THAT THE RIGHT QUESTION?

As a generation we are disenchanted with interpretations. We find it hard to believe that listening to people and then telling them something will transform their life. We doubt that being told something is a cataclysmic event. We think interpretation was oversold, that what really affects patients is a mélange of personal forces. We may think our doubts prove us to be either demoralized Freudians or proud pioneers. These doubts, I think, show no such thing. They have troubled analysts from the start.

In fact, as soon as he discovered psychoanalysis, Freud (1914) was plagued by the same doubt. He had seen minds loosened in the acid of hypnosis. He had seen minds shaken by the blast of catharsis. But now he appeared to be just telling patients something. What could he possibly expect from that? Freud kept trying to figure out what it was inside the new, nondirective treatment that packed a punch like abreaction. One thing was certain: It was not mere words. In terms of my title, Freud believed that we must go Beyond Interpretation. Of course, Freud said, the patient's loving trust is a pre-condition for any influence. But he knew that love will not tear patients out of their old world – in fact, it sometimes keeps them there. Then what does have the needed impact? Freud's answer is revivifying old attachments (in the relationship to the analyst), and then killing them off. And how do you kill them off? Freud said, in effect, "Don't think you can do it by pointing something out. It can only happen through an intense experience." The intense experience, Freud said, was the experience of wrestling with opposing wishes as expressed in the torments of analysis. He called it "working through." It was something the patient was experiencing, not something he was listening to.

Of course, one could choose to look on psychoanalysis as an intellectual enterprise. Who can deny that, historically considered, interpreting means providing edifying information? But I remind you that already in 1923 Ferenczi and Rank (1923/1925) reported that playing teacher was a well-known error. Were they,

**84** The idea of Freudian therapy

then, the rare exception? It might be argued that other analysts often fell into the error of pedantry. Mention Ferenczi today, and one thinks of the war between cognitivists and emotionalists. But despite a little theoretical warfare and its tactical expression in technique, psychoanalysts were never divided on the *principles* involved, because nobody ever finally signed off on the problem. They simply emphasized different aspects of one single rationale: Ferenczi and Rank were elaborating Freud's emphasis on infantile desire; their critics were extending Freud's emphasis on the patient's unrealisticness. Championing each aspect at one time or another, Freud himself never abandoned either element. In 1937, Fenichel observed that analytic fashion always fluctuates between too much talking and too much experience.

Well, then, what did our forebears think it was that lies beyond interpretation? Many thought that patients are subtly induced to copy the analyst's attitude, for instance, imitating his tolerance (Strachey 1934), or his objective problem-solving (Sterba 1934), or his way of articulating and integrating (later emphasized by Loewald 1960). Edmund Bergler (1937) even suggested that the analyst's seemingly sexual engagement shows the patient the way out of his repressions. The skeptic will say that it is easy for analysts to acknowledge that sort of personal influence because it blends so respectably with the act of interpreting. But that is not the end of the story. Analysts were also aware of untidy, emotional clouds of personal influence hovering out there beyond interpretation – even emotional blackmail, according to Nunberg (1928/1948). Reviewing the literature, we are always surprised to see how many old, mainstream analysts declare that, at the end of the day, everything depends on the analyst's true, overall feeling for his patient, including his unconscious attitude, which, obviously, he cannot control.

Anyway, my point is that there was nothing secret or scandalous about such talk of nebulous personal forces that are essential to treatment. By and large it was taken for granted. Nobody was shocked in 1937 when Glover teased analysts for preening themselves on the exquisite refinement of a procedure that, in reality, packages so many inadvertent forces that they can never all be known. In the same years, Fenichel (1937) declared that the analyst's affects were always taking part in the exchange. And nobody cringed when Bibring (1954) made a list of five separate types of analytic doings, of which four were Beyond Interpretation and the main one – the analytic setup – was a manipulation. Only the early Kleinians shunned these questions, thinking that interpretations put pieces of the patient's mind back into him, and that oversimplification was corrected by Bion.

Why, then, is there such a ferment of reforming zeal today? Is there really a new issue before us? I believe there is. Whatever the myriad forces are that have always been acknowledged, there is now a challenge to the image of the analyst's *deliberate* doings. It was the idea of deliberateness that used to be embodied in the ideal of "interpretation only." To locate our new worries, we must therefore look beyond questions of what goes on "besides" interpretation to some thornier questions about the analyst's intentions, specifically what his intentions are, how much conscious control he has over them and in what domains, and what the net effects are of the analyst having those intentions.

Before deciding those issues, we should recall what a psychoanalytic interpretation was supposed to be, at least after the early enthusiasm for peripatetic dream interpretation. Definitions differ slightly, but Freudians always agree that a psychoanalytic interpretation is never just something said. Interpretations are certain words that emerge from the mouth of a free-floating, anonymous, objective figure watching a free-associating patient, with all the feelings and forces attending such an event. Never mind for the moment whether an event like that is possible. Call it hypothetical, if you like, but you must imagine that, conceptually, the entire analytic format is rolled up and squeezed into the term "interpretation."

And, whatever one may argue is actually going on, there is no doubt that the setup does induce a range of attachments and passions with little reciprocity. Stone (1961) and Tarachow (1963) call it closeness in distance. The important thing to note is that this is not a natural way for human beings to be together. We are designed for social relationships. But a social reaction would confirm some particular relationship. And analysts believe that any particular relationship will be fitted into the patient's habitual image, thus discouraging other experiences. That is why patients need an analyst and not just an honest friend. Analysts have sometimes come right out and *defined* interpretations as efforts to head off a social relationship that a patient thinks he is making (Tarachow 1963). Correspondingly, the act of interpreting heads off the analyst's own social impulse, so that the patient is exempted from the demands the analyst makes on other people (Klauber 1971/ 1981). Interpreting is the analyst's way of resisting nature.

Theoretically, an interpretation is an accurately responsive action that can be repeatedly and consistently taken by someone who otherwise has no fixed shape, and thus seeks no particular relationship. The patient finds no single aspect of himself officially endorsed at the expense of another, and none forbidden. With this nonsocial way of calling something to attention, the analyst intends to describe something *about* the patient, or something in the patient, instead of definitively characterizing the whole patient morally and dramatically, as all our actions do with social partners. Interpretation allows the analyst to wear an infinitely flexible persona while yet consistently orienting the patient in self-inquiry. At least that is the principle, which means that whatever the analyst actually ends up doing, the patient can see that he was *hoping* to occupy that unsociable position.

Still another way of putting this has special relevance to some noninterpretive ideologies. As Freud (1915) warned in 1915, analysts must be prepared to be at once both tempting and frustrating. That is exactly what a consistent interpreter is doing – he is preparing and warning – preparing himself and his patient for the weirdness of a relationship that is both tempting and frustrating. He says, "this is what I have to offer, and not what you would naturally expect from your partner." The interpreter is constantly advising patients (and himself) of the limits of his commitment. Interpretation throws an honest wet blanket over hopes and expectations – as well as fears – while the rest of the treatment is busy firing them up.

**86** The idea of Freudian therapy

Inside himself, a consistent interpreter is relieved of some worry about the intimacy of treatment, because he is constantly disowning promises he cannot keep. Meanwhile, as John Klauber (1971/1981) pointed out, interpretation is the analyst's pacifier, substituting for the social recognition he craves. And we all know that interpreting habituates the courage needed to march into the patient's inevitable knives. The more interpersonal forces there are at work, the more useful an interpretation is as a broom. Interpretations are a straightforward, up-front declaration of intentions in what is otherwise a murky business. At least that is how they make analysts feel.

So the act of interpreting carries the whole psychoanalytic situation on its back – but only implicitly. We all know that is not what interpretations look like on their face. Explicitly, interpretation refers only to the analyst's specific, intentional action. That is important. By thinking of interpreting as a separate action, analysts dissociate themselves from the manipulative forces that they train on the patient. Customarily, if you asked an analyst what he did, he would say, "I interpret." He would not say, "I make patients lie down and lose control. I haunt them with silence and hide my face. I make them think I know them better than I really do, and that I carry an authority nobody really has. I confuse them about where we are heading. I creep daily into their life but keep them guessing about where they fit in mine." These actions are all done by The Analysis, while the analyst personally confines himself strictly to interpreting. Interpretations allow analysts to take personal responsibility only for deliberate actions that are supposedly not manipulative. Manipulation would be a form of social activity, and analysts practice not being social.

In the process, it is not surprising that some psychoanalysts developed a special pride in their Spartan self-restraint. Perhaps in the 1940s, 1950s, and 1960s some acted a little like Clint Eastwood with a couch. But machismo was not the driving force; it was fear. Analysts feared a particular shadow lurking just beyond interpretation. From Freud on, the implicit forces of treatment were most often thought to be passionate parent–child forces. In a sense, the effort to avoid manipulation was specifically an effort to disrupt the inevitable parent–child configuration of treatment. Any deliberate use of the silent forces would deliberately infantilize patients. And please note: The trouble with deliberately infantilizing lay not so much in the infantilizing as in the deliberateness. As to the infantilizing alone, it might be inevitable. The analytic setup might automatically put the analyst in a parental position. The parental aura might even be essential to the cure, as an implicit invitation to regrowth (Balint 1932/1953; Loewald 1960; Winnicott 1971; but also, Bibring 1937). But it is quite another matter if the analyst personally *tries* to be – or *wants* to be – seen as a parent. Freudians thought that would reinvigorate the patient's original problem. By restricting himself to interpretation only, analysts declared their personal intention to avoid being like parents, and that intention was a fact in its own right, whether or not it succeeded. The visible intention to avoid a parental role advertised the ideal of self-responsibility and freedom, and, I might add, honesty (because the analyst is not a parent).

All of which is to say that previous Freudian conferences revered interpretation not as a fetish, but as the only deliberate, nonsocial, nonmanipulative, non-infantilizing way of directing attention inside an otherwise uncontrollable inter-personal field. It was (ideally) a minimal action, so (ideally) it left the patient free from social constraint. Well, not exactly free. It was still, after all, an interpersonal action, so the patient's freedom was not total. There was one demand left. The form of interpretations revealed the analyst's interest. Patients recognized it as a demand for drastically honest self-contemplation and self-confrontation. That demand was the one social structure left standing. But even that demand was unique in that it was actually framed as an appreciation of the patient's good reasons for refusing it.

So much for the definition of interpretation. Now, let us ask "what's new?" What's new is this: The Freudian rationale is both indirectly undermined by a shift of zeitgeist, and directly assaulted by many specific challenges. Altogether, these admonish the old interpreter: "You are wrong about what sorts of things you can control, and wrong about how much you can control anything."

To begin with, many see less structure in the mind. Consequently, the target of interpretation has become harder to identify. In fact, the target was beginning to blur already in 1900, when analysts stopped fishing for neatly defined traumas. It was not as easy to delineate targets such as complex affects and patterns of rela-tionships (e.g., in the transference) as it had been to delineate memories. And the target of interpretation got blurrier still when mental *processes* were described. It is a different thing to be telling a patient what he is doing with his insides than it had been to evoke a forgotten memory already inside him. (After all, a natural-born unconscious does not contain an index of defense mechanisms.) If you tell some-body what he is doing to protect himself, you can no longer pretend you are offering an exact replica of what he would say to himself if he were "normal." In this situation, it is harder for an analyst to claim that his saying just replaces some-thing missing from the patient's own stash of sayings (as Kurt Eissler [1953] required it to do). Already in the 1930s, even before Anna Freud, Glover (1937) pointed out that interpretation could no longer claim to be the one way out of the woods, as there was no longer a simple path that led into the woods. And that is not all. It is not just that the targets are fuzzier. The targets also refuse to stand still, or they may be totally shielded from the words that are hurled toward them: On the one hand, fantasies have many versions. Narratives can be told every which way. In fact, ultrasophisticates no longer believe there is any matter of fact at all in the patient, no, and not any objective relationship, either, that we could con-ceivably be deliberate about, even approximately, even tactically, even narratively. And at the opposite extreme some say that the conduct of life is so thoroughly objective in the physical sense – so much a neurological matter of habit training (procedural memory, etc.) – that the analyst's talk is like a speech addressed to the patient's kidneys.

And, even as the target was evaporating, the message flying toward it – I mean the psychoanalytic interpretation – wavered in the target's gravitational field,

## 88 The idea of Freudian therapy

swelled into a blunt instrument, and finally exploded in a cloud of context. Mind you, context itself is not a new discovery. At least from the time Edward Glover (1931) wrote about inexact interpretations, analysts realized that most of what they said got its meaning from the patient's own desires. And analysts had never been so stupid as to think that their interpretations drifted impersonally toward a patient. Starting with Freud, they recognized that interpretations are understood in terms of their perceived intent, which, in turn, depends on who the patient thinks is uttering them. Who speaks? Is it a fostering figure or a punishing one? Does the interpretation appear to hold out promise or foreclose it? Does it suggest an opportunity or pronounce a doom? Obviously, everything in the relationship contributes to the meaning of an interpretation. And by the same token, everything in the relationship has interpretive significance, including the nature of the analyst's motives and the overall drift of his behavior.

All that was well understood. But nowadays some say that context is not just important; it is everything. Some think speech conveys no propositional information whatever. Some people say that language is just socialized behavior. As Ted Shapiro (2002) has shown, thinkers have shifted attention from the truth-value of speech to its practical effect in moving people. Looking at the pragmatics of speech, today's analyst might view interpretations as just another way of pushing or petitioning patients. Speech, it would seem, simply joins forces with other personal reactions to express the analyst's own feelings and to make himself comfortable. In other words, it is really just the opposite of its old nonmanipulating, nonsocial appearance.

Analysts are told that the relationship does not just color meaning; it determines the whole of what is heard. Not only is every interpretation a social act; it is an act whose meaning is made up entirely of countless other, imperceptible acts by both parties. Since nobody can describe a complete context, or view a moment while in the middle of it, how can the analyst ever specify a meaning? The art of interpreting is beginning to look like the Mikado's punishment, a game played "on a cloth untrue with a twisted cue and elliptical billiard balls."

Analysts have therefore been grateful for new trends that legitimize noninterpretive actions. They think observations of child development show that the Hungarians were right: Childhood wishes are not necessarily passionate; they may not be dangerous traps for the analytic relationship after all. On the contrary, patients' childlike wishes may be flexible, forward-moving quests, similar to cognitive explorations. It is thought that such relational needs can be safely shepherded deliberately in a progressive direction without fear of consolidating a child–parent relationship. With that, the analytic world is turned upside down. Analysts used to think that what they could not control was the vague, interpersonal forces, and what they could control was their deliberate speech. Now many analysts feel they have no control over their message, but a fair chance of managing the overall machinery of growth. They think the relationship is the only thing they can govern, at least in collaboration with the patient – certainly not an interpretive message.

Now, you may ask how an analyst can accept a social bond without unwittingly responding to the old passionate demands of infancy, for nobody denies that there are such demands. How does an analyst make use of progressive attachments without being used by regressive ones? If he does not shun relationships in general, how can he know which relationship he is actually encouraging? The answer is that today's analysts hope to dig out those aspects that are passionate and confining – call them enactments – and then – what else? – interpret them. Thus, when push comes to shove, most analysts have never given up their faith in interpretation, and especially the importance of their *intention* to interpret. The new specialists in enactment show how important the analyst's intention is. When they confess their regular lapse into enactment, what they are advertising is not their success in bonding with the patient, but their contrary intention – that is, an intention to stay unsocial, or at least *get* unsocial after all. Relationally-minded analysts might phrase their intention differently. They might talk about clarifying rather than interpreting, and they may picture its purpose more as articulating what was previously amorphous or mysterious. But I think these are all roughly equivalent in their format. Though they do not say so, analysts are still putting their money on an intention – on a direction – on the therapeutic importance of the unrealizable ideal of objective interpretation. They tell the patient over and over again: "You see, I do not *wish* to settle for the perspective we have fallen into."

All these challenges to interpretation go to the question of deliberate control. Unfortunately, it is often debated in terms of absolutes: Can we conceal reactions or are we always giving ourselves away? Can we speak objectively or are we just reacting personally? That is the wrong sort of question. The practical question is one of degree: Can we govern our vision enough to make decisions? Can we govern our self-awareness enough to know, roughly, what our decisions actually are? Can we govern our speech to get across something of what we intend? If not our speech, then can we govern our behavior a little, and, through behavior, influence the relationship more or less in the direction we want? And at the very least – and perhaps it is not so little after all – can we veer *toward* a chosen professional stance? In a nutshell, the question is this: Can we deliberately lift anything out of the jumble of inputs and outputs, and can we give to that jumble some coloring of our choosing? And finally, what sort of professional habits are most likely to free our vision from social constraint?

By definition, all professionals make choices. Analysts must try for something and, considering the human condition, they will probably fall short. When we think of ideals, we should think of the effects of *trying*. We must ask, what happens if we try for this instead of for that? What happens within us as we try; how does it constrain our own feelings; how does it constrain our other choices? But also, what does it signify to a patient when he sees us trying for this or that, and what difference if he sees us trying openly or covertly? No matter what we end up doing, an important message is conveyed by what we are seen to be trying for, and how we seem to feel about it.

**90** The idea of Freudian therapy

Analysts have always recognized that much of their impact comes from just hanging in there – from constancy and familiarity. But if an analyst has even the vaguest idea of what he hopes to achieve by it, then his hanging in is an effort to orient the patient's attention to something, overtly or subliminally.

Clearly, some ways of directing attention are broad and open-ended, while others are more focused. And obviously, communication induces some degree of both. Every act of sharply focusing somebody's glance is partly decoded by reference to the interpersonal situation and its history. But despite the new challenges, practice has followed old common sense in taking words to be the easiest and most precise way to orient a person's attention. Now, analysts know that in the very act of focusing the patient's attention, words are also building a relationship, and older analysts were wary of that. They wanted only so much relationship as would get the partners looking in the same direction. They wanted to point, not to schmooze. And they prized the fact that just as words can build a relationship, they can also extricate one from it. For example, you can use words to disrupt a personal situation by describing it impersonally, or by commenting on what is supposed to go unmentioned. (Goffman [1974] called it breaking the frame.) As I indicated, that bit of old wisdom has been retained. Even analysts who believe they are always and inevitably socially entangled look to words to help them break loose now and then, which proves that they have even more confidence in words than the older analysts who thought that, once formed, social roles are not so easily dissipated by words.

But, as noted, attention is also oriented in nonverbal ways. The general setup of the analytic treatment is broadly interpretive: it embodies a theory of the mind and of interpersonal relations, and an implicit theory of what the patient needs. If the setup glorifies interpretations, that glorification has an interpretive significance of its own. In other words, the procedure itself says a lot in addition to what is said by the interpretations. (For instance, besides warning the patient about the analyst's distance, interpreting also says, "Look more honestly at yourself. It's good for you.") And we should not fail to note that a treatment that glorifies what is beyond interpretation will also be saying a lot to a patient, something quite different, and let us hope it is not a message about the analyst's exceptional humanity.

Finally, I want to emphasize that the most powerful and least conspicuous way of directing attention is by setting up a problem. Emphasizing interpretation was one way to do that. (As though the patient must ask himself, "How do I wrestle my way out of this dilemma between getting what I want and giving my game away by talking about it? Or how do I put up with feeling something to be happening that also seems 'perpetually out of reach?'" [e.g., Bird 1972; French 1958; Macalpine 1950].) Beyond that, what kind of productive problem does an emphasis on interpretation set the *analyst*? (He may wonder, "How do I manage to think all at once about what the patient is seeing and also how it exemplifies his mental routines and also what he's trying to recruit me for?") Similarly for non-interpretive settings. What different problems do they set for patient and analyst?

In summary, when we think of actions that go beyond interpretations, we should consider how they meet the technical challenges that inspired the old ideal of "interpretation only." For instance: The interpreting analyst tried to focus the patient's attention on more comprehensive ways of getting a sense of himself and his world. The interpreting analyst tried to focus the patient's attention where it feels dangerous to both parties, but not so dangerous as to be unacceptable. He tried to sketch a paradigm of honest self-scrutiny and responsibility. He tried to focus the patient's attention particularly and partially, without characterizing him as a whole. He tried to offer neither criticism nor approval. He tried to refuse all social roles, tried not to want to be seen any one way more than another, tried to say, in effect, "You can't please or displease me; you can think anything you want of me." He assumed there is a hidden rank order of momentary fears; he tried to deal with them according to their urgency and relevance. He tried to make evident what he could and could not promise, by making his offering as explicit and consistent as possible. Whatever lies "beyond interpretation," we should make it speak one way or another to those concerns.

## REFERENCES

Balint, M. (1953/1932). Character analysis and new beginning. In: *Primary love and psychoanalytic technique*. New York, NY: Liveright, pp. 159–173.

Bergler, E. (1937). Symposium on the theory of the therapeutic results of psychoanalysis. *International Journal of Psycho-Analysis*, 18: 146–160.

Bibring, E. (1937). Symposium on the therapeutic results of psycho-analysis. *International Journal of Psycho-Analysis*, 18: 170–190.

Bibring, E. (1954). Psychoanalysis and the dynamic psychotherapies. *Journal of the American Psychoanalytic Association*, 2: 745–770.

Bird, B. (1972). Notes on transference: Universal phenomenon and hardest part of analysis. *Journal of the American Psychoanalytic Association*, 20: 267–301.

Eissler, K. (1953). The effect of the structure of the ego on psychoanalytic technique. *Journal of the American Psychoanalytic Association*, 1: 104–143.

Fenichel, O. (1937). *Problems of Psychoanalytic Technique*, trans. D. Brunswick. New York, NY: The Psychoanalytic Quarterly.

Ferenczi, S. & Rank, O. (1923/1925). *The Development of Psycho-analysis*, trans. C. Newton. New York, NY: Nervous and Mental Disease Publishers.

French, T. (1958). *The Reintegrative Process in a Psychoanalytic Treatment: The Integration of Behavior* (Vol. 3). Chicago, IL: University of Chicago Press.

Freud, S. (1914). Remembering, repeating and working-through. Standard Edition, 12.

Freud, S. (1915). Observations on transference-love. Standard Edition, 12.

Glover, E. (1931). The therapeutic effect of inexact interpretation: A contribution to the theory of suggestion. *International Journal of Psycho-Analysis*, 12: 397–411.

Glover, E. (1937). Symposium on the theory of the therapeutic results of psychoanalysis. *International Journal of Psycho-Analysis*, 18: 125–132.

Goffman, E. (1974). *Frame Analysis: An Essay on the Organization of Experience*. Cambridge, MA: Harvard University Press.

Klauber, J. (1981/1971). The relationship of transference and interpretation. In: *Difficulties in the Analytic Encounter*. New York, NY: Jason Aronson, pp. 25–43.

## 92 The idea of Freudian therapy

Loewald, H. (1960). On the therapeutic action of psychoanalysis. *International Journal of Psycho-Analysis*, 41: 16–33.

Macalpine, I. (1950). The development of the transference. *Psychoanalytic Quarterly*, 19: 501–539.

Nunberg, H. (1928/1948) Problems of therapy. In: *Practice and Theory of Psychoanalysis*, Vol. 1., New York: International Universities Press, pp105–119.

Shapiro, T. (2002). From monologue to dialogue: A transition in psychoanalytic practice. *Journal of the American Psychoanalytic Association*, 50: 199–219.

Sterba, R. F. (1934). The fate of the ego in analytic therapy. *International Journal of Psycho-Analysis*, 15: 117–126.

Stone, L. (1961). *The Psychoanalytic Situation*. New York, NY: International Universities Press.

Strachey, J. (1934). The nature of the therapeutic action of psycho-analysis. *International Journal of Psycho-Analysis*, 15: 127–159.

Tarachow, S. (1963). *An Introduction to Psychotherapy*. New York, NY: International Universities Press.

Winnicott, D. W. (1971). *Playing and Reality*. Harmondsworth, UK: Penguin Books.

# 5

# IS THERE LIFE AFTER ENACTMENT?

A practicing analyst will naturally take certain features of his daily work for granted. They seem part of the natural rhythm of things, hardly worth scrutinizing. One example is the sense of a patient "working at" or "not working at" treatment. But can an analysand deliberately work at treatment? And if so, how does such deliberate work fit in with the specifically psychoanalytic rationale of treatment? How is the patient's cooperative work different from – and how is it like – an enactment?

The problem here is only partly the difficulty of defining a patient's proper work; the grim truth is that it is much easier to argue on purely psychoanalytic grounds that there is no such thing as a patient *not* working at treatment, which means that a patient *cannot* have the sort of proper, deliberate work to do that we all find ourselves expecting as a matter of course in practice. That very observation will remind the reader that the question of a patient's deliberate work is just one more path into that old quagmire: the problem of "cooperation" in psychoanalytic treatment.

## PERENNIAL PROBLEMS POINT TO THE ESSENCE OF TREATMENT

Old quagmires are precious. At a time when psychoanalysis seems to morph from shape to shape, a good old quagmire may be the clearest sign of an essential "knot" or "navel" in the tradition. In this case, we recognize the stubborn bite of arguments about the therapeutic alliance (Zetzel 1958, 1966), the unobjectionable positive transference (Freud 1912), the working alliance (Greenson 1965), etc. As I will indicate, old problems can also be newly shaped by interests of the times.

There are ways, however, in which this problem has been finessed rather than discussed. To some extent, the notion of a patient's work is one way to finesse the question of how much the treatment depends on the patient's reactive affiliation and how much on his autonomous understanding. Nor is it a dishonorable strategy to disguise the intractable old question in this way, since it serves a worthy purpose. The familiar concept of work grabs hold of the slippery theoretical problem (relational satisfaction vs. acquired knowledge)[1] and wraps it in a neat action package that we can visualize. Such images are profoundly stabilizing for the practitioner. Like Samuel Johnson kicking a rock and saying of the philosophical idealist Berkeley, "Thus I refute him," the practitioner welcomes a patient's good work, groans at the lack of it, and leaves the old worry about suggestion for theorists to chew on as they please. I think this is just as true of sophisticates who accept Sullivan's sentiment, "God save me from a treatment that is going well," as it is of those who were never tempted to knock a good thing in the first place.

## EARLY RELIANCE ON "THE EGO" AS CONVENIENT SHORTHAND FOR WORK

Classical theory includes a drama of wishes and fears, and practitioners valued it chiefly as a no-nonsense field guide for spotting those wishes and fears. What the theory said about the rest of the treatment – what happens after the wishes and fears are labeled – was usually taken care of by rough reference to "the ego." The patient's "ego" represents pure work: reality testing, integration, adaptation, objectivity, even courage, stoicism, and love of truth. The analyst does his work, and then the ego does *its* work. The patient himself is always motivated by drives (and thus is continuously subject to skeptical analytic scrutiny); it is only the ego that is doing plain old (nonanalyzable) work. When we persist today in respecting the patient's deliberate work in the face of our eternally skeptical analytic rationale, we are doing what early analysts did when they labored to distinguish between persuasion and insight. To the extent that we can count on the insight of an unaltered ego we do not need to resort to suggestion. And to the extent that the patient is doing his proper work we are not engaged in an enactment. I will elaborate this comparison in what follows.

I do not suggest that theorists had nothing specific to say about what the ego does. Freud indicated that intensified introspective attention is a force in its own right, especially – and perhaps only – if it is directed by a beloved teacher, and Loewald (1976) showed how useful Freud's concept of hypercathexis is in accounting for therapeutic action. Moreover, analysts have always assumed that interacting layers of representation turn on each other and recast themselves in many dimensions as treatment progresses (as in the "observing ego," the ego's ability to split itself, etc.). Those who regarded the superego as a specialization of the ego (Waelder 1936; Schur 1966) were suggesting that the mind automatically surveys itself whenever it gets the chance. (One task of the ego, according to Hartmann [1939], is to anticipate one's own likely reaction to one's contemplated action, a notion recently revived by Damasio [1999].) And familiar terms like "the realistic ego" and "the function of reality testing" preserve Freud's earliest picture of the mind as scouting for features of external reality that are simultaneously relevant for psychic reality. It was thought that the physiology of the ego includes tension between "the ego ideal" and the "ego," which builds a steady aspiration to accuracy and honesty. (On the superego as the placeholder for the sense of the future, see Loewald [1961].) Further details of the ego's work include the blending and balancing of purposes, as captured in phrases like "the synthetic function of the ego" (Nunberg 1930) and the "the integrative function of the ego" (Hartmann 1950). And from Freud's early days, the work of languaging was seen as the chief instrument of mental integration.

Despite this extensive theorizing about the ego, the impression remains that analysts never regarded general psychology as their proper business. Freud apologized for digressing from depth psychology to talk about the ego. Hartmann is roundly abused for dabbling in unconflicted, undynamic, "superficial" matters best left to academic psychology, and even charged with killing psychoanalysis as a result. When Hendrick (1943) made too much of the ego (as having energies of its own), he was quickly forced onto the defensive. For these and other reasons, I believe, analysts have until recently been happy to read the ego's functions by title, so to speak, rather than show an unseemly interest in its details.

## NEW INTEREST IN EGO FUNCTIONS

For some time, however, it has ceased to be acceptable for theorists to use the term *ego* as lazy shorthand for all the deliberate and undeliberate ways that the stuff of analysis is processed. Earlier critiques (e.g., Klein 1976) long ago exposed the term as a convenient wastebasket for miscellaneous "functions." And the modal thinker of today snickers at the "reality ego," which older practitioners would clutch at like a security blanket when asked just who they were addressing with their interpretations. As a consequence, the problem of a patient's autonomous task must now be discussed in different terms. And those new terms are not hard to spot. We see the old issue at play, for instance, when the new analysts debate the extent of their "authority," or when they postulate a "co-creation" of meaning, or visualize an analytic "third," or imagine themselves "containing" a patient's anxieties and conflicts. Most recently, most helpfully, and most provocatively, the quixotic nature of the ideal that is projected as the patient's autonomous task has been illuminated by Smith (2004), who asks analysts to acknowledge their personal stereotype plate of the Ideal Patient (see also Friedman on the therapeutic alliance [1969] and the realistic ego [1973]). And now there are two new theoretical developments that bring the notion of work to focal attention, where it can be scrutinized and theorized – namely, neuroscience and countertransference theory.

### *Will and automaticity in neuroscience*

Actually, cognitive psychology never left psychoanalysis alone, but its voice has become increasingly respected over the years. If Hartmann was once chastised for contaminating depth psychology with nonconflictual cognitive psychology, he is now (such being the fate of the mediator) more frequently condemned for the

96 The idea of Freudian therapy

sin of tainting cognitive psychology with libidinal schematisms. Infant observation long ago slipped quietly into accounts of ego psychology (see, e.g., White 1963; Hartmann 1939, p. 52 [where Bühler is cited]). Many contemporary psycho-analysts in North America are no longer bashful about consorting with academic psychology, now that it is embellished with neurophysiology. Watching images from neuroscience, psychoanalytic sophisticates lose their scorn for the jumbled collection called ego and repent their earlier accusations of reification. We are readier to take seriously an autonomous work-agent inside the patient when told that decision making and effortful attention light up a prefrontal-cingulate gyrus circuit. The ego's reality testing seems a genuine activity when a PET-scan shows how deliberate attention modifies cortical metabolism and emotional intensity in tandem. The ego's ability to split itself no longer seems a merely convenient verbal formula when it can be paired with the neurocognitive models of Damasio (1999), Lane (2000), and Karmiloff-Smith (1994), which feature multilayered representations of representations. The organizing function of the ego seems less philosophical and more concretely equivalent to affect regulation when devel-opmentalists like Gergeley and Watson (1996) show how mothers teach infants to define and evaluate their feelings by "marked" matching responses. (That sort of shaping has inspired Fonagy [1991] to specify a function of ego in treatment as refining feeling and imagery, representation and symbolization, etc., and ultimately facilitating affect regulation.)

But neurophysiology has been a two-edged sword in the matter of the ego. While cognitive neuroscience has with one hand been restoring dignity to notions of deliberation and choice, its other hand has been taking more away from con-scious volition than it had given. For each image of executive function, neu-roscience offers twice as many images of either drivenness or automaticity. As to the former, no better example can be found than Panksepp's "seeking system" (1999), which reimports lust into the very nature of cognition. As for the latter, one thinks of the nonconscious shortcuts between perception and emotion men-tioned by LeDoux (2000); the extremely popular mirror neurons that seem to equate perception with action (Nelissen et al. 2005); the apparent lag of conscious intention behind the actions they supposedly started (Libet 1985); and the massive machinery of procedural knowledge. The congeries of pathways for blind habit, interpersonal passion, and mendacious rationalization (Gazzaniga 1998) overshadow any neurological basis for an innocent work ethic that we might have wished we could rely on for brave, hardworking effort.

### *Countertransference and enactment*

Nor is it just neuroscience that challenges the independent ego. Within their own precincts, psychoanalysts have been thinking more and more about compelled reactions, as they follow the implications of exuberant countertransference theory. Having recognized their own libidinal involvement with patients, analysts could not refuse to confess their many subtle collusions. And having gone that far, they were bound to wonder whether enactments aren't, in fact, omnipresent (Smith 2006) – whether, in fact, analytic treatment isn't altogether a continuous game of catch-up, a constant chase after the always escaping (drive-motivated) enactment (Levenson 1972). But if enactment is part of the very fabric of analysis and not just an occasional snag, the question logically arises, What would *not* be an enactment? Why use the word at all? What was the error we would have fallen into without the term? If recognizing our enactment means realizing that we have been laboring under an illusion, what was the illusion that fooled us? Given the contemporary climate, the handiest answer might be this: "Not-an-enactment is both parties doing their proper work." And if that's what not-an-enactment would be (were it possible), then we might say that an enactment (were it separable) is the analyst helping the patient avoid doing his assigned work (were there such a thing).

The current interest in enactment reflects a tendency to experience the analytic interchange as a continuous libidinal interplay. Feeling thus swept about by irresistible tides, the analyst welcomes the possibility of a patient's proper work as a stable underlying seabed, even while he is allowed less justification for believing in it. In this chapter I will discuss enactment as the contrasting correlative to assignable work, distinct from the inner psychic work that we may hope for but cannot assign or presuppose.

## WHAT IS THE SPECIFIC INNER PSYCHOANALYTIC WORK THAT A PATIENT'S DELIBERATE WORK IS SUPPOSED TO PROMOTE?

By definition, the common baseline of all talking treatments is the act of talking about oneself. For all we know, the mere talking about oneself, together with a few other nonspecific factors, dwarfs in significance any sophisticated twist psychoanalysis might give it. In their heart, many practitioners may suspect that everything else is decoration (if not, indeed, an interference). Even those therapists who prize a psychoanalytic difference of some sort may, for practical purposes, implicitly count on the work of verbal expression and self-examination to do the heavy lifting.

If, however, psychoanalysis wants to reflect on itself as a special subset of talking treatments, it is obliged to say what it adds to the already profound experience of ordinary self-examination-in-colloquy-with-another. Psychoanalysis must point to something special in its plan beyond features common to all psychotherapy and counseling; i.e., something beyond the mastery and dignity that one naturally feels in serious self-reflection, the power gleaned from discovery of new perspectives, the enhanced sense of oneself as the focus of another's interest, the widening of one's world in the act of continuous narrative, etc. We must look past aspects of treatment that are central in all psychotherapies not because, being common, they are banal and trivial. On the contrary, nonspecific phenomena require especially close study, for not only is a pervasive climate harder to make out than a particular device, but the commonness of the common factors testifies to their central importance in human life, and hence to treatment. From moment to moment,

**98 The idea of Freudian therapy**

psychoanalysts will always be mostly aware of the nonspecific advantages of inducing a patient to talk relevantly and reflectively. That sort of deliberate work can be relied on to be profitable. But I repeat (and I ask the reader to keep it firmly in mind, since the narrowness of my aim may be forgotten along the way), that we are investigating how a patient's deliberate work fits into the *special* action of psychoanalysis.

We cannot answer that question without first saying what the special action of psychoanalysis is, though a summary statement is bound to be somewhat arbitrary. Like all human interactions, the analytic interaction has more aspects and levels than can ever be exhaustively surveyed. We will probably each have a different formula for the essence of psychoanalysis. Each of us privately translates our shared technical jargon into the ordinary language of inner thought to capture what we individually regard as special to psychoanalysis. I don't think it is defeatist to recognize that we will never have either a full or agreed-upon account of even the commonest features of specifically psychoanalytic treatment, much less a final description of an actual treatment encounter. Nevertheless, we must keep trying to capture the specialness of analytic treatment or else give up all claim to a procedure.[2]

I think the specialness of psychoanalytic treatment is most starkly illuminated at its birth. What was the original uniqueness of psychoanalysis; how did it depart from other psychotherapies at the beginning? As it happens, an assigned task was what first marked psychoanalysis as a special sort of talking treatment. The patient's earliest, most fundamental, and most explicit work assignment was to try to resist the social temptations (libidinal and defensive) in the relationship. That hard discipline paradoxically required the patient to put himself into an uncaring mood, embodied in the Zen-like rule (!) of free (!) association. Adherence to that discipline and an attitude of abandon defined a goal-directed determination to "work through" resistance, that is, to freely associate while at the same time feeling an urgent need to avoid doing that. The work thus required a self-undercutting motive. (This was the work Freud referred to in 1914 as "working-through.") In and of itself, this work is a constant discipline. It is no exaggeration to consider it a kind of endurance test, a little like trying to see how long one can hold one's breath under water.

One can see here an operation on two mental functions: attention and intention. In normal life attention and intention are fused: A person's net, overall intentions ordinarily direct his momentary, focal attention, and his momentary attention assigns priorities to his various intentions. What makes psychoanalytic procedure tormentingly peculiar is its relentless pressure to split these apart. It does that by (1) immobilizing conscious attention (in free association), (2) allowing the untethered (unconscious) intentions to reveal their focus on the analyst, and then (3) refocusing the patient's attention onto the covert intentions that had temporarily escaped attentional control. This way, patient and analyst can see how transference images are determined by wishful and fearful intentions. Of course, such an ideal process can only be approximated, but catching a glimpse of disguised intentions and noticing how they shape one's vision is the essence of a non-directive, interpretive method. Analytic procedure approaches the ideal insofar as it stubbornly interferes with attention ("free association"), irresistibly draws out buried intentions ("transference"), and effectively directs newly focused attention to those newly visible intentions ("interpretation and insight"). The analyst's ambiguity ("neutrality" and "abstinence") acts both to dislocate attention and to lure out hidden intentions.

Treatment forces are psychoanalytically effective when they prevent the patient's wishes from biasing the way he views those same wishes, while nevertheless sustaining the wishes in a vivid transference. In other words, the patient must be brought to simultaneously immerse himself in, and estrange himself from, his experience. Closeness in distance has long been recognized as the hallmark of psychoanalytic treatment. Other ways of describing the same effect include taking an objective look at subjectivity, being playful with serious matters, and gaining a new perspective on old mental contents. They all refer to the same activity.

As mentioned, one main psychoanalytic force that was found to foster this attitude is the analyst's ambiguity. By presenting himself as a blurred image for the patient's attention, the analyst works to shake intentions free from attentional control.[3]

Trying for social formlessness is what the analyst must do to shake patient's wishes loose from self-conscious control. That is the analyst's work. But what is the patient's corresponding work? What can we possibly ask a patient to do that would separate his own wish from his control? Freud had an answer: he exhorted patients to suspend prudential control precisely when they felt the greatest need to exercise it. As the patient loosened attention he began to feel certain needs, but was required nonetheless to relinquish the impression management (vis-à-vis himself and the analyst) that these needs almost reflexively dictated. In this situation, the patient would viscerally experience all the conflicting wishes involved. It was a self-imposed, revelatory disruption of his normal attention and intention. Freud was relieved to identify that self-wrenching act as the experiential dynamite that would do for the new, drifting treatment what catharsis had done for the old, dramatic protopsychoanalysis. He called it "working-through" (Freud 1914). That was a big part of the deliberate work that Freud assigned patients in order to foster the peculiar action of psychoanalysis.

But what would induce the patient to perform it? According to Freud, love for the analyst was what prompted patients to work this way. For later analysts, it remained an open question whether such a motive doesn't undermine the very work of independence it is supposed to prod. This is by no means a simple question. Most analysts would agree that a great deal is accomplished when a patient deliberately works at analysis, regardless of whether it is done for the analysis or for the analyst. A useful working posture may be inspired by many motives, and reflective "work" in analysis has, all by itself, many profound cognitive and emotional effects conducive to independence and wellness. Furthermore, most analysts

**100** The idea of Freudian therapy

probably agree with Freud that a work begun for the purpose of pleasing the analyst may gather autonomous motivation as it rolls. I believe each of these situations should be studied separately and in detail; we should catalogue in conscientious detail the various motivations, as well as the various benefits that result from a deliberate work assignment. I will mention just a few of the ways that a work assignment, even if transferentially motivated, helps sustain the specifically psychoanalytic project of closeness in distance, and I will dwell principally on the relationship of a work assignment to the subject of enactment. (I emphasize again that my specific goal requires me to ignore the even more important nonspecific benefits that accrue to all talking treatments when a patient deliberately works at treatment.)

## SPECIFIC USES OF THE WORK MODEL BY PSYCHOANALYSTS

*Assigned, mutual work softens the feelings of inequality between analytic partners.* Mutual work brings a measure of equality to a relationship that often seems overbearing. That reassurance makes patients more confident and allows the required dislocations to proceed more smoothly.

*Analysts are less perplexed about how treatment works if they think the patient has a job to do.* As mentioned, the "job" stands in for a mechanism of therapeutic effect, and so analysts can forget that question and just get down to the business of analyzing.

*Assigned work makes the analyst's ambiguity more tolerable.* If the analyst thinks he could in principle assign the patient a straightforward task (even if he doesn't actually do so), he will feel a little less slippery when, inevitably, his intense, selfless attention falsely signals an enduring, family-type relationship to the patient. (See Chapter 6 and Chapter 9.) And, correspondingly, when the patient worries in the back of his mind about just what is going on in this undefined relationship, he can make himself comfortable by telling himself that he is engaged in a proper work and is not involved in the sort of shady and uncertain personal bonding it otherwise feels like. In other words, the work format disguises the essential ambiguity of the situation and makes it more tolerable. It cushions the moral strain on the analyst, allowing him to believe he is more straightforward than he really is (seeming to be "playing his cards face up," to use Renik's phrase [1999]). And patients who might otherwise play it safe, either by remaining aloof from the illusion of closeness or by demanding its clear actualization, can abandon themselves more freely to what seems to be a tangible and respectable job of work. They have somewhat less reason to feel cautious about how they present themselves. They will be freer to reflectively "split" their mind, as the analytic method intends them to do. Under those conditions, all the ways patients reach for the analyst (including their rhetoric and the dramatic, illocutionary, and perlocutionary force of their self-presentation) can be held at a distance and given a different value as simply part of the work.

*Work interferes with the ordinary governance of attention.* This was the original rationale for the work assignment. The fundamental rule is a kind of Zen training in emptying the mind of purpose, but unlike Zen practice, psychoanalysis uses the rule to allow hidden purposes to pop out. Perhaps we should say that the usual activity of trying to look good (to the analyst and to oneself) in ordinary ways, or to be safe, or independent, or to feel hopeful, is distracted by a divergent effort to look good as a worker.

*Work gives patients a guaranteed way to please the analyst.* I have noted that much good work can be accomplished even if it is done for the "wrong" reasons. But that is an understatement. Pleasing the analyst by "working at analysis" is of no small moment in securing a long-term treatment relationship. A "working" patient guarantees that the analyst will enjoy a proper satisfaction even when the work is saturated with transference meanings he is pledged not to enjoy. A work program is a way the patient can reliably please the analyst in reality, no matter what he is doing in fantasy. Many factors contribute to the analyst's pleasure in the patient's work, and his consequent gratitude: there is the sharing of enthusiasm; the patient's visible endorsement of the value of the analyst's profession; the reassurance (warranted or not) that the treatment is "going somewhere"; and help in sustaining the analyst's interest in the long haul. One major source of the analyst's pleasure is the universal delight we take in witnessing the crystallization of knowledge *in statu nascendi*. Just as we marvel at budding scientific breakthroughs and innovations in the arts, it is exciting to watch the actual movement in someone's mind toward a sharpened grasp of an underlying reality. I think this joy is related to the human abstractive imperative (see Friedman 2002) and to several Kantian principles concerning the aesthetic response to a vision of reality that vividly illustrates the mind's adequacy to its task (Kant 1793). In any event, no psychotherapist can resist enthrallment when a patient is in the process of genuine personal discovery. We all know that it was Freud's principal tie to his patients (1912), despite his painful discovery that even this noble dependency on the patient can backfire in treatment.

## ENACTMENT – A CONVENIENT CATEGORY MADE POSSIBLE BY THE IDEA OF WORK

It must be granted at the outset that analysts do not need to assign a task to patients in order to accept one for themselves. There is no logical need to share with patients a procedural discipline, or the blame for its lapse. It may be inevitable that the analyst feels seduced when lulled (as it seems to him) into departing from his intended attitude, and analysts do frequently feel misused by a patient's persistent and successful intent to undermine their poise and neutrality. But at least in the Freudian tradition, that is not a theoretically mandated – or perhaps even theoretically sensible – attitude to take. The analyst may wish, as I have suggested, that the patient had more uninterruptedly split his intention (his desire) and his attention (which throws cold water on his intention). The analyst may hope to restart the patient's inner psychoanalytic work. But he doesn't need to think that the patient, too, should have been trying for that goal, that he has temporarily failed, and will return to his work when reminded.

**102** The idea of Freudian therapy

But though the analyst doesn't *need* to imagine a patient's dereliction in order to recover his own discipline, it can *help* him to fault the patient, openly or silently in his own thinking. It makes the analyst feel less helpless (or rather, to feel less ashamed of his helplessness). And it makes him feel less manipulative when he deliberately turns against the enactment (by objectivizing it), for then, instead of feeling that he is deliberately and provocatively disrupting a comfortable relationship (and one, moreover, that he has inadvertently been encouraging), he can think he is simply asking the patient to get back to the work he signed on for.

The emotional balm for the analyst is obvious, but it is not the only benefit he gets from thinking that the patient should be attending to his work. There is an important cognitive advantage, as well. The analyst's image of being misused by the patient's "non-work" purpose graphically helps him to define his enactment. No matter how theoretically gauche it may be, an inner feeling that the patient is "getting away with something," is not doing his work, may be the analyst's first warning that he himself has slipped. We might wish that we could count on unremitting analytic curiosity to rescue us from tides of enactment, but we may find that it helps more at the moment to grab hold of positive, shared work than to rely on an idealized abstinence to rebalance us. With his sights set on a mutual work relationship, the erstwhile enacting analyst is not limited to asking himself, "What have I not been looking at in our interaction?" (i.e., How am I not doing my job?); he can also ask, "What relationship have I been accepting from the patient *instead of the work* he has promised to participate in?" (How is he not doing *his* job?).

Speech acts being what they are, the analyst who hears himself talk to the patient about an enactment may be persuaded by his own grammar that the patient should shift to a better sort of behavior. Moreover, once he has "called" the patient (and himself) on an enactment, he may feel he *owes* the patient an image of an alternative, that is, the "work" that he should have been doing. When the analyst says to himself, "I should not be wholeheartedly sharing this archaic mini-world with the patient," he may need to offer the patient (explicitly, as Gray [2005] does, or implicitly, as others do) some semblance of another world to share.

So it might be argued that the analyst cannot simply pull the rug out from under the patient without implicitly offering him some other rug to stand on – something else the patient could be doing, at least by taking a look at what he's been doing. But psychoanalysts are not cognitive therapists. They dare not assign a very specific other role, such as the role of the analyst's pupil, for that would simply encourage another inflexible enactment. Small wonder, then, that at the moment when the analyst calls himself to account for an enactment, he fancies a very *general* alternative, namely, a world of work that the patient could instead be sharing with him – an alternative not confined (he hopes) to any single, picturable world, but an elastic world that would liberate both of them to explore many other worlds. He hopes that the patient, now alerted to an enactment, will pick up his assigned work again, just as the analyst himself is trying to do. I doubt that even the most nondirective analyst is entirely free of such a background image.[4]

And is the analyst wrong to think he owes the patient such an image of "proper" behavior? Doesn't the patient, too, need a crutch to help him out of an enactment, and won't he get it one way or another? Suppose the analyst does not imagine an assignable task: What does a patient resort to when the analyst simply detaches himself from an enactment and moves into a more analytic position without any implication that the patient has been derelict? How does the patient *read* such an evasive analyst's role flexibility? Doesn't he just assimilate *that* to his own transference? And if so, wouldn't he have succeeded in transforming the analyst's simple professionalism into one more picturesque enactment, again seeing his wishful imaginings instantiated in the analyst's own (professionally) wishful activity? (For an example, see Smith 2004.) In other words, even if the analyst doesn't offer a positive alternative (proper work) in place of the enactment, the patient is likely anyway to think he has been told to get back to work, and he will give that vague command a personal, dramatic form shaped by his own fantasies. Insofar as the fantasy is shared by the analyst, it would be another enactment. The analyst is likely to think of that as a therapeutic alliance, which then becomes a name for the baseline enactment of that particular analytic pair. A work assignment, explicit or implicit, will be hard to escape in a psychoanalytic treatment.

Still, we want to ask, is enactment absolutely inescapable? Can we, perhaps, imagine a situation in which no fantasy of interaction is shared between patient and analyst to any appreciable extent?

That is an outstanding question for psychoanalysis at this time. In the old days, many who accepted the omnipresence of transference believed that it dovetails only occasionally with the analyst's own attitudes and motivation. For the most part, the analyst's neutrality was thought to protect him from sharing the patient's meanings. The analyst ensured his neutrality by continuously superimposing on the patient's personal, social appeal an outline of a mental mechanism that evokes stoical patience rather than a social response. In this way the "Teflon" analyst would avoid being "actualized" as a consistently defined social partner. Of course, the patient might tendentiously misperceive even neutrality as evidence that the analyst shares his motive, but it was thought that the patient could be persuaded to do a little "work," cease indulging his motivated misperception, and gaze instead upon the action of his own mind. In this older psychoanalytic paradigm, the analyst moves about pretty freely, swayed but not bent by interpersonal pressure. We see him dispassionately observing a mind in lawful action. We see his patient moving about almost as freely – and generally going about the work of observing his mind in lawful action. At times each party might slip from this ideal situation, and very occasionally the two might slip in tandem, but it was thought that at least some of the process was conducted austerely and that a joint fantasy was rarely realized simultaneously.

But is it reasonable to think of enactments as episodic? Henry Smith (2006) has argued persuasively that it is not. We must recognize that to communicate is to act and be acted upon. Actions establish and reinforce relationships, at least by implicitly asking for reciprocal attitudes and acknowledgment. Insofar as they manage to

**104** The idea of Freudian therapy

communicate with each other, patient and analyst continuously mold and modulate their relationship (call it "negotiation," "projective identification," "constructing," "containing," "empathizing"). One can be as taciturn as one likes and just point "here" or "there," but eventually one's perception must rent space in the other person's receptive field or there is no communication.

Many psychoanalysts shield themselves from the patient's "impression management" by turning a deaf ear to his ordinary speech in order to listen undistractedly to his unconscious meaning. It might even be argued that the common function of all theories is to chatter in the analyst's distractable ear, saying never-mind-what so long as it interferes with his social hearing and thereby immunizes him against the manipulative force of the patient's speech. The cliché that psychoanalysts are united by their belief in the unconscious may in this way prove true even if their definitions of the unconscious have little in common. *Anything* designated as the unconscious interferes with ordinary listening, which guarantees a shared efficacy. A wag might say that the defining feature of analytic treatment is a persistent past-pointing responsiveness to the patient's overt appeal.

Freeing himself from enslavement to the patient's conversational entrainment, the analyst can attend to the unconscious message and, by the act of noticing it, partly sidestep its impact. The analyst's own analysis is supposed to give him a measure of awareness and self-control, celebrated in the term "trial identification" (Fliess 1942). But even if, as seems unlikely, an analyst could listen clear "past" the patient's ordinary speech, and even if he could focus a purified, objective attention on the unconscious "speech" itself, the unconscious message would have to fit somehow into the analyst's inner world or it would have no meaning (that being a hermeneutic principle), and we are now brave enough to concede that the analyst's personal meaning will then find its way back to the patient, at least minimally, in his responsive interventions. And that sets the stage for enactment. Is there any escape from this mutual contamination of meanings? Perhaps if we could picture the patient as suffering from a kind of aphasia, with the analyst replacing a missing word or two from a shared unconscious, a storehouse of universal symbols, we could imagine the "unconscious telephone" exchange to be free of every sort of emotional collusion. But even then we would have to acknowledge that it is one thing for an analyst to privately register an objective meaning, and another to fashion a response. An intervention, like all personal action, will draw on every part of the analyst's psyche and acquire meaning from the momentary context. For that reason alone, we must agree with Smith (2006) that at some level there is a continuous array of enactments in the flow of treatment. If we conclude that human relationships always involve some sort of enactment, and that enactments are not discrete episodes, then the idea of work as an alternative to enactment becomes problematic, no matter how comfortable – or even necessary – it may be for the analyst's working orientation.

But that is a somewhat abstract way of considering work and enactment. Practical life is rarely a matter of all or nothing; it usually involves a measure of more and less. We may have to grant that the most an analyst can do is to favor mobility

Is there life after enactment? **105**

and laminate new enactments over old ones, each suited to destabilize the others. Still, that leaves ample room for standards of technique by which we can measure *degrees* of analytic circumspection. We can see the difference between stronger and weaker discipline in an analyst, observe his drift into greater or lesser indulgence. We can note the consistency of his professional wariness, recognize his greater or lesser tolerance for loneliness, chart the different proportions of tact and courage that characterize his work, etc.

Nor, perhaps, is it only the analyst's abstinence that can be measured in degrees. It may be that patients' immersion in enactment meanings also lies on a spectrum. Some patterns of interaction may be so passionately invested and so easily mapped onto dominant themes that they seem to distill a patient's entire life. These would be the sort of repetitions that astonish an analyst when he suddenly becomes aware that he has collaborated with them. Other interactions, while necessarily reflecting the patient's patterns, may, *relatively speaking*, be less blatantly reminiscent of defined life patterns, less plausibly translatable, more of a stretch to make a case for. They may look like fleeting, or conventional, or experimental interactions. Some behaviors may be especially fine copies of core patterns, while others can be seen only as vague and approximate analogs. While conceding that every personal meaning is related to every other, analysts are unlikely to regard regular payment of their fee as revelatory, or their own silent acceptance of it each month as an enactment, unless some marked association calls attention to the exchange. Indeed, many a practitioner may secretly wish he could leave the pestilential universality of enactment to the philosophers and go back to the good old days when a red-blooded enactment meant a vivid copy of a significant relationship startlingly partnered with a matching performance by a delinquent analyst, in which both parties share the same, joint satisfaction in a folie à deux that is neatly distinguishable from ordinary transference and countertransference. To the extent that an analyst still thinks of enactments that way, he is free to imagine them as distinct episodes like beads on a string, the string being the thread of a "proper" and deliberate collaborative work. Other analysts, for whom an enactment is an enactment, whether of the eye-catching bead sort or the humdrum string type, will have less justification for assigning patients a deliberate task.

But even without strong justification for assigning such work, an analyst may, for the reasons given, find it useful to preserve the idea of a job the patient should be tackling. Even skeptical analysts may allow themselves one of those self-contradictions that psychoanalysis seems to count on, in this case continuing to believe that dramatic, interpersonal motivation is never negligible, while at the same time imagining that one can work against its hegemony. They may think in terms of effortful *direction* and imaginary *ideals* (which is what the possibility of technique ultimately depends on). Even if we are never without enactments, the notion of a patient's endorsed work can serve as the ideal image of a *minimal* enactment. We could define a minimal enactment as the analyst's most professionally motivated (and least personally tinged) behavior, collaborating with the patient's most objective, open-ended motivation. As an ideal asymptote, this assigned, deliberate work,

**106** The idea of Freudian therapy

despite its residual dramatic and collaborative transference overtones, would constitute the least directive instruction a patient can read into the analyst's social elusiveness and distancing maneuvers. (The residue of enactment might, for example, be the patient's sense that "he wants me to be independent," or "he is challenging me to show how independent I can be," or "he wants me to see/think that he doesn't want to dominate / adopt / be responsible for me.") According to that definition, joint work may be the one enactment that is amorphous enough to be minimally entrapping. For his part, the analyst may feel that the best compromise he can make between pulling away from the patient, on the one hand, and promoting a vividly personal alternative relationship, on the other, is to set up a collaborative work on the assumption that it will retain enough generality and amorphousness to ensure therapeutic efficacy, despite the personal dramas it nevertheless draws in.

When an analyst with this idea of a patient's work designates a situation as "an" enactment, he is telling himself that he and his patient have been sampling each other socially when they "should" have been doing their work, although he has learned a valuable lesson during their "holiday." In the subsequent process of understanding the enactment, patient and analyst will in fact have disrupted one form of enactment and substituted another (labeled a joint work) that offers greater freedom – trying as long as possible not to see it as another social relationship. A work assignment here refers to a minimum, default enactment.

An analyst who thinks of work as an ever present, minimal play of enactments will never trust it to remain minimal. He will be eternally wary of the tendency for the innocent, joint *basso ostenuto* to swell into a sentimental duet. Not that there is anything wrong with a little harmonious part-singing. It is not satisfaction per se that "contaminates" the analytic process. Rather, what we should regard as a "departure" from "proper" process is the endorsement of one particular satisfaction (to the exclusion, for example, of conflicting wishes), and the protection of the (defensive) stasis that it seals. Whether we consider a particular satisfaction to be an undisturbed transference or an enactment, the reason we worry about it is not that it has happened, but that it may prevent something else from happening. Since fantasy is intrinsic to social perception as well as to desire, we expect that patients will always get some particular satisfaction from the relationship they find themselves in, and that will always militate to some extent against their internal work of splitting their attention in order to examine their wish. When we recognize that we have allowed or encouraged the patient to come to rest in a gratifying relationship, we need not – and I think should not – say that he failed at his assigned work. What we must say is that we failed, at that moment and in that regard, to give his *internal* work a stimulus. To the degree that we have actively participated in the patient's drama, we have undoubtedly obtained "inside knowledge" of it, but as long as the enactment lasts, we have lost the power to produce the therapeutic split. Enactments, then, would be those occasions when the analyst, by subtly sharing the patient's aim, is encouraging the patient to not divide himself in its pursuit.

I conclude from these observations that it is useful but optional, and potentially hazardous, to share with a patient the subtle sense that he has a deliberate work to do.

## SUMMARY

We have seen that a social relationship of joint work serves both cognitive and comfort needs of the analyst and facilitates many deep purposes of analytic treatment.

But we have also examined the quicksand this notion rests on. Isn't mutual "work" confounded by the same problems as the therapeutic alliance? How is it not just another transference-countertransference enactment? What could be more unanalytic than looking for actions and relationships that are "innocent"? Instead of patronizing Freud for naively believing in an unobjectionable positive transference, perhaps we should admire his frankness in plainly calling it a transference.

Though not merely a convenient illusion, a work project is problematic. We feel obliged to say there is a sense in which everything is an enactment. And yet we want to say that A is more of an enactment than B because B looks more like a patient "working at" treatment. But allowing a more and less of the matter puts us in danger of expecting or demanding unnatural behavior from patients. We should not fall into the habit of expecting patients to behave without drives and without satisfaction. ("Work is the last refuge of a transference.") Nor can we say that joint work is less an enactment because it expresses only the patient's transference satisfactions without engaging the analyst's. The whole of treatment is a genuine joint enactment. Even apart from inescapable subtle social responses, the drama that weaves together the analyst's professional and personal commitment, his professional pride and personal obligation, and all the primitive and personal motives that resonate with these, make him a ready stand-in for figures in the patient's early life who had comparable wishes.

The idea of assigned work, like the idea of enactment, is a bridge concept. It connects ordinary living to extreme disruption, so that the analyst can function in the uncertain middle as common sense dictates. But we should never forget that psychoanalysis is – or at least was at its inception – an experiment in living close to the end of the bridge, as far to the extreme end as feasible. While its rationale must in the end be a form of common sense, as Schafer (1983) says, its conduct is anything but common. The bridge concepts of work and enactment (and therapeutic alliance) normalize – and thus obscure – its uncommonness. They make the best – or almost the best – of a bad deal, which is nothing less than an intolerable and impossible nonsociality. But the bad deal is exactly what analysis is supposed to offer: the almost impossible fragmentation of desire; the almost impossible withholding of confirming social responsiveness. Success in that endeavor depends, first and last, on how far the analyst can go toward suspending his social desires, which, unless he is able to fool himself, means all his desires. Of course, he could obtain no human knowledge and have no human effect if he were to achieve that ideal.

## 108 The idea of Freudian therapy

But if the analyst forgets that in principle he is not supposed to want anything from his patient, that he is not supposed to want his patient to satisfy his interest, be it an interest in collaboration or in gathering knowledge (like Freud's interest in dreams, or figuring out the patient's pathodynamics), or an interest in achievement, or a wish for companionship – if he forgets that he is supposed to at least lean away from all his demands and desires, at least from time to time, then he has lost touch both with ordinary reality (which brands him ridiculous for expecting patients to temporarily put aside their humanity to satisfy his needs) and psychoanalytic reality (which tells him that his wishes guarantee an enactment). The analyst's tough task is to recognize both of those realities.

It is unlikely that the working analyst will ever shake out of his head the notion of a complementary work that he wishes his patients would undertake (and just as unlikely that patients will ever fail to express unanalyzed intentions and wishes in terms of that very work). And it may be useful on occasion to "remind" a patient that he has a job to do. And it may be inevitable that analysts will catch themselves wondering why on earth the patient isn't doing what "everyone knows" a patient is supposed to do. And we may always shake our heads, bewildered (and a trifle annoyed) by patients who cannot "appropriately" and "realistically" see that, for heavens' sake, we are, after all, just analysts, and why not just use us for what analysts can do (namely, help the patient in his work)? But a moment's genuinely psychoanalytic reflection will in each case pull us up short with the question: "Why on earth should I expect any of that?" Interrupting our own best intentions with that sort of question is the psychoanalyst's secret formula.

## Notes

1 We cannot contrast "relationship" with knowledge, since relationships, besides being sometimes an end in themselves, often (or always) impart knowledge, and, conversely, the act of imparting knowledge always establishes a relationship.
2 I am aware that many analysts today are offended by the manipulative connotation of "procedure," "technique," and even "treatment," and prefer to think of psychoanalytic practice as just an especially thoughtful and benevolent human relationship. Obviously, these analysts may be excused from discussing the specialness of psychoanalytic procedure.
3 This is equivalent to offering a broad array of temptations to the patient's intentions, thereby seducing desires and resuscitating hopefulness.
4 Exceptions are the cryptic sort of analysis we find in France, the continuous, running, interpretive commentary practiced by some early Kleinians and at one time by Winnicott (1972), and the seamless, perspectival deconstructing of Levenson (1972).

## REFERENCES

Damasio, A. (1999). *The Feeling of What Happens: Body and Emotion in the Making of Consciousness*. San Diego, CA: Harcourt Brace.

Fliess, R. (1942). The metapsychology of the analyst. *Psychoanalytic Quarterly*, 11: 211–227.

Fonagy, P. (1991). Thinking about thinking: Some clinical and theoretical considerations in the treatment of a borderline patient. *International Journal of Psychoanalysis*, 72: 1–18.

Freud, S. (1912). The dynamics of transference. Standard Edition, 12: 97–108.

Freud, S. (1914). Remembering, repeating and working-through. Standard Edition, 12: 147–156.

Friedman, L. (1969). The therapeutic alliance. *International Journal of Psychoanalysis*, 50: 139–153.

Friedman, L. (1973). How real is the realistic ego in psychotherapy? *Archives of General Psychiatry*, 28: 377–383.

Friedman, L. (2002). Symbolizing as abstraction: Its role in psychoanalytic treatment. In: *Symbolizing and Desymbolizing: Essays in Honor of Norbert Freedman*, ed. R. Lasky. New York, NY: Karnac Books, pp. 204–230.

Gazzaniga, M. (1998). *The Mind's Past*. Berkeley, CA: University of California Press.

Gergeley, G. & Watson, J. S. (1996). The social biofeedback theory of parental affect-mirroring: The development of emotional self-awareness and self-control in infancy. *International Journal of Psychoanalysis*, 77: 1181–1212.

Gray, P. (2005). *The Ego and Analysis of Defense*. 2nd ed. Lanham, MD: Aronson.

Greenson, R. (1965). The working alliance and the transference neurosis. *Psychoanalytic Quarterly*, 34: 155–181.

Hartmann, H. (1939/1958). *Ego Psychology and the Problem of Adaptation*. New York, NY: International Universities Press.

Hartmann, H. (1950/1964). Comments on the psychoanalytic theory of the ego. In: *Essays on Ego Psychology: Selected Problems in Psychoanalytic Theory*. New York, NY: International Universities Press, pp. 113–141.

Hendrick, I. (1943). Work and the pleasure principle. *Psychoanalytic Quarterly*, 12: 311–329.

Kant, I. (1793/2000). *Critique of the Power of Judgment*, ed. P. Guyer. Cambridge: Cambridge University Press.

Karmiloff-Smith, A. (1994). Precis of beyond modularity: A developmental perspective on cognitive science. *Behavioral & Brain Sciences*, 17: 693–745.

Klein, G. (1976). *Psychoanalytic Theory: An Exploration of Essentials*. New York, NY: International Universities Press.

Lane, R. (2000). Neural correlates of conscious emotional experience. In: *Cognitive Neuroscience of Emotion*, eds. R. Lane & L. Nadel. New York, NY: Oxford University Press, pp. 345–370.

LeDoux, J. (2000). Cognitive-emotional interactions: Listen to the brain. In: *Cognitive Neuroscience of Emotion*, eds. R. Lane & L. Nadel. New York, NY: Oxford University Press, pp. 129–155.

Levenson, E. A. (1972). *The Fallacy of Understanding*. New York, NY: Basic Books.

Libet, B. (1985). Unconscious cerebral initiative and the role of conscious will in voluntary action. *Behavioral & Brain Sciences*, 8: 529–539.

Loewald, H. (1961/1980). Superego and time. In: *Papers on Psychoanalysis*. New Haven, CT: Yale University Press, pp. 43–52.

Loewald, H. (1976/1980). Primary process, secondary process, and language. In: *Papers on Psychoanalysis*. New Haven, CT: Yale University Press, pp. 178–205.

Nelissen, K., Luppino, G., Vanduffel, W., Rizzolatti, G. & Orban, G. A. (2005). Observing others: Multiple action representation in the frontal lobe. *Science*, 310: 332–336.

Nunberg, H. (1930/1960). The synthetic function of the ego. In: *Practice and Theory of Psychoanalysis*. New York, NY: International Universities Press.

Panksepp, J. (1999). Emotions as viewed by psychoanalysis and neuroscience: An exercise in consilience. *Neuro-Psychoanalysis*, 1: 15–38.

Renik, O. (1999). Playing one's cards face up in analysis: An approach to the problem of self-disclosure. *Psychoanalytic Quarterly*, 68: 521–539.

Schafer, R. (1983). *The Analytic Attitude*. New York, NY: Basic Books.

## 110 The idea of Freudian therapy

Schur, M. (1966). *The Id and the Regulatory Principles of Mental Functioning*. New York, NY: International Universities Press.

Smith, H. F. (2004). The analyst's fantasy of the ideal patient. *Psychoanalytic Quarterly*, 73: 627–658.

Smith, H. F. (2006). Analyzing disavowed action: The fundamental resistance of analysis. *Journal of the American Psychoanalytic Association*, 54: 713–737.

Waelder, R. (1936). The principle of multiple function: Observations on overdetermination. *Psychoanalytic Quarterly*, 5: 45–62.

White, R. (1963). *Ego and Reality in Psychoanalytic Theory: A Proposal Regarding Independent Ego Energies*. Psychological Issues Monograph 11. New York, NY: International Universities Press.

Winnicott, D.W. (1972). Fragment of an analysis. In: *Tactics and Techniques in Psychoanalytic Therapy*, ed. P. L. Giovacchini. New York, NY: Science House, pp. 455–693.

Zetzel, E. (1958/1970). Therapeutic alliance in the analysis of hysteria. In: *The Capacity for Emotional Growth*, ed. E. Zetzel. New York, NY: International Universities Press, pp. 182–196.

Zetzel, E. (1966). The analytic situation. In: *Psychoanalysis in America*, ed. R. E. Litman. New York, NY: International Universities Press.

# 6

# THE DELICATE BALANCE OF WORK AND ILLUSION IN PSYCHOANALYSIS

By definition, treatment is an action on a patient. Before the advent of psychoanalysis, all treatments were conspicuously active. Coming onto this scene, analysts became notorious for their inactivity, and did indeed sometimes caricature their own passivity. Despite current interest in the analyst's actions, analysts remain, at least in comparison with other therapists, mainly reactive. Analysts are self-employed workers who get down to work by waiting for another person to forward their project.

This strange, expectant attitude seems to suggest that the patient has a job to do, that something is up to him, that his help is needed. Analysts tend to think about patients as workers, especially when a question arises as to who has how much responsibility for treatment; or when the air is full of uncertainty about "What is going on around here?" or "How is this thing supposed to work?" And the issue of patients working or not working escalates when treatment is frankly failing.

At these times, analysts find themselves thinking that patients should be – or at least could be – working at treatment. Beyond that, we tend to think of psychoanalysis as fostering a kind of integrity, and that context also suggests a deliberate work for the patient.

Please note that when I say *work*, I mean the program that the patient knows he should follow, and I mean the goal that the analyst believes that the patient must deliberately aim for if his own work is to be successful. The patient says to himself, "I can try harder in this way." The analyst says to himself, "If he will not do that, how can I be expected to do my part?" *Work* can mean many other things, as well, but when I use the word alone, I mean this overt, deliberate effort, which at other times I contrast with inner, undeliberate psychic work.

Does the analyst prototypically regard deliberate work as a good thing? In other words, is he happier when the patient is "working" than when he is doing something else? Should the patient pursue a shaped, prefigured project? Or will his

## 112    The idea of Freudian therapy

project at any given moment always be part of an enacted fantasy? Should the analyst encourage a work, or should he undercut the patient's fascination with it so it can be examined? (See Kris's [1956] bad examples.)

How does the psychoanalytic tradition answer this question? Initially, as a hypnotist, Freud took full responsibility for his treatments. He did not begin by saying to himself, "If the patient is not willing to do such-and-such, I cannot be expected to help her." Instead, when Miss Lucy R. "cannot" answer Freud's question, he performs an action that "makes" her see an answer.

Things changed when Freud abandoned hypnosis. Indeed, psychoanalysis came into being as Freud accommodated himself to his patients' directions. Many scholars (Ellenberger [1970], Gay [1988], Macmillan [1990], and others) have noted that Freud allowed his patients to teach him analytic technique. But it should not be thought that Freud was a dutiful student; what he learned from patients was not how to cooperate better on their mutual task. What happened was far more complicated.

Reading about those early patients in *Studies on Hysteria* (Breuer & Freud 1895, p. 110), from whom Freud was learning, we are struck by how certain they sometimes seem to be about what they are up to. We are impressed by their often substantial, ambitious, sometimes imperious agenda. Nowadays we would be very suspicious of that aspect of their work. Anna O. is the most extreme example. She is engaged in recalling three different time spans from three different years, all within one interval of treatment. This first analysand – as Freud thought of her – has her own ideas about how pathogenic experiences are stratified and how they are to be eliminated. Her physician, Breuer, is midwife to her amazing work, merely trying to deliver out of it a finite etiology that will bring him profit from her labor.

Inspired by that account, Freud comes to his patients with the belief that suppressed memories cause hysteria. He tries to persuade patients to tell him what events have caused their symptoms. But some of them do not want to simply answer his questions. These patients, along with Anna O., have a work of their own that they want to pursue. No doubt, catharsis is part of it, since catharsis was a popular concept at the time. But catharsis is not all that these patients are engaged in. They are not always satisfied to answer the therapist's questions about causes; they want to ruminate about fears. They are intent on accomplishing a marvelous feat or commanding a methodical project. They demand that Freud hear them out on whatever they want to talk about, and they express all sorts of feelings about the day's events. They want reassurance; they react to the physician's attitude; they assert their independence against him. And they frequently try to turn the relationship into a social one.

Freud deliberately assumed that, in doing all this, his patients were really working to answer his own questions. He insisted on reading their work as a better way of doing what he was trying to do. In other words, no matter what they did, he imagined that they were still working to give him his answers – merely showing him by their digressions that those answers were not as simple and handy as he had

The delicate balance of work and illusion   113

assumed. He thought they were just teaching him that memory clues materialize piecemeal and at their own pace.

But, now, having equated the patient's new work with his own, old work, Freud took over the responsibility for maintaining it. With patients' miscellaneous behaviors having been labeled as a search for causes, Freud now took responsibility for seeing that they continued their search – yes, in their own miscellaneous way, but now at his command. When they stopped the work, he would "make" them do it by suggestion. He would "make" them picture something and presumed that what he had made appear was a piece of the answer to his question about the cause of symptoms. He figured that the causal memories were ready at his call to arise from their layered web, and emerge, one by one, through what he called the "defile of consciousness" (Breuer & Freud 1895, p. 291) – according to their complex, previously hidden order, like Indians trooping through a canyon.

Freud had appropriated the patient's plan for his own purpose, given it his own meaning, and then taken the responsibility for seeing that it was carried out. It was no longer the patient's plan in any obvious sense. Indeed, from that point on, the patient's planning became an obstacle. Freud tried to force plans out of the patient's mind and keep her distracted by getting her to concentrate on minute-to-minute proceedings (a process known as free association; see Breuer & Freud 1895, p. 271). It was his program, but by the time the idea of work had passed from therapist through the patient and back to the therapist, it had been soaked in the patient's drivenness. By identifying his own investigative program with the patient's overpowering effortfulness, Freud had framed his own program as a shared one. That's why he could picture the resistance as something that both he and the patient were trying to overcome.

Freud always counted on some sort of automatic process within the patient to be his ally. As mentioned, his original ally had been the natural momentum of memories marching through that defile of consciousness – I picture somebody regurgitating a thread from a swallowed ball of twine (and I apologize for the image). If patients didn't seem to be cooperating, Freud could assure himself that deep down inside them, the physiology of memories was doing Freud's work. But by 1914, Freud had to admit that even that inner automatic process wasn't doing his (Freud's) work. Inevitably, as patients insisted on showing him more than just the memories he asked for, Freud was gradually forced to accept every kind of phenomenon that popped out of the defile of consciousness, and he could not go on forever pretending that all these assorted behaviors were simply memories in various disguises. After all, it would have been odd, wouldn't it, if evolution had carved a defile of consciousness just to process sick memories?

To be sure, pathogenic memories never lost their pride of place in psychoanalysis, but, obviously, it is not memories per se that are pushing at the patient's thoughts: People do not live in order to remember. And so, Freud eventually came to think of the automatic process within the patient more as a set of dispositions – cravings and prejudices – largely focused on the patient's mother and father.

**114   The idea of Freudian therapy**

That changes the whole picture of treatment. The patient is no longer working – not even deep down and not even inadvertently – to express smothered memories. He is working to reenact a hidden drama, an aim that is accomplished in the transference neurosis. It is the analyst who seeks memories. The patient wants to act and not to remember. His private work is diametrically opposed to the analyst's, and it is the analyst's job to see that he fails.

Surely, by now, you are wondering why I haven't ended my search for work with the discovery of working through. I'll tell you why. Like *acting out*, the phrase *working through* has been saddled with almost every schoolmarmish meaning it can lexically bear. And like every other moralizable term from psychoanalysis, it is even dragged outside the treatment situation. Though he later used the term variously, Freud introduced it for one specific purpose. Let's look at that.

What did one work through when one was "working through"? One did not work through material, interpretations, or problems. One did not work through symptoms, dreams, or defenses. One did not work through a long inventory of instances that proved how right the analyst was. One did not work through the tedium of repeated interpretations. One worked through a *resistance*, and that's it.

Freud (1914) described working through as the way a patient gets to know his resistance (p. 155). Freud was telling us that a patient doesn't get to know a resistance by talking about it or even by sensing its action. He has to become familiar with the impulse that feeds it. The patient may recognize a departure from what's expected of him, but he doesn't begin to know his resistance until he identifies with it. Here Freud, the technician, was reminding us that resistance is not an abstraction but a specific aim of a particular person.

For instance, the patient has to feel not just a duty to speak his mind, but also his good reasons for not wanting to do so; he has to identify with both perspectives at once. Behind the treatment difficulty, the patient is experiencing dangerous inclinations, which warns him not to cooperate, but he perseveres. By continuing to follow the rule, he may be risking disappointment and derision. He is thus required to have two feelings about his audience – one that would cause him to rebel and the other that makes him continue. Working straight through that danger, he has to be willing to sabotage some hopes that would have been best served by rebelling against the procedure.

This amounts to acting against interest. The patient is caring and not caring about consequences. For instance, some inner purpose would be better served by silence, and yet he wittingly frustrates that purpose for the sake of his treatment. He is worried about the response of the parent figure/analyst – yet he also doesn't give a damn, and that indifference allows him to risk it.

Encouraging a patient to work something through does not so much invite him to undertake a work of his own as it calls on him to possess a certain kind of attitude – an attitude of partial indifference in the analytic situation. But indifference is a state, not a work; you cannot assign indifference.

The delicate balance of work and illusion    **115**

Indeed, a considerable portion of analytic theory and most of its technique is focused on the patient's misunderstanding of what he is doing. He may think he's working on one thing, but analysts are likely to think he's up to something else. Indeed, it would be difficult to assign the patient anything but a nominal task, because the work he really has to do is to move in and out of caring about his analyst/audience. I'll save more about that for later, except to say that we scarcely know how to describe such a task, let alone how to *pre*scribe it, and even if it should turn out to be partly under voluntary control, it can't be prescribed by the analyst since it consists of being indifferent to the prescriber, at least in part. Work that is done on demand – or, strictly speaking, done because the patient thinks it's demanded – is something we insist on dealing with as food for thought rather than as a thoughtful performance. No matter how much it looks like the right sort of work, we analyze it as an enactment – as Kris (1956) did in his discussion of the "good analytic hour" (p. 446). Even Loewald (1980), who makes the least of this distinction, discounts work that's done to please the analyst (p. 296).

Yet, although every deliberate effort to accomplish something gets a cold stare from the analyst, who suspects covert motives, nevertheless, we are all inclined to privilege the working posture in general. And please don't mistake that for a triviality, as though all human activity must look like work. There are some very interesting psychotherapies that do not encourage or applaud a work format. Thus, analysts and analysands must have their reasons for picturing the whole project and the overarching intention as a joint work, and I believe that one of their reasons has to do with safety.

Patients who are scared of the lasting, intense relationship that the analyst seems to offer will find the idea of work very reassuring. And patients who are under the illusion of being lastingly important to the analyst will be relieved to hedge their bets and secure some freedom by noting that, whatever is or isn't developing of a personal nature, they are also visibly working at something.

And how about the analyst? Doesn't he also benefit from the work format? Surely, he's pleased to see the patient count on something besides the relationship mirage. And what a boon to be able to demonstrate tangible respect for the patient's autonomy by appointing him a co-worker! Indeed, the work format may even reverse the dependency, as the analyst humbly records the patient's discoveries.

In a nutshell, "working on something" distracts attention from the constant illusion of a mutually sentimental relationship.

We are specialists in dangerous illusions. Everything in treatment happens in and about illusions. Most of its profit, all of its disasters, its high seriousness, its moral and spiritual riskiness, the bitterness and fatigue of both parties, the need for professional comradeship that draws us together at meetings – all come from the fact that psychoanalysis is a procedure of encouraging illusory expectations. The role of analyst is simply not a good place for a person to be. It is not a healthy job (Freud 1909, p. 210; 1915, pp. 170–171). It is not what would ordinarily be called wholesome or honorable (as the general populace recognizes).

**116** The idea of Freudian therapy

This is obvious from the psychoanalytic stage-setting alone. The standard features of classical analysis – couch, fee policy, frequency and regularity of sessions, etc. – are all designed to regulate and limit illusion. The official drill concerning regression and its management – interpretation of transference, vacation and termination procedures, etc. – is set up to keep illusions from getting infected, in the same way that operating room protocol guides surgeons through a perilous journey.

And yet, I think, one aspect of illusion has been deliberately neglected. Analysts have preferred to conceal that aspect, and they do that by emphasizing two other aspects instead. First, analysts have dwelt mainly on the active and desiring aspect of illusion – typically, what the patient wants from the analyst – rather than what the patient comes to expect as a result of how he's treated. Second, analysts are happiest when they study those illusions that the patient can be expected to grow out of in the course of treatment, rather than illusions that are built into the analytic relationship itself.

It is these latter illusions that I am talking about – illusions that inevitably arise when someone selflessly and earnestly attends to another person's feelings. Socially and psychologically, such behavior signals a relationship of great intensity. It says more clearly than words: "You mean an awful lot to me"; "You mean as much to me as my family." This sort of attention is a tacit promise of a relationship, and it is a promise that stands in stark contrast to the analyst's real intention.

By *illusion*, then, I mean the tacit, implicit promises that the analyst has no intention of keeping: the analyst knows that nothing will happen until the patient comes to think that the analyst is not merely doing his job. This illusion is a sine qua non of the work, but the analyst would rather not accept responsibility for its creation. It is hard enough for him to cope with illusions *after* they have come into being (as transference). He would certainly prefer to overlook those that he *plans* to create (safely labeled *regression*, as though regression "just comes," and as though it isn't equivalent to expectations induced by an atmosphere of tacit promise).

Of course, these tacit promises have not gone completely unexamined. Ever since they were described in *Studies on Hysteria* (Breuer & Freud 1895), analysts have tried to separate earned affection and honest caring from transference and countertransference, so that at least the face that they deliberately put on can ultimately be shown to be sincere. So analysts write about a real relationship, the realistic, parental role of the physician, etc. One of the reasons that object relations theory is popular is that it makes analysts comfortable with their seductiveness. In its crudest form, object relations theory allows an analyst to imagine himself to *be* a caring parent, rather than a con man promising to be a caring parent. And there are many other persuasive arguments for the analyst's truthfulness.

Beyond all these theoretical excuses, however, our strongest support – as always in carrying out disagreeable tasks – is convention. Convention warrants an image of analysis as a mutual work rather than a deceptive manipulation. Custom allows us to go on telling ourselves – and some of us to go on telling our patients – that we do not assume complete responsibility for the work; that the patient also has a job

The delicate balance of work and illusion **117**

to do, which could be put into words, and that, although both of us have a sneaking suspicion that an extraordinary promise of intimacy is playing hide-and-seek in the consulting room, we could alternatively draft a perfectly ordinary, businesslike, matter-of-fact, above-board, mutual contract about our respective tasks, with a signed release that all illusions are byproducts of our mutual work for which we both share responsibility – or even (as many prominent analysts hold), that the illusions are entirely the patient's inventions, which it is his job to work "on," or "through," or what have you.

But what's the point of all my irritating provocativeness? Suppose we do cover up our teasing with a pretty picture of mutual work. That doesn't mean our cover story is wrong. Even if work does sweeten unsavory aspects of treatment, the patient's work may nevertheless be important in its own right.

The question is not whether the patient's hard work is partly an enactment. The question is whether a patient's deliberate work – even if it is illusory – fosters the inner, undeliberate work that psychoanalysis counts on. Does it move the patient to both care and not care about his internal audience and his listening analyst? Does it inspire him to orbit away from the analyst, to stretch his emotional tie, acknowledge the analyst's brand of indifference, and nevertheless continue to court or battle the analyst and care intensely about his imagined love?

Of course it does. I'm sure you can all think of ways that deliberate work produces flexibility.

I'll just lump the items into three categories. How does work *work?* Let's say it activates esthetic, ludic, and mastery motives. It's not hard to see how mastery motives might make a patient eager to take on the inner challenge of the analyst's closeness-in-distance – inspiring him to face frightening thoughts, wrestle with the transference. Esthetic motives? Not only might this kind of motive build connections; it might also increase the patient's fortitude. In the simple image of doing a work, a patient finds credit for a creative accomplishment that compensates for discomfort.

And as to play, well, that's the very thing that we pray for – acceptance of the analyst's teasing illusion as a good thing, almost fun. And a vague work may be the best structured simulacrum of play. Indeed, it seems to me that one of the most valued services of the work format is to keep at bay the useful but scary sense of an improvised, unstructured, playful interaction, and post it around with signs of pre-destined, orderly dissection. One can play wildly if supervised by an adult goal. In this regard, the work format does for patients what theory does for analysts – it makes play look serious. Related to play is the sheer satisfaction of mutual influence, as described by Stern (2004).

Do you like me better when I praise work this way than when I natter on about illusions and seduction? Your preference warns us again that our enthusiasm for a patient's work is – how shall I say it? – slightly overvalued, albeit helpful to us in doing our job.

What do I mean about our necessary self-soothing? One way in which *every* patient can appeal to *every* analyst, at least a little bit, is by simply wrapping his

**118** The idea of Freudian therapy

personal yearnings inside a work format. The admiration and affection this evokes in the analyst have their own therapeutic value. And, conversely, the analyst's weird expectation that the patient should partly court him and partly dismiss him – that inhuman demand – will make just a little more sense to patients if it is slipped inside a socially defined work assignment.

Let me summarize: a work assignment acts as a bridge between motives and a bridge between persons. As regards motives, work mediates between incentives based on illusion and incentives that are "realistic." A joint work blends passionate demands with creative and playful urges; it makes some kind of sense of things, stretches out a field for refined evaluation, and encourages the patient to orient toward problems.

And work brings the two parties together. It mediates between analyst's wishes and patient's wishes, that is, between the patient's wish for affection and the analyst's wish for a creative enterprise. It mediates these by allowing each partner a little of what he wants while inspiring a little of it in the other. What excuse do I have for taking up your time with all this? I think we can use the interplay of work and illusion to evaluate current trends. What will the future do with the psychoanalytic tradition? The Freudian prescription was to induce the patient to use the analytic relationship as a tool for exploring his nature, and to accomplish it by modeling the delicate balance between an illusory attachment, on the one hand, and a program of working together, on the other hand.

That venerable plan is now stretched out on the operating table. What will happen to work and illusion? Even before the advent of managed care, these delicately balanced aspects were roughly torn apart, each half being cultivated in isolation. In one corner, we see analysts encouraging work and dispelling illusions. In the other, we find analysts disdaining work assignments and celebrating illusion.

Let's look first at the pro-work faction. It's no mystery why work is newly popular. We've all felt the wind of egalitarianism sweep through family, professions, and society at large. Egalitarianism has torn through analytic institutes, thrown analyst and analysand close upon each other, scrubbed away the awe and mystification that used to veil analytic technique, and left nothing but honest, mutual work. Gone is the esoteric theory that once justified asymmetrical maneuvers. The analyst's old, secret assurance is now denounced as preposterous and elitist; his once-mythic aura is mocked by economic insecurity and shriveled prestige. (Do you remember when analytic meetings were closed even to general psychiatrists?)

Analytic neutrality is roundly abused as a pompous myth. Nobody stands up for the old blank screen. Many analysts believe they can have no secrets, that their personal reactions will always be accurately read by their patients. Others believe that the patient's feelings about the analyst are provoked by the analyst's feelings about the patient, with the consequence that what used to be described as an illusory drama (transference) is now taken to be a more or less accurate perception of the analyst's real collusion.

In fact, we are sometimes told that there isn't *any* hidden reality at all in the relationship – nothing over which the analyst could claim authority or even pretend to have a learned guess. We are lately assured that the nature of the treatment relationship is simply whatever the parties construe it to be at the moment.

These popular beliefs put patient and analyst on an equal footing, which means that treatment proceeds by joint decisions about what will promote understanding (Renik 2006). Naturally, such an egalitarian approach will emphasize the work side of treatment – the joint working together on understanding. Manipulative illusions have little place in such a treatment, for if the analyst really doesn't know what he's expressing, and is therefore unable to manipulate even himself, he is certainly in no position to manipulate the patient. Honest, mutual work is what remains.

That's one side. But this extreme rationalism and its program of mutual work is not the only game in town. For one thing, there's the opposite: the romantic effort to bypass the patient's work and celebrate the treatment illusion. Kohut rebelled against a truth morality (1977, pp. 64–65; 1984, p. 54). In a sense, he facilitated illusions of adoption.

Nor is it only romantics who put all their credence in illusion and question the idea of work. Brenner (1998), nobody's romantic, refuses to privilege any action of the patient as a disinterested work; everything is as much an illusion as it is reality. Schwaber (1984) doesn't exactly revel in illusions, but she, too, cuts work out of the picture by refusing to foist any project on the patient. Her patients are left grasping in vain for an assignment. Half the world is Kleinian, and, in my opinion, the Kleinian tradition has logically no place at all for a working-together project. (I think one of Bion's contributions was to invent a work for Kleinian patients.)

If in the future all analysts have signed up with one or the other of these parties – if they throw in their lot exclusively with work or illusion – psychoanalysis might lose its special interest in the fostering of separation-in-closeness. Treatment might mellow out into a settled project – featuring, in the one case, a comradely pair of investigators and, in the other case, a nurturance couple or a hypnotic team.

I hasten to remind you that I am talking about the future. The living analysts I have cited are still working within the great tradition, which is why my comments about them are wild caricatures. I am imagining what would happen if, besides their vital research into basic ingredients, their models should become the full program of treatment. I am trying to picture what a psychoanalytic treatment would look like without the old ambiguity of purpose that has been its hallmark.

There would be one conspicuous gain: it would be a cleaner treatment. The analyst would no longer confuse himself and his patient by whispering, in effect, "Are both of us simply looking for patterns? Or am I really exerting a healing influence? Or am I also doing something weirder and indescribable, which you as a patient can neither take over nor simply accept?" In short, if the purifying trends were to win out, analyst and patient would no longer have to live under the shadow of manipulation.

What would be lost? Let's worry about each possibility in turn. Take the relationship model first, where the patient's work is considered an illusion. If all responsibility is flatly retained by the analyst, will that infantilize patients, encourage their passivity, and offend their dignity? With no work to do, will patients

**120** The idea of Freudian therapy

lack the exercise that stimulates internal change? Will discovery be limited because only one person is doing the discovering? If a treatment is identified specifically as a relationship, will it harvest unbearable disappointment when it ends? If an analyst looks down on all collaboration, will he puff himself up in grandiosity – or, in the absence of a collaborator, will he try to avoid grandiosity by becoming timid and tentative? Is it possible for an analyst to believe *anything* he is told if he always regards the patient's report as a personal maneuver rather than a piece of honest self-inquiry? Could analysts sustain interest in a prolonged treatment without an image of mutual work?

So much for the no-work side. Now let's worry about the all-work model of treatment (where what is discouraged is the illusion of the relationship). If the analyst certifies this one activity – this work of understanding – if he comes right out and says, "This is what I want," wouldn't that make it impossible to analyze what the collaboration means to the patient? It will seem as though the work of understanding is accepted as a good thing, unlike everything else in the patient's life. (And, after all, who really knows what "understanding" means, and therefore what the analyst is asking for or what he's getting?)

And what about those illusions that the analyst *can't* get rid of – the sense that he is more attached than he really is, for example? What about the ways and means of treatment that, deep down, never really make sense to a patient even after they have been explained and accepted? In short, what happens if the analyst has prematurely cleared his conscience about mystification, and, worse, actually comes across as being on the level? Will that make such deception as remains even more profound, more manipulative? ("See? I have nothing up my sleeve!")

Will the flagrantly unmysterious analyst seem to say that he doesn't like being thought of as manipulative? Will the patient feel that the analyst is uncomfortable with the strains and unfairness of treatment, and can't really see any justification for complaints? Will the arrangement seem to tell the patient that he has no cause to feel toyed with? Will an all-work format, in fact, take away the very vocabulary needed to express such feelings? If we behave like people who are forthcoming without being able to follow through as forthcoming people do, might we confuse our partner and deceive him still more?

These are fairly obvious worries. I'm sure we all worry this way about the other person's leanings. But I'll tell you one worry of my own about both leanings: *I worry that we'll stop worrying.*

I fear that we will lose the private research into the analytic process that goes along with every treatment. I suspect that – in regard to what's really happening – a consistent treatment will be an opaque treatment. Getting us to think about our patients is no problem at all; it is our job. But thinking about what we're doing – that's another matter. We are only human, and it would be just a slight exaggeration to say that the only reason we ever think really hard about the treatment set-up is that it feels so treacherous. Just once, give us some permission (let alone a mandate) to picture our analytic treatment as a plain, safe, visible work, or as a straightforward, healing relationship, and you'll never again persuade us to agonize about what we're involved in. We have more than enough other worries of a practical kind. (To tell the truth, I think this danger is greater for the all-work model. Gravity pulls the analyst's world to a plain, joint work, and I am afraid that if it lands there, it will never take off again.)

If it seems that I have been making a hole in the ocean, as the Greeks say, it is because we all know that almost everyone profits from a work assignment of self-understanding, as well as from a wholesome relationship. It stands to reason that, if analysis means changing and enlarging contexts of meaning, there will be as many ways to go about it as there are styles of human interaction. Some ways may be more useful for some people than for others.

For instance, people who feel safe only if they can clearly visualize a nearby opportunity will thrive on either a work format or a relationship. Others, who are richer in fantasy solutions or in confidence that they can find their way home, may be shortchanged if they are handed an explicit work assignment or provided with a compassionate companion, rather than being bewitched into discovering their own opportunities within the therapist's obscure manner.

Psychoanalysis has historically presumed that there are many people who are able to use the therapist not as a friend and not as a co-worker, but as a hobbyhorse – a living experiment, a device to explore freedom. Those people might profit most from a treatment that manages to preserve some of the old, analytic illusion, some of the closeness-in-distance, the sport, the game, the radically alone honesty, that psychoanalytic therapy was built on.

## REFERENCES

Brenner, C. (1998). Beyond the ego and the id revisited. *Journal of Clinical Psychoanalysis*, 7: 165–180.

Breuer, J. & Freud, S. (1895). *Studies on Hysteria*. Standard Edition, 2.

Ellenberger, H. (1970). *The Discovery of the Unconscious. The History and Evolution of Dynamic Psychiatry*. New York, NY: Basic Books.

Freud, S. (1909/1974). Letter Jung, Letter 134F. In: *The Freud-Jung Letters: The Correspondence between Sigmund Freud and C. G. Jung*, ed. W. McGuire. Cambridge, MA: Harvard University Press, pp. 209–211.

Freud, S. (1914). Remembering, repeating and working-through. Standard Edition, 12.

Freud, S. (1915). Observations on transference-love. Standard Edition, 12.

Gay, P. (1988). *Freud: A Life for Our Times*. New York, NY: Norton.

Kohut, H. (1977). *The Restoration of the Self*. New York, NY: International Universities Press.

Kohut, H. (1984). *How Does Analysis Cure?*Chicago, IL: University of Chicago Press.

Kris, E. (1956). On some vicissitudes of insight in psycho-analysis. *International Journal of Psychoanalysis*, 37: 445–455.

Loewald, H. (1980). Psychoanalytic theory and the psychoanalytic process. In: *Papers on Psychoanalysis*. New Haven, CT: Yale University Press, pp. 277–301.

Macmillan, M. (1990). Freud and Janet on organic and hysterical paralyses: A mystery solved? *International Review of Psychoanalysis*, 17: 189–203.

## 122 The idea of Freudian therapy

Renik, O. (2006). *Practical Psychoanalysis for Therapists and Patients*. New York, NY: Other Press.

Schwaber, E. (1984). Empathy: A mode of analytic listening. In: *Empathy II*, eds. J. Lichtenberg, M. Bornstein & D. Silver. Hillsdale, NJ: Analytic Press, pp. 143–172.

Stern, D. N. (2004). *The Present Moment in Psychotherapy and Everyday Life*. New York, NY: Norton.

# 7

# HOW AND WHY DO PATIENTS BECOME MORE OBJECTIVE? STERBA COMPARED WITH STRACHEY

What Richard Sterba described in his influential paper was not, as some have thought, a lasting alliance between patient and analyst but a momentary dissociative state, accompanying the analysis of transference resistance, in which the patient detaches himself from his strivings and views himself objectively before lapsing back into normal coherence. We also find in the paper a hinted answer to the vexing question of what motivates patients to engage in characteristically psycho-analytic self-scrutiny. Sterba implicitly proposes a problem-solving incentive acti-vated by transference. A comparison with Strachey leads us to ask whether patients progress only by disinhibition of particular strivings through particular resolutions of particular fears, or whether patients also experience a more general liberation that fosters their own, deliberate search for integration.

Richard Sterba's "The fate of the ego in analytic therapy" (1934) is the earliest elaboration of the concept of the therapeutic alliance; it is the respected ancestor of all subsequent considerations of the subject.

Unfortunately, a primal paper in psychoanalysis is fated to be dragooned into alliance with successor discussions, its particular slant gradually bending to the developing trend. I have contributed to that bias (Friedman 1969), and I hope to make amends in this chapter.

To begin with, Sterba was not describing a general collaboration between patient and analyst as we now define the therapeutic alliance. His alliance was a far more specific phenomenon: He was describing something that happens during the interpretation of *transference resistance*. The alliance Sterba had in mind occurs when the patient temporarily stretches himself away from conflicted involvement with the analyst and looks at his transferential behavior objectively. Thus: no transference resistance, no alliance!

Looking at this fact in more detail, it is noteworthy that for Sterba the alliance is at once more ephemeral and more universal than the alliance imagined by later

**124** The idea of Freudian therapy

writers. We first note its transience. Like Strachey's mutative interpretation at the "point of urgency," Sterba's alliance, although requiring continuous preparation, is not a working contract but a happening – an immediate dissociation within the patient who experiences himself as simultaneously in (resistant) disguise and as seeing through his disguise. Furthermore, it is a genuine dissociative state, not merely an act of reflection or the flexing of a perspective. Patients recover from this abnormal quasi-alliance and assimilate the double vision to a normal – but now enlarged – coherent awareness, with long-forgotten memories summoned to cement the new coherence. Indeed, the alliance is so transient that it may lead to an *intensification* of libidinal demands on the analyst (p. 125). What tends to endure and grow is an at-home-ness with the *sequence* of depersonalization and repersonalization, and an ease in falling back into it:

> When analysis begins, the ego is subject to a process of 'dissimilation' or dissociation, which must be induced by the analyst by means of his interpretation of the transference-situation and of the resistance to which this gives rise. As the analysis proceeds, the state of 'dissimilation' in the ego is set up again whenever the unconscious material, whether in the shape of instinctual gratification or of defensive impulses, fastens on the analyst in the transference. All the instinctual and defensive reactions aroused in the ego in the transference impel the analyst to induce the therapeutic process of ego-dissociation by means of the interpretations he gives. There is constituted, as it were, a standing relation between that part of the ego which is cathected with instinctual or defensive energy and that part which is focussed on reality and identified with the analyst, and this relation is the filter through which all the transference-material must pass. Each separate interpretation reduces the instinctual and defensive cathexis of the ego in favour of intellectual contemplation, reflection and correction by the standard of reality.
>
> However, once the analyst's interpretations have set up this opposition of forces – the ego which is in harmony with reality versus the ego which acts out its unconscious impulses – the state of 'dissimilation' does not last and a process of 'assimilation' automatically begins.
>
> *(pp. 122–123)*[1]

By coining the term, "dissimilation," as an antonym for assimilation Sterba makes it clear that the ego split he has in mind is not a life style fashioned to the couch, but a repeated abnormality that is progressively displaced by normal, integrated functioning.

Yet, compared with the specialized psychoanalytic task that today's authors call therapeutic alliance, Sterba's ego split has unspecialized, universal significance. Sterba saw it as a variant of the normal, characteristically human capacity of reflection, the sort of thing a Piagetian might describe as operating upon one's operations, or a philosopher might refer to as abstracting from one's abstractions, or a man in the street might say amounts to looking hard at oneself.

The therapeutic dissociation of the ego in analysis is merely an extension, into new fields, of that self-contemplation which from all time has been regarded as the most essential trait of man in distinction to other living beings.

*(p. 125)*

In support of the naturalness of this faculty, Sterba invoked the authority of one of Freud's most beautiful paeans to humanity's capacity for an infinite series of self-reflections (p. 120, n. 2).

As subsequently developed, the concept of the therapeutic alliance has been shadowed by a dismaying problem: The alliance seems to require, quite implausibly, the creation *ex nihilo* of a unique motive for a prolonged, intense human relationship. Or else it seems to postulate an attitude of unmotivated opposition to motives (Friedman 1969). When we notice that Sterba is referring to a different phenomenon – a *common* variety of thought occurring in an exaggerated fashion at a *particular* moment in treatment – we become hopeful that he may have something more believable to tell us about the *motives* involved in a patient's psychoanalytic work, something missing from later teachings about the therapeutic alliance.

By 1934, psychoanalysis had developed structural concepts that made it easier to say without inconsistency that the transference is both a reaching out to the analyst and a pulling back, that it expresses both desire and prohibition, that it tries to use the treatment to achieve satisfaction and tries to abort it to achieve safety. Explicating what Freud (1914) had folded into his concept of working through, Sterba identified the clinical problem that analysts were up against when they confronted transference and its avoidance:

The function of the transference is twofold. On the one hand, it serves to satisfy the object-hunger of the id. But, on the other, it meets with opposition from the repressive psychic institutions – the super-ego, which rejects it on moral grounds, and the ego, which, because of unhappy experiences, utters a warning against it.

*(p. 118)*

Where the transference-situation is intense, there is always the danger that one or other of the conflicting forces may prevail: either the analytic enterprise may be broken up by the blunt transference demands of the patient, or else the repressive institutions in the mind of the latter may totally repudiate both analyst and analysis. Thus we may describe the transference and the resistance which goes with it as the conflict-laden final result of the struggle between two groups of forces, each of which aims at dominating the workings of the ego, while both alike obstruct the purposes of the analysis.

*(p. 119)*

**126** The idea of Freudian therapy

As to how this problem can be solved, analytic theory was making it increasingly clear (it was never really all that obscure) that patients can be changed only by utilizing their native powers of self-rearrangement.

> In opposition to this dual influence, the object of which is to inhibit the analysis, we have the corrective influence of the analyst, who in his turn, however, must address himself to the *ego*.
>
> *(p. 119, italics in original)*

The words, "who in his turn, however, must address himself …," remind analysts that, no matter how well attuned they are to the patient's unconscious desires, it is not their attunement that makes the therapeutic difference, but rather some capacity patients have for shifting the way they experience themselves.

The conceptual task that lay before analysts at that time was to understand what prevented and what facilitated that ability: Where did the analyst fit into the patient's self-shifting machinery? How does the analyst ensure that the patient will experience himself in a heretofore prohibited fashion?

James Strachey (for instance in the pages immediately following Sterba's article [Strachey 1934]), argued that the patient's prohibitions would have to be modified before the analyst could be seen, let alone followed into a new experience. The analyst would have to modify the superego if he hoped to have his message received. Sterba, on the other hand, pointed out that superegos are not formed every day: the superego is a peculiar developmental achievement of the immature human being. Viewed from Sterba's perspective, it might seem a bit disrespectful of the superego's uniqueness as a structure, its fateful historicity, its rootedness in phase-specific readiness and Proustian memory, to imagine that an analyst can take up superego modeling as a handicraft.

Sterba suggested a more modest role for the analyst. He said that the faculty of mind which had been drawn into superego formation remains always at a person's disposal. It is because we are *generally* capable of reflecting on ourselves as though we were somebody else, that we can create a *particular* superego at one stage of our life. The superego is the "prototype" of self-confrontation; it pairs a person's own spontaneous attitudes with supervisory attitudes derived from identifying with somebody else, and it is a permanent structure within the unified mind. But although such structuralization happens only once, we always retain the capacity to temporarily separate ourselves from our outlook and identify with another person's view of us. When the other person is an analyst, the view taken up lacks the moral coloring characteristic of the superego.

> Whilst the super-ego demands that the subject shall adopt a particular attitude towards a particular tendency in the id, the demand made upon him when therapeutic dissociation takes place is a demand for a balancing contemplation, kept steadily free of affect, whatever change may take place in the contents of the instinct-cathexes and the defensive reactions.
>
> *(p. 122)*

The effect of this new experience may be to fortify the patient against superego restrictions.

> In overcoming the transference-defence by the method of therapeutic ego-dissociation we were not merely attacking that part of the ego which was using the patient's unhappy experience with the physician in her childhood to obstruct the analysis; we were, besides, counteracting part of the super-ego's opposition.
>
> (p. 125)

Analysts have framed various pictures of the fate of the superego in treatment. Some, such as Franz Alexander (1925), have regarded the superego as a primitive irrationality, a sort of universal core neurosis requiring removal or replacement. Although most writers do not take such an extreme view, they vary in the degree to which they expect to make the superego "realistic" as against wishing simply to make it less automatically dispositive. In his 1934 paper, Sterba emphasizes the latter aim, and narrows even that aim to the therapeutic moment. He suggests that analytic technique is designed not so much to change standards as to suspend their force long enough to allow the patient to grasp his internal situation; and the outcome of analysis is not a new set of standards but a new disposition achieved by progressive, naturalistic glimpses of oneself. Sterba leaves us free to imagine that after treatment the same old superego functions less unrealistically only because it reacts to a more accurately discriminated psychic field.

Unlike Strachey's thesis, this is intended as a description of what the analyst does with transference resistance. Although it is not unreasonable to regard it as a general theory of therapeutic action, Sterba is more modest:

> Now amongst all the experiences undergone by the ego during an analysis there is one which seems to me so *specific* and so *characteristic* of the analytic situation that I feel justified in isolating it and presenting it to you as the 'fate' of the ego in analytic therapy.
>
> (p. 117, italics added)

I do not mean to exaggerate Sterba's difference from Strachey. For both, a successful interpretation of transference resistance is a kind of epiphany. But for Strachey, it permanently changes the patient's values, while Sterba regards it as a temporary suspension of "oughts" – a brief holiday in which the patient can compose a new mental balance and glimpse the way analysis can help.

> Through the explanations of the transference-situation that he receives the patient realizes for the first time the peculiar character of the therapeutic method used in analysis. Its distinctive characteristic is this: that the subject's consciousness shifts from the centre of affective experience to that of intellectual contemplation. The transference-situation is interpreted, i.e., an explanation is

**128** The idea of Freudian therapy

given which is uncoloured by affect and which shews that the situation has its roots in the subject's childhood.

*(p. 121)*

Mindful that this most characteristic and peculiar analytic experience occurs only in the context of transference resistance and its interpretation, we suddenly realize that Sterba is not describing a general attitude of dispassionate contemplation, but the disruption of a state of conflicted attachment.

Why does the patient allow himself to be thus disrupted? For Strachey, that is the basic question, and his answer is that the disruption is *forced* on the patient by the immediacy of the analyst's helpful response. No special motive is required of the patient other than the simple functioning of his sense organs.

Sterba's answer is more complex. At first he seems to be counting on the power of transferentially reinforced suggestion. For instance, he supposes that the patient comes to identify with the analyst because the analyst has been deliberately cultivating a collaborative transference.

The use of the word 'we' always means that the analyst is trying to draw that part of the ego over to his side ...

*(p. 121)*

But we must not lose sight of the fact that a general spirit of cooperation is not the alliance Sterba had in mind. Sterba's alliance, we recall, is a momentary, dispassionate identification with the analyst at a time of transference resistance.

As mentioned, Sterba's alliance comes about because the patient allows himself to be disrupted in an intense conflict. The positive transference – the cooperative spirit – precedes that and simply makes it *possible* for the patient to identify with the analyst when the disruption occurs.

If it were just a matter of cooperative spirit, perhaps that could be taught. But in referring to a dissociation, Sterba is not describing an ordinary learning experience (as Strachey was). Sterba's ego split is a flickering experience that quickly alternates, for instance, with starkly contrasting manifestations of attachment. And positive transference leads in many directions: it cannot alone account for the split in the ego. So, the crucial question is this: If the disruptive self-scrutiny is only facilitated, and not *driven*, by the positive transference, and if that new perspective is truly affect-less, *why*, at those moments, does the patient let himself be disrupted at all? Why does the patient shift his style of experiencing from intense involvement to partial indifference?

I do not think that Sterba answers this question clearly. He is inclined to invoke the motiveless formulas of "strengthening the ego" (p. 121) and "identification." Yet there is evidence in his paper that Sterba sensed a real and lively goal that inspires patients to *use* their positive feeling for – and identification with – the analyst, *to effect* a dissociation.

One very small clue is Sterba's reference to the encounter of the patient's passion with the analyst's objectivity, which faintly suggests that Sterba may have been impressed by the same considerations that moved Strachey:

> The transference-situation is *interpreted*, i.e., an explanation is given which is uncoloured by affect and which shews that the situation has its roots in the subject's childhood.

> *(p. 121, italics in original)*

Now, Sterba may only mean that the patient is impressed by an objective account of his state of mind. But since *anything* the analyst says is always and everywhere bound to be free of the *patient's* affect, there is at least a possibility that in writing about these strange moments, Sterba has in mind the powerful effect analysts have on patients' stereotyped perceptions when they react in a dispassionate way to passionate incursions.[2]

But even if Sterba shared Strachey's interest in the shock created by meeting the patient's passion with calmness, it seems to me that there is a significant difference between Strachey's and Sterba's description of what happens as a *result* of the analyst's neutral response. Although the intensity of the transference moment is crucial to both Sterba and Strachey, it is important to them for different reasons.

Strachey observed that patients ordinarily assimilate their analyst to a prefigured role in their life drama. Whenever the analyst imparts information, it is regarded as an interpersonal attitude or a social action rather than information about reality. With his every movement the analyst comes across as positioning himself in the patient's real life. And if he comments on that fact, that comment is construed in the same way. Only the intensity of a personal confrontation can distract a patient from "hallucinating" a fantasy analyst and allow the real analyst to be seen. Strachey's point, as I would phrase it, is that it takes a social action to change a social perception, and it is only when the analyst's "just informing" is also an action (specifically a reaction of tolerance) that it will inform as intended. Moving toward the patient's thrust, the analyst acknowledges that he is being wrestled with (i.e., indicates that he has felt the patient's impact), and the patient learns the lesson in his own language.

As I understand Strachey's argument, the transference-intense moment is crucial just because at that point the analyst is taking an action in the social field and not trying in vain to speak without acting. I have in mind Irwin Hoffman's (1983) principle, which I would paraphrase this way: We know, roughly, how another person feels when, for example, we attack him. Since we know the internal experience that we have made the victim deal with and then see his overt response, we can interpolate a truth about his attitude to us beyond his deliberate communication. It would follow from this principle that, no matter what the analyst's professional demeanor, when he explicitly faces into the patient's gesture, he reveals a variety of real (i.e., social) responses to the patient. At the very least his inner reaction is revealed as self-restraint, and even that meager response is arresting

**130** The idea of Freudian therapy

because the restraint is real and not imaginary. (It may, indeed, be patronizing.) The same cannot be said, for instance, about the analyst's response to a story that the patient tells because the patient has fewer primordial clues to a hearer's reaction. Strachey believes that at the point of direct, personal impact there is something that cannot be misconstrued. A logical gloss on Strachey's principle would be that, when the analyst welcomes stressful approaches, even though he may be generally unrevealing, he rules out several *misconstruals* of his attitude – namely, those misconstruals that would predict his avoidance or retaliation. By eliminating those few misconstruals the analyst has objectively cleared the way for at least some permissive perspectives.

Now, turning to Sterba, we observe that, although generally speaking he is more confident than Strachey that he can make the patient see him as benevolent, it is not an issue that especially interests him in interpreting transference resistance. He does not seek to demonstrate his real permissiveness. The perspective he recommends is neutral. No doubt he would have agreed with Strachey that he is caught up in the patient's fantasy as a real player in the drama of life. However, Sterba escapes this psychic trap not by *adding* a little normal reality, but by *subtracting* a little subjective reality. He does not modify the patient's ordinary perception but encourages a totally different sort of self-experience. According to Sterba, what the patient needs in order to entertain a new perspective is not safety from a *specific* threat (emanating from a feared analyst); what he needs is to be momentarily freed from *identification with (all) his fears*. That is done by interpreting transference resistance.

What is there about interpretation of transference resistance that makes that possible? Part of the answer seems to be that the moment of transference resistance (if one can call it a moment) is at once more confused and more easily sorted out than other moments.

> Through this interpretation there emerges in the mind of the patient, out of the chaos of behaviour impelled by instinct and behaviour designed to inhibit instinct, a *new point of view of intellectual contemplation*.
>
> *(p. 121, italics in original)*

Perhaps it is the exemplary quality of the problem that not only recommends it to Sterba but makes it attractive to the patient: transference resistance is an acute but workable problem. It is also examplary in being synoptic, since "the personality of the analysand passes first of all under the domination of the *transference*" (p. 118). We may suspect that immediacy, difficulty, solubility, and illustrativeness are the features of the situation that make it exemplary for Sterba, and that these same features attract the patient's interest. We might say that the analyst, exploiting a situation of this sort, *suggests* and *models* for the patient a way of pushing his own natural faculty of self-observation to a near-pathological extreme at a time when the need is maximal, the challenge greatest, the solution clearest.

How and why do patients become more objective? **131**

According to this reading, the *co-presence* of passionate and dispassionate visions is more important to Sterba than to Strachey. For Strachey, passionateness ("urgency") is only incidentally important: It is useful only because it forces attention away from the fantasy analyst and onto the real analyst. But for Sterba, passionateness is important for two other reasons that have nothing to do with the real analyst: (1) transference passion is a painful but masterable challenge, and as such, it illustrates the usefulness of dissociated dispassionateness in analysis; (2) the passion contains the material that the patient needs to learn about.

Strachey's problem was, "How can I point out something to the patient when all he will look at is my finger? I guess I'll have to find a way of gesturing toward my finger." Sterba's problem was, "How can I get the patient to point to himself objectively? Let me give him an example at a time when he needs desperately to master a difficult problem." In contrast to Strachey, it is a way of looking at oneself – rather than an awareness of some features or an experience of an impulse – that Sterba is trying to induce.

The theme that Sterba inscribed in psychoanalytic theory remains with us, along with the questions and debates that attend it. Psychoanalysis asks that patients dissociate themselves from earlier figures toward whom they direct their conscious and unconscious reactions. The interesting question is: To what extent can the patient deliberately intend a useful dissociation? Sterba suggests that, given the proper encouragement, human beings have the capacity to observe themselves consciously and preconsciously in progressively less restrictive ways. In short, Sterba does not regard it as absurd for an analyst to *ask* a patient to take some distance from both himself and the analyst – to look down from the ceiling, so to speak – whereas Strachey implicitly argues that this is not a reasonable request even with suggestive encouragement. According to Strachey, the patient will always see the analyst in the way his history inclines him. The analyst's job is to introduce some new history and thereby incline him differently, by providing an experience so "hot" that it makes the analyst's true attitude inescapably clear. Thus, for Strachey, the style of the patient's experience is not changed, only its content. For Sterba, on the other hand, the exact opposite is true at the moment of dissociation.[3]

On the issue of motives, Strachey does not need to invoke anything but passion, which will follow the paths newly opened by the analyst. Sterba, on the other hand, was the first in a line of theorists who suggested that analysis sets the patient a problem (chiefly through transference), the efforts to solve which lead to health.

Had he been asked to elaborate on this point, perhaps Sterba would have said that the analyst shows his patient how he can immediately begin to resolve a painful conflict. Furthermore, we have reason to suppose that Sterba would have said that unclarity is a kind of pain, and the promise of clarity is by itself an incentive for trying out the recommended experience (see also Myerson 1981).

Perhaps the most tantalizing question raised by Sterba's rationale is whether there can be such a thing as an affect-less view of oneself – or of anybody else, for that matter. Should we, instead, agree with Strachey when he implies that, for better or worse, a superego of some sort will always influence one's view? It is not

**132** The idea of Freudian therapy

a question of whether a non-attitudinal description can be made. We can easily formulate an impersonal account of a person; we do it all the time when we write a case history. But that is not the same thing as taking a non-attitudinal view of an acquaintance (including ourselves). Is there, perhaps, something in the *experience* of personhood that places it outside the realm of objectivity? Or are some dissociative states truly impersonal?

And does it matter? By itself it probably makes little difference whether we adopt Sterba's rationale or Strachey's, whether we fancy that the patient's new access to himself is obtained with the superego's blessing or without it, i.e., with a more tolerant superego or with a more "realistic" use of the superego, since both Strachey and Sterba have their eye on the new synthesis that the ego makes in each case. But Sterba's rationale evolved into a major tradition of technique, different in important respects from Strachey's. And the difference does not hinge on the belief that it is possible to see oneself objectively, popular as that belief may be within the tradition. Even if human beings can see themselves only in terms of attitudes, of morally tinged perspectives and dramatizations, etc., it can still be argued that a particular new, therapeutic way of seeing oneself has as its principal *significance* that it *generally* loosens restrictions of fear, and is not merely one additional, useful, perspective. A certain type of psychoanalytic self-scrutiny might be said to function *mostly* as a freeing example – a demonstration that safety can be enjoyed even while perspectives shift.

Many treatment attitudes will be determined by how we answer this question: Is a therapeutically split ego important because it leads one to a more promising view of oneself, or because it shows that one can shift perspectives indefinitely without desperate loss? When the patient accepts a transference interpretation, is he shifting to a more satisfactory perception (Strachey), or is he gravitating to a more abstract confidence (Sterba)?

Depending on how the analyst answers this question, he will see his role differently and will count on different motivations in his patient. If, like Strachey, he thinks of himself as clearing the way for a repressed id expression, an analyst will trust the id impulse to move the patient forward. If, on the other hand, the analyst follows Sterba and presents himself as a foil for the patient's use in untangling internal knots (perhaps to retangle himself more adequately afterward), that analyst will be making a peculiar demand on the patient's problem-solving motives. Although Sterba did not suggest that this builds a life-long skill, others in the tradition have explored that possibility. In particular, Gray (1973) hopes for a lasting self-ownership, so to speak, in which the patient has the option of using the mind's creative resources for their own sake, rather than for their social consequences.

Can we combine passionate and mastery incentives into one theory? We might suppose that each movement in treatment is evoked by the new prospect of a libidinal satisfaction but that the progressive assimilation of those movements yields a sense of power which then becomes attractive in its own right. In that sense, we could say that the libidinal struggles serve as tools. (I understand Myerson [1965] to be describing the patient's fantasy repertoire as a problem-solving tool kit; see also French [1958] who maintained that patients enlarge their "integrative fields" by successively revising their fantasy solutions to the problems encountered when new hopes are stirred by the analytic situation.) I think this has been the common trend of the Freudian tradition.

We must be careful with this image precisely because it is so congenial. Freudian theory has had good reason to keep "mastery" motives at arm's length. The power of Freudian theory comes from its relentless hunt for particular, earthy motives and its refusal to be soothed by bland generalities. The theory grants the mind its constant integrative tendency, but it views integration as reactive to more particular demands. In the light of recent infant observation, some authors (e.g., Lichtenberg 1989) have postulated original impulses corresponding to what used to be called "effectance motives." But Freudian theory tends to define those motives according to what at any time they are trying to effect so that practitioners can avoid being fooled into endorsing a particular, conflictual compromise. Analysts have usually felt that it is tactically wisest to let hypothetical, general growth "motives" take care of themselves. The irony is that when analysts are allowed absolutely no picture of an endorsable motive – no nonconflictual activity of the patient that tends toward independence – they deprive themselves of a standard baseline of neutrality from which to measure their unwitting collusions.

Sterba offers us a standard. It is his stark picture of a dissociative state, by contrast with which other analytic events, including his own rhetorically encouraged alliance, can be seen to be the product of suggestion and manipulation. And in recent years, Gray (1973, 1991) has used a related picture of reflective independence as a treatment goal, by comparison with which many perfectly ordinary analyst behaviors, such as routinely interpreting dream contents or speaking in a kindly voice, may be judged to be unthinking endorsements of conservative motives of the patient.

In general terms, psychoanalysts labor to disrupt an equilibrium. (That is just rephrasing the goal of change.) In doing this, they have little choice but to see themselves as either impressing something on the patient, or withdrawing something from him, or both. Strachey explored the possibility of imposition, forcibly pulling the patient close enough to impose a new perspective on him. Sterba is sometimes read as recommending a similar approach, and surely there is truth in that. But perhaps Sterba should be principally credited with exploring the other aspects of disruption, i.e., how to undermine *all* the patient's convictions and help him *estrange* himself from the person of the analyst.

These are not just alternative abstract formulas describing one, complex therapeutic event. They refer to two different practical forces in treatment: the analyst's wish to impress the patient with his vision, and his contradictory hope that the patient will not care how the analyst sees him. There is a faint irony in the fact that the paradigm of patient alienation (in both the ordinary and psychiatric sense of alienation) should be the ancestor of the concept of therapeutic alliance.

**134** The idea of Freudian therapy

## Notes

1 Unless otherwise specified, all page references are to Sterba (1934).
2 Sterba (1940/1929, p. 376) had made this more explicit in a paper that was preliminary to the one we are examining. But while noting his emphasis in that paper on the analyst's soothing efforts, we should not fail to also note his unusual reference to the *disappointment* a patient feels in the analyst's detachment. Of course, that feature of analytic treatment was always well known, having given rise to Freud's original discovery of transference. But it is surprisingly overshadowed in the literature by images of the analyst's benignity and reassurance. I find it remarkable that the father of the Therapeutic Alliance was more sensitive than most to the sadness of the progressive features of treatment; the original Therapeutic Alliance was not a jolly comradeship.
3 Again, I am exaggerating the difference between these two theories: Very likely what Strachey has in mind when he imagines the patient internalizing features of the analyst's superego is the same thing that Sterba visualizes as the patient's identifying with the analyst's observing ego. And it prescribes the same action for both analysts.

## REFERENCES

Alexander, F. (1925). A metapsychological description of the process of cure. *International Journal of Psychoanalysis*, 6: 13–34.

French, T. M. (1958). *The Integration of Behavior, Vol 3. The Reintegrative Process in a Psychoanalytic Treatment.* Chicago, IL: University of Chicago Press.

Freud, S. (1914). Remembering, repeating and working-through. (Further recommendations on the technique of psycho-analysis II.) Standard Edition, 12.

Friedman, L. (1969). The therapeutic alliance. *International Journal of Psychoanalysis*, 50: 139–153.

Gray, P. (1973). Psychoanalytic technique and the ego's capacity for viewing intrapsychic activity. *Journal of the American Psychoanalytic Association*, 21: 474–494.

Gray, P. (1991). On transferred permissive or approving superego functions: The analysis of the ego's superego activities, part II. *Psychoanalytic Quarterly*, 60: 1–21.

Hoffman, I. Z. (1983). The patient as interpreter of the analyst's experience. *Contemporary Psychoanalysis*, 19: 389–422.

Lichtenberg, J. D. (1989). *Psychoanalysis and Motivation.* Hillsdale, NJ: Analytic Press.

Myerson, P. G. (1965). Modes of insight. *Journal of the American Psychoanalytical Association*, 13: 771–792.

Myerson, P. G. (1981). The nature of the transactions that occur in other than classical analysis. International Journal of Psychoanalysis, 8: 173–189.

Sterba, R. (1940/1929). The dynamics of the dissolution of the transference resistance. *Psychoanalytic Quarterly*, 9: 363–379. First published in German as: Sterba, R. (1929). Zur Dynamik der Bewältigung des Übertragungswiderstandes. *Internationale Zeitschrift für Psychoanalyse*, 15(4): 456–470.

Sterba, R. (1934). The fate of the ego in analytic therapy. *International Journal of Psychoanalysis*, 15: 117–126.

Strachey, J. (1934). The nature of the therapeutic action of psycho-analysis. *International Journal of Psychoanalysis*, 15: 127–159.

# 8

# A RENAISSANCE FOR FREUD'S *PAPERS ON TECHNIQUE*

It is one of the great peculiarities of psychoanalysis that Freud's *Papers on Technique* (1911–1915) – a work finished in 1914 – is still the backbone of treatment. Here, between 1911 and 1914, the shape of psychoanalytic treatment was definitively mapped. Here the concepts were named that made the immaterial stuff of practice tangible and teachable for the profession's lifetime. There is no other way to talk about psychoanalytic treatment than with the vocabulary born in the *Papers on Technique*, and that is as true for those who would modify or reject it as for those who take it as canonical. *Papers on Technique* floats the buoys that mark out psychoanalysis from other human relationships. You can argue about whether to steer this way or that around those markers, but without them you have nothing but open sea.

## RECOGNITION OF DESIRE IN THE FIRST MODEL

I want to emphasize that Freud crafted these crucial terms to cope with painful, practical problems that entangled him as he tried to sustain the strange new treatment. The terms mold a cognitive style for an unusual inquiry, but also an attitudinal posture for unusual stress. Bitter experience taught Freud that this style and posture are what keep the peculiar treatment going. Writing these papers, Freud is in the process of discovering something, not inventing something. Moreover, what he is discovering is not at all what he wanted or expected.

To begin with, Freud had to give up his main ambition, which was to read out the hidden meaning of dreams. That was his claim to immortal fame. That was what he considered his competence. That was what psychoanalysis was supposed to be in the early days. And Freud had to just junk it. His first lesson, then, was: "Don't be so interested in dreams!" From there, the admonition broadens to the starkly shocking: "Don't be so interested in anything!" Why did he write that? His

## 136 The idea of Freudian therapy

account shows that it is not because he wanted to, and not because theory told him to, but because he had discovered the trouble he got into when patients were able to use his own interest against him, so to speak – that is, against the process of analysis.

Freud was discovering that the analyst's strange power was connected to his will-less-ness and role-less-ness. And he saw the ramifications: the patient should try to give up purposes, and the analyst was supposed to do that, too. We have become so accustomed to it that we may not realize how odd is this mysterious require-ment of nondirectiveness – the requirement that the analyst leave the patient to his own natural devices. Freud could not have reached that peculiar principle without a stepladder, though it was one that had to be kicked away after it was used. The stepladder was the old, simple memory-retrieval model of treatment. The irony is that Freud's overwhelming wish to hear memories is what had made it possible to discover the effect of suspending all searching.

What I mean is this: Freud's early ideas about how memories are processed allowed him to sit back and wait for memories, of their own accord, to make themselves evident. By supposing that the patient produces memories through a natural process and heals himself by disgorging them, Freud automatically crossed the threshold into a nondirective treatment. If memory and healing are like that, all the analyst need do is nontendentiously clear away obstacles (resistances) to natural self-healing.

The trouble is that remembering isn't so natural after all. In fact, analysis isn't natural, and patients don't really want to be analyzed (Freud 1912, p. 108). As Freud writes *Papers on Technique*, psychoanalytic treatment is shaping up as a giant paradox. Think about it: it is a nondirective treatment directed against the patient's will! You can see Freud glimpsing that paradox out of the corner of his eye from the first of the *Papers* onward, trying over and over again to push it into a closet, until it simply would not fit there any more. At that point, he faced a choice: one option was to picture the patient as being opposed to the aims of treatment, in which case the analyst would have to fight back, giving up the power of his neu-trality, together with his free-floating attention and abstemious, nonmanipulative posture. Freud tried out that option at the end of the second paper, "The dynamics of transference" (1912), where we see him battling with the patient to force her to get well (p. 108). Alternatively, he could go on as before, supposing that patients *really* want to cooperate, and what *seems* to be their unwillingness is the almost impersonal protectiveness called *"the" resistance* – something that sounds like the inflammatory reaction a doctor has to shrink in order to free a patient's airway (see Freud 1912, p. 105).

Looking at the interaction in this second way, Freud was able to retain his neutral position, but now he was at a loss to say why, among all the many things that could obstruct memory, transference was so often the culprit. Nor could he say why the transference – so helpful in eliciting memories in his previous, sug-gestive practice – functioned instead as an obstruction in the new treatment (Freud 1912, p. 101). And after making several efforts to answer the question in just those terms, he realized he could not do it.

A renaissance for *Papers on Technique* **137**

There was only one path left. If Freud wanted to maintain his nondirective role as facilitator of a natural process (remembering), while nevertheless acknowledging that patients naturally want something else altogether, he would have to *redefine* memory, remembering, transference, and resistance. He would have to redefine them in a way that would make what uncooperative patients visibly want coincide in some way with the very different, natural process he thought he was liberating. The labels had to be changed if the nondirective attitude was to be saved. The well-known result is that passionate action in the transference is now labeled "memory," and "resistance" now refers to the patient's refusal to admit that his wants are (in a sense) only what he used to want (Freud 1914, p. 155).

Now, viewing what one *wants* as really a memory of what one *wanted* is to place a momentary desire in a past framework. And that, in turn, amounts to separating oneself from one's momentary desires by objectifying them. This wrench is called *working through* (Freud 1914, p. 155). (That is the first meaning of working through, not quite understood by Strachey – who, therefore, in his translation, rejected Freud's own clarification in his second edition [Freud 1914, p. 155n].)[1]

In working through, the patient has to work against interest – against the interest of the moment – and forfeit the advantage of insistence aimed against the analyst's neutrality. The patient is required to tear himself away from effective, whole-hearted effort, right in the middle of wishing, and instead observe the inappropriate, unintegrated longings as though they were mere memories. In that position, he will feel both the current wish or need and his analytic obligation to treat it as though it were currently invalid. The outcome is that he will know the wish more articulately but will no longer press for its gratification.

The violence of that self-alienation was sufficient to satisfy Freud that he had at last found what it was in this new, undramatic treatment that had a power comparable with the old, cataclysmic catharsis – a treatment force capable of shaking a mind (Freud 1914, p. 156; see Friedman 1991). Instead of a liberation of memory, there was now a transformation of desire.

Like the patient, the analyst reacts to the scene as though it were a display of memories, even while he honors the reality and genuineness of the current feeling (Freud 1912, 1915). This strange fractured vision results from insisting that memories are slyly hiding, while at the same time acknowledging that they are straightforwardly seeking – seeking out the analyst in a most vigorous manner (called transference). The patient is and is not expected to be on the side of the analyst. A hundred years later, we recognize our enduring commitment to that paradox in our work.

With the retreat from the naturalness of the simple memory retrieval paradigm, this first novice discovered, like all who would follow, that some forcible means was required to effect the treatment. We are all familiar with Freud's view that treatment is propelled by attachment to the analyst. Yes, a split in the ego was needed, but it was not something to be assumed (as many modern analysts do when they consider playfulness to be a prerequisite for treatment rather than its effect). Freud taught that patients are drawn forward by transferential longing. Desire would be used against desire.

**138** The idea of Freudian therapy

## DESIRE OBSCURED IN THE SECOND MODEL

At this point in my account, the reader may object that a hundred years have, after all, made a significant difference. True, you may say – the physical set-up prescribed in *Papers on Technique* has remained in place, but our sense of it shifted after the 1920s. Informed by the structural and signal anxiety theories, we now find it easier to sympathize with resistance. We can visualize the patient's fears more specifically and see the reasonableness of his defense more concretely. We no longer believe that a single, protean enemy ("the" resistance) is always waiting in the wings to scuttle our enterprise. We can empathize with the immediate, particular causes of treatment difficulty.

In point of fact, those changes represent less a theoretical shift than a clarification of what was already implicit. But taken together, the structural theory did bring about a genuine reorientation toward patients. After the 1920s, analysts would think of themselves as dealing primarily with fear (anxiety). In contrast to the analyst of the *Papers on Technique*, the later analyst is a liberator – not just in his aim, but in the actual conduct of treatment. The analyst is not curing the patient by administering bitter medicine. The ongoing procedure itself consists in constantly freeing the patient from the unnecessary grip of unrealistic fears. The analyst brings the good news that danger situations are not really dangerous.

In contrast to the analyst depicted in Freud's early paper "The dynamics of transference" (1912), the analyst who has read *Inhibitions, Symptoms, and Anxiety* (1926) is really working with his patient, not against him, and he doesn't have to fudge his definition of memory in order to persuade himself that he is being unqualifiedly kindly. He has discovered a genuinely organic, natural process that he can fit right in with, and needs no contrived, paradoxical physiology as an imaginary ally in his work. He can tell himself that he is actually the patient's buddy. Nobody wants to live in fear, and so, in principle, everybody will welcome analytic help.

To be sure, some attachment to the analyst may be necessary to persuade patients to look at their fearful fantasies in the first place, but once the dangers are seen in their infantile context and shown to be harmless to adults, they cease to be fearsome. The protection of the transference will then not be needed; the patient's discovery of his own adult strength will be incentive enough to draw him forward, and he can, without regret, relinquish the transference bridge that brought him to freedom. A therapeutic alliance is now a reasonable expectation en route.

What is played down in this picture is desire. That is the first part of my argument.

After the 1920s, the emphasis on anxiety allowed practicing analysts to believe that infantile wishes are infantile only because repression has not allowed them to mingle with the rest of the personality. The popular formula is that overcoming the fear leads to conscious awareness, which in turn leads to an automatic modification of infantile wishes.

From this point on, analysis develops in directions that vary theoretically, practically, and geographically. I shall deal mainly with North American ego psychology. But I do want to observe that British Kleinians and French analysts such as Laplanche (1989), each in his own way, retain the older emphasis on desire. Neither of those traditions encourages the idea that patients suffer simply because they fail to understand their currently safer position in the adult world. In both Kleinian and French traditions, some essential aspect of the patient's striving is itself considered troublesome and will remain troublesome until it is given up. When French analysts criticize North Americans for being too practical, and when Kleinians fault North Americans for being distracted by external reality, it may be their way of saying that Americans do not appreciate the stubbornness of desire (though they put it in terms of "forgetting the unconscious" or of promoting social adaptation).

My second thesis, then, is that later analytic theory made treatment seem more harmonious, at least in principle, at the cost of muffling the insistence of the patient's wishes in the analysis.

## RENEWED RESPECT FOR THE PATIENT'S DESIRE (ENACTMENT THEORY)

But times are changing in North America. American analysts are rediscovering the phenomenon Freud described in his first model of treatment, namely, the patient's passionate and not-entirely-defensive cross-purposes with the analyst's efforts – in other words, the struggle in treatment. Analysts today are just a little less inclined to view patients as fearfully hiding, more inclined to see them as greedily grabbing. What is responsible for that shift?

One influence is the large body of holistic elaboration of Freudian theory that goes by the name of ego psychology. Contrary to popular opinion, that holism has made it harder for American analysts to discount the patient's approach as purely defensive. Instead of supposing that the patient's demands on the analyst are merely protective maneuvers just waiting for a safe chance to turn into objective intro-spection, ego psychologists actually join the English and French in thinking that every act and gesture has its wishful significance. This tough-minded view of the patient's thrust brings them straight back to the *Papers on Technique*.

The sense of a genuinely oppositional patient also comes from the new appreciation of countertransference. Hyperalertness to countertransference has led directly – some would say, inevitably – to America's current preoccupation with *enactment*, which is further aggravated by an epistemological crisis that has gripped the nation. The obsessive, self-critical skepticism so characteristic of con-temporary American psychoanalysis saps the analyst's confidence in his readings and demands more acceptance of the patient's own experience of the relation-ship. The new American analyst is shy of judging what is real and what is not – shy even of supposing that there is an objective reality. If the patient takes the analyst to be mixing with him in a social rather than a psychoanalytic way, well, it is not easy for the American analyst to say he isn't. If the analyst doesn't admit to an enactment, he can be sure that his colleagues will pounce on him for his defensiveness.

**140** The idea of Freudian therapy

When today's analyst calls something an *enactment* rather than a *transference*, he is implicitly acknowledging that the patient has not merely sought or imagined a satisfaction but has in fact been granted actual satisfaction by the analyst's response. In this way, today's analyst accords "reality" to the patient's current experience of the relationship, just as Freud granted that transference love is as real as any other, and just as he observed that patients want from the analyst what they want from anyone else. And when today's analyst deconstructs the enactment, he is sharing the same experience Freud reported in *Papers on Technique:* he finds himself asking his patient to give up something valued, not just something feared. Like Freud back in 1914, he vividly experiences the full force of the patient's wanting and the patient's demanding, and he acknowledges the patient's primary interest in obtaining satisfaction from the person of the analyst.

Indeed, today's analyst registers that pressure for satisfaction even more vividly than Freud did (if that is possible) because he believes patients actually succeed in obtaining it from the analyst. For that reason, you will hear American analysts speak of enactment almost as frequently as they speak of transference. (Some, in fact, seem to think it a logical error to regard these two as separate.)

But analysts are hired to make something new out of the old. And it has to be done without overt manipulation. Even before conceiving of signal anxiety, Freud expected that his struggle with unrenounced wishes would be less arduous when patients are finally brought to see the contrast between the archaic context and the current reality. But many of today's postmodern analysts cannot hope for that. When they rediscover that they are struggling not just with blindness but also with passion, they cannot hope for reality to come riding to their rescue. Sophisticated transference theory makes *everything* in life seem to be a memory in the form of action, and analysts cannot argue that transference wishes and entanglements are cut from a different cloth. (For example, see Brenner 2006.)

An analyst who no longer believes he is solely in the business of disproving infantile dangers must find an alternative, nonmanipulative way of changing infantile desires. Faced with the same adversarial pressure Freud reported in *Papers on Technique*, today's North American analysts grope for their own way of translating the patient's heedless wishes into something therapeutic and mapping the analyst's therapeutic demand onto the patient's inclination. In other words, they need to find something that will serve them the way working through served Freud.

I suggest that North Americans hope to achieve this negotiation of cross-purposes by the disruption of enactments – that is, by repeatedly dislodging covert relationships. This episodic sidestepping of inadvertent roles is designed to avoid what Fairbairn called being *press-ganged* into the patient's relational world. The rationale is the same as it has always been in psychoanalysis, namely, to objectify what has happened in the relationship. But today many analysts hope to accomplish that by simply wriggling out of the relationship, by unmasking it and failing to play, rather than by treating the relationship as a misplaced memory. Of course, these analysts will go on from there to delineate the organized fantasies that inform the enactment, and most of them will trace the patient's participation in the enactment back through mnemic representatives and personal history. But they will be doing that for the purpose of understanding the passions, not in order to unmask their inappropriateness to "reality." For postmodern analysts who no longer have confidence in a contrasting reality, the thrust of current enactment theory is to deprive them of all complacency, subjecting them over and over again to the sudden awareness of the satisfactions they are inadvertently providing the patient (see Smith 2006).

This sudden awakening shocks both parties and fuels the treatment. In order to achieve this sort of disruption – this pulling oneself free from a role enactment – it is not necessary to claim authority over truth and reality, or even to re-label action as a memory. To critics, it may seem that today's introspective analysts (e.g., Jacobs 1991; Levenson 2005) turn Freud's instruction on its head, as though it is less important for the analyst to see the patient's action as a memory than to view his own participation as a memory. What such critics often fail to appreciate is that the analyst who looks on an enactment as his own memory not only recognizes details that might have escaped notice; he is probably also disrupting the patient's thrust more effectively than he would by observing it from the "outside," and managing to do that without depending on rhetorical appeals to reality and appropriateness.

So my third conclusion is that postmodern North American analysts have again allowed themselves to boldly confront the cross-purpose in the patient's desire, just as Freud did in *Papers on Technique*.

## RENEWED RECOGNITION OF CROSS-PURPOSES ENTAILS NEW RECOGNITION OF CLASSICAL IDEALS

It is not at all my purpose to argue for the postmodern skepticism about reality. I have explored that issue critically elsewhere (see Friedman 1999, 2000a, 2000b, 2002). Here I am engaged in description and inference, not advocacy. I refer to a revival on the current scene of the earliest and therefore rawest experience of psychoanalytic treatment as it was recorded in Freud's *Papers on Technique*. I describe a psychoanalytic trend in North America that has revived Freud's original sense of the work, but with a changed epistemology – or rather, has revived it *because* of a changed epistemology. That restoration of awareness of the patient's desire – and not just his fear – would seem to call for a restoration of Freud's earliest principles of technique.

I think that implication has been overlooked because of a paradox in postmodern thinking. In view of American doubts about reality and the analyst's ability to define it, it is not surprising that the old ideals of anonymity, abstinence, and neutrality would come in for heavy criticism. If the analyst cannot know what he is really doing or what the patient is really doing, let alone how to compare it with a memory and with current reality, how can he pretend to be a blank screen?

And yet once it is acknowledged that patients want something different than analysts provide, as early reported in *Papers on Technique* and newly recognized in

## 142 The idea of Freudian therapy

current enactment theory, the original ideals of detachment that were framed to deal with that cross-purpose would seem to be even more crucial than they were during the long interval after the 1920s when analyst and patient were thought to share a common interest in a reassuring reality. Of course, ideals such as neutrality persisted during those intervening years, but they were not especially linked to the structural model or the theory of signal anxiety. If one doubts that, one need only trace the reasoning of Alexander (1925), who, having learned that the superego's distorted view of reality is responsible for neurosis, could first seek to abolish the superego, and then go on to fit himself out with specific, tailor-made roles and relationships to calm his patient's fears and correct his vision of reality (see Alexander 1956). You may fault him for this approach on clinical grounds, but you cannot say that it is, strictly speaking, illogical on the basis of his model. But if (as today) there is no reassurance about reality to be had, and all one has to go on is the disruption of fixed roles (by calling attention to enactments), then clearly, no clarifying role will fill the bill, and only neutrality, anonymity, and abstinence will serve as beacons.

This has been hard for many analysts to accept – partly, I think, because they have forgotten, or never understood, the original function of these ideal terms in *Papers on Technique*. If you take anonymity, neutrality, and abstinence as free-standing terms, they will absorb their meaning promiscuously from whatever context you currently have in mind. You may suppose that the ideals derive from an antiquated "drive theory," a mental mechanics, a hydraulic apparatus, or whatnot. If, however, you look again at the actual *birth* of these ideals in the *Papers on Technique*, you see that they are not derived from theory. They are warning flags planted on thin ice; they record Freud's bitter experience. He was telling us that if we disregard anonymity, abstinence, and neutrality, patients will use us as they wish. (See Chapter Two.) Absence of these ideals puts the analyst at the mercy of the patient and subverts his ability to introduce newness.

That is the message of the *Papers on Technique*. And where do these ideals show up in today's treatment? Aren't they the silent self-images that an analyst implicitly reaches for as he tears himself loose from an enactment? Always visible in Freud's striving, though mostly absent from his lips, the ideal principles of 1914 have become even more indispensable to the contemporary analyst. The original ideals are the analyst's sole remaining leverage in a treatment that once again struggles to take patients' wishes seriously, but this time without a contrasting reality to offset them.

## Note

1 Ellman (1991), in his excellent comparative exegesis of the *Papers on Technique*, is one of the few to recognize Freud's intention here.

## REFERENCES

Alexander, F. (1925). A metapsychological description of the process of cure. *International Journal of Psychoanalysis*, 6: 13–34.

Alexander, F. (1956). *Psychoanalysis and Psychotherapy: Developments in Theory, Technique, and Training.* New York, NY: Norton.

Brenner, C. (2006). Conflict, compromise formation, and structural theory. In: *Contemporary Psychoanalysis in America: Leading Analysts Present Their Work*, ed. A. Cooper. Washington, DC: American Psychiatric Press, pp. 5–20.

Ellman, S. J. (1991). *Freud's Technique Papers: A Contemporary Perspective.* Northvale, NJ: Jason Aronson.

Freud, S. (1911–1915). *Papers on Technique.* Standard Edition, 12.

Freud, S. (1912). The dynamics of transference. Standard Edition, 12.

Freud, S. (1914). Remembering, repeating, and working-through. Standard Edition, 12.

Freud, S. (1915). Observations on transference love. Standard Edition, 12.

Freud, S. (1926). *Inhibitions, Symptoms, and Anxiety.* Standard Edition, 20.

Friedman, L. (1999). Why is reality a troubling concept? *Journal of the American Psychoanalytical Association*, 47: 401–425.

Friedman, L. (2000a). Modern hermeneutics and psychoanalysis. *Psychoanalytic Quarterly*, 69: 225–264.

Friedman, L. (2000b). Are minds objects or dramas? In: *Changing Concepts of Psychoanalysis: The Legacy of Merton M. Gill*, eds. D. Silverman & D. Wolitzky. Hillsdale, NJ: Analytic Press, pp. 145–170.

Friedman, L. (2002). Symbolizing as abstraction: Its role in psychoanalytic treatment. In: *Symbolization and Desymbolization: Essays in Honor of Norbert Freedman*, ed. R. Lassky. New York, NY: Karnac, pp. 204–230.

Jacobs, T. (1991). *The Use of the Self: Countertransference in the Analytic Situation.* Madison, CT: International Universities Press.

Laplanche, J. (1989). *New Foundations for Psychoanalysis*, trans. D. Macey. Oxford, UK: Basil Blackwell.

Levenson, E. (2005). Interview of Edgar Levenson, by I. Hirsch and V. Iannuzzi. *Contemporary Psychoanalysis*, 42: 593–650.

Smith, H. F. (2006). Analyzing disavowed action: the fundamental resistance of analysis. *Journal of the American Psychoanalytical Association*, 54: 713–737.

# PART THREE

# The psychoanalytic phenomenon

## INTRODUCTION TO PART THREE

While the central point of *Papers on Technique* may have been largely missed by the analytic community, the individual papers were lodged in the profession's bedrock as a sort of rule book. When it has surfaced in that form, the collection has been treasured as a pearl collection, or reproached as an embarrassment, but always, always felt as a challenge that analysts have to come to terms with.

In this section I will focus more particularly on the demands *Papers* makes on analysts, and the various ways analysts cope with an assignment that could easily be a torment (partly because it is somewhat of a torment for their patient). My underlying theme is that analysts always meet that challenge one way or another because it is impossible to simply ignore *Papers on Technique* without leaving the tradition altogether.

In previous chapters I have dealt with the strain of accommodating the weird perspectives, contradictory attitudes, and cognitive paradoxes that evoke the analytic phenomenon. As I take them up again in the following chapters, I will emphasize the shiftiness of the personal relationship that *Papers* recommends for analyst and patient. That is the most disquieting of its legacies and may be said to sum them all up.

# 9

# FLIRTING WITH VIRTUAL REALITY[1]

We live very odd work lives, you and I, groping our way through mists of virtual reality. In what follows, I will recall how analysts got themselves into that vaporous landscape and how they have felt about it – how they have felt about maneuvering people to regard them as virtual objects while looking for actual truths and alternate virtualities. And I will discuss how analysts tailor their job description to make themselves more comfortable in doing that. Thus, you will mainly hear about how analysts prefer to picture themselves, but I will also mention a kind of motive in the patient that might be best exploited by the old-fashioned custom in which the analyst, and not just the patient, flirts with virtual reality.

A couple of warnings: I love scholarly writing but I hate fussy speech, so be prepared for rough and facetious characterizations. And most unwelcome to your ears, I confess that you may come away from my harangue none the richer in treatment ideas. The reason for this is that I don't know to what extent the analyst's own sense of what he's doing (which is what I describe) leaks out into his behavior and technique. Maybe it leaks a lot; maybe just a little. If you like, you may regard this as merely a gallery talk for voyeuristic analyst watchers, rather than a technical deliberation. But as I go on about the analyst's attitudes toward virtual reality, I rather suspect you will find yourself thinking about practical issues of neutrality, abstinence, and self-disclosure, as well as relativism, constructivism, objective reality, and so on.

I begin with the fact that, long before the advent of the computer, Sigmund Freud invented an instrument for studying virtual reality. Catharsis was achieved by hallucinating an event that no longer existed. It was an experience of a virtual reality. At first, it happened in a trance. But some patients couldn't be hypnotized, and those patients, therefore, could not be made to reexperience the past as a virtual presence.

Then Freud discovered that even without catharsis, the virtual world could be made to appear in the actual world. It only needed to be given the chance. (The

**148** The psychoanalytic phenomenon

chance was the transference.) There was a difficulty: there is no simple way of telling which part of the patient's behavior is virtual and which is actual. It isn't clear-cut, like the difference between a trance state and waking, or between a memory and a current perception, or the obvious difference between a dream symbol and its meaning. On the couch, it's all blended together – virtual and actual.

Nevertheless, even if it's hard to draw a line around what's only virtual, Freud did find that the virtual world would come alive if patients abandoned their customary self-protection. Then they would begin to live in the virtual reality of their childhood, to the point of dragging their analyst into it. Freud thought that when patients were forced to flip attention back and forth between their virtual world and the actual world of treatment, they would experience something equivalent to catharsis, though without the mighty cataclysm that had formerly blasted cathartic memories into the present. In both cases, the trick was to make the patient feel both realities at once – the virtual and the actual, in competition with each other (Freud 1914, pp. 155–156).

But that is easier said than done, because virtual reality is the stuff of *wishes*. Indeed, as Freud observed, virtual reality is everybody's most intimate reality, as witness the phenomenon of romantic love. Why would anyone give it up?

Mindful of that question, Freud, as early as 1914, was forced to admit that memories and affects were not the whole story of treatment. Something new had to be factored in. It was something that philosophers call *conation* and we might call *striving* (Freud 1914). Strivings mark the values in a person's world. Strivings now became as important as emotion and memory. The problem wasn't just a sick memory here and there; patients were doing their entire living, struggling, and wanting in terms of virtual reality. So it was not sufficient for patients to remember and emote. Their *wishes* had to be changed along with their reality. And then they had to compare and contrast the one kind of wanting with another. (That was the first meaning of "working through" [Freud 1914].)

In those early days of 1910–1920, something powerful was drawing Freud toward a frank understanding of the situation. He was captive to an extremely odd encounter with virtual reality – an odd encounter that became known as *psychoanalytic treatment*. Freud's *Papers on Technique* (1912–1915; Friedman 1991) show what a tough meeting it was. As I mentioned, Freud discovered that virtual reality infiltrates actual reality in all the important scenes of life. To be psychoanalyzed one had to stop the normal mixing of the two. Patients were required to separately incubate virtual and actual worlds in pure culture for study, while suffering the dislocation of their wishes. Not illogically, Freud supposed that the only way people could be made to do that is under the influence of the transference, since it, like all virtual worlds, has strivings already built into it. Thus, in designing psychoanalysis, Freud set up a mixed state in which the virtual experience of the analyst as a transference figure intermingled with the actual experience of him as a professional technician. The two would later be sorted out (although Freud recognized that some virtuality always remains – for example, a virtual father dwelling forever in the professional technician).

Some will say we are more sophisticated nowadays. We know that you can't eliminate a transference by using transference. Or do we? Some would say that Stone (1961) didn't accept that principle, nor do most analysts, according to Gray (1994). Indeed, the question of how to use the power of wishes without confirming them remains the great puzzle of all talking treatments. But there was no need to wait for us clever moderns to perceive the contradictory requirements of this weird occupation. The paradoxes were carved into the foundation stone of treatment. The very act of defining psychoanalytic treatment, Freud's *Papers on Technique* (1912–1915), consisted precisely in a display of paradoxes. I would call them the three great paradoxes of virtuality:

1. Transference is a virtual reality, but it's hard to tell it apart from the actual relationship.
2. Transference is universal, but there's a sense in which it's peculiar to analysis.
3. Transference is a retreat from actuality, but it's also what engages people in actuality – it's what makes actuality valuable.

The nubbin of Freud's inaugural report was these three paradoxes, which suggests that they, and the problems that spin off them, are the essence of treatment insofar as it is psychoanalytic. As a result of these paradoxes, analyst and patient are in a state of uncertainty. For instance, patients never know how much and in what way the analyst is attached to them. Will the analyst love the patient? Will the analyst protect the patient?

Now, I ask you: What happens in such a close relationship when one party knows that hope and protection are merely virtual, while the other party is never quite sure? As the patient probes and feigns, the analyst's answer sticks in his throat: "No: I will not protect you; I will not stick by you for your whole life; I will leave you more easily than you will leave me; I will walk out on you if I am not paid; I would not respect you in every way in other contexts." How does one person feel when he encourages uncertain illusions in another?

And the analyst has his own uncertainties: He cannot easily determine what in himself the patient is seeing, a virtual or an actual aspect, especially since he, too, partly sees himself as a virtual figure – as a figure of his own fantasies, for instance, or at least as a socially defined virtual figure, such as a parent surrogate, as Freud saw a virtual father in the physician (Freud 1912, p. 100). And the analyst must ask himself whether and how much he is responsible for what the patient thinks he is. Is he deliberately misleading patients (for example, to see him as passionately engaged with them)? Is he, perhaps, actively impersonating a virtual figure, either inadvertently (as in an enactment), or because he really fancies the role (for instance, of a mother)?

The uncertainty crackles in the air. There's bound to be plenty of challenge going on, inward and outward, by both parties at all times.

Psychoanalysis tends toward a critique of the virtual (though not a complete escape from it). And nothing could be more awkward than waffling between

**150** The psychoanalytic phenomenon

virtuality, loaded as it is with human meaning and wishes, and nonvirtuality, with its cold-blooded critique of meanings, its disappointment of strivings. No wonder psychoanalysis has been said to be a process of loss and mourning, and thank heaven there is a limit to how far that can go (Tarachow 1963).

Even faced with this unpleasant tension, Freud disdained a facile solution, though later analysts were not always so tough-minded. As mentioned, Freud allowed the analyst to retain his virtual image alongside his actual image during treatment. He permitted virtuality to reign (in the unobjectionable positive transference) as long as it allowed him to direct the patient's attention. He hoped to exchange a virtual for a real appearance at termination, but modern analysts nevertheless fault him for exploiting his virtual image en route. (Suggestion is nothing but the power of the virtual.)

Beginning with Ferenczi (1933; Ferenczi & Rank 1925), experiential analysts have made themselves more comfortable with their virtual come-on by declining to distinguish sharply between virtual reality and actual reality (while in the meantime stretching the blurred virtual-but-also-real image to cover the mother role). Gitelson (1962), Stone (1961), Racker (1968), Winnicott (1971), Zetzel (1966), and others have continued that tradition. To be sure, this softening of the contrast between virtual and actual captures a deep truth of human life – the overlap between imagination and brute fact. My point is that relaxing the distinction also serves to ease the burden on the analyst; it reassures him that he is not tantalizing the patient with an illusion, an illusion that he himself secretly sees through – an illusion, moreover, that he is secretly sworn to back out of. Instead, he can feel that actuality and illusion blend harmoniously, with promise and fulfillment united. (Here I am deliberately oversimplifying these theorists.)

That's one way the analyst can make himself comfortable, but it's not the only way. Ego psychologists can comfort themselves not by blending the two worlds, but by downplaying the analyst's virtual image and emphasizing his objective reality. They may assume the role of foreman in an ongoing work project. They look beyond virtual illusions to the actual job at hand; they summon the patient's actual exploration and investigation and emphasize their own objectively real act of pointing things out and directing attention, as well as the patient's objectively real acts of weighing and scrutinizing the findings. (One thinks of Gray [1994], and especially of Busch [1996].)

Those are two ways of being more comfortable. For a third, we can turn to the older Kleinians, who opted for the one remaining alternative: Instead of emphasizing the overlap of virtual and real, in the fashion of Ferenczi and other experiential analysts, and instead of emphasizing the actual workproject as the ego psychologists were inclined to do, the older Kleinians imagined themselves to be moving entirely in the virtual world (Spillius 1988). You could see this attitude in bold relief when they argued with Anna Freud about whether the child analyst was a real or a transference figure.

The Kleinian choice was also Kohut's (1977). In fact, self-psychologists are even happier to think of themselves as wholly virtual figures in the patient's mind.

Indeed, Kohut's contribution was to catalogue the universal virtualness of all human relations and human strengths, and he alone, among contemporaries, criticized Freud for using his virtual powers too little rather than too much.

Let me recapitulate. Analysts who didn't want to flirt with virtual reality had three logical alternatives: They could blend virtual and actual; they could stay entirely with the actual; or they could stay entirely with the virtual. I don't say that analysts adopt these views simply to make themselves more comfortable. But neither do I think that comfort is a negligible incentive, or, indeed, an unworthy one. And, for the purpose of this talk, I will artificially treat comfort and discomfort as the main issue (earning, I fear, the enmity of most of my friends). So let me speak loosely and say that what I've outlined are the ways that analysts pictured the scene in order to diminish the discomfort of a flickering virtual reality.

If I may mix art-historical and cultural metaphors, I would put it this way: There is the baroque portrait painted by Freud (not classical in this context), in which the ornate complexities of treatment are emphasized and played off against each other. There is a clear, simple, Enlightenment model in which treatment is flattened out as a plain, straightforward inquiry, with no murky depths. And there is a romantic vision of treatment as an inspirational creation that is unique to each couple (similar categories have been used by many commentators). To some extent, the Enlightenment and the romantic portraits were painted to ease the discomfort of living with the uncertain virtuality of the baroque model, with its deep shadows. But I have the impression, and this is the crux of my talk, that many contemporary Anglo-American analysts are still not sufficiently comforted even by these easier ways of thinking, and they wish to get rid of the last vestige of ambiguity.

The earlier analysts allowed themselves to flirt with a flickering virtuality in order to study it, but today's analysts, though naturally happy to study virtuality when it occurs in the transference, are less willing to actively flirt with it, by which I mean that they model their beliefs, and perhaps their actions, on a steadier image of their role.

Why now? What is it about our times that has made a flickering virtuality more uncomfortable than it used to be?

To begin with, philosophical and social assaults have demolished the old tools that analysts relied on to help them live simultaneously in both the actual and the virtual world. Let's look at those bygone tools. Obviously, the most important was the very distinction between virtual and actual reality. As I mentioned, the slipperiness of the distinction has been known since Freud's time (Freud 1912). Nevertheless, the older analysts thought it possible in principle to separate what they were really offering from what the patient *thought* they were offering, though they recognized that they might be mistaken in any particular ruling. That certainly made them less uneasy about the patient's expectations.

Secondly, the old-time analyst thought he could rely on his patient's lawfully functioning mind to do a real – nonvirtual – work of recognition. That machinery would ultimately correct the virtual image of the analyst and vindicate the real one. Together, these two pillars of strength – the philosophical distinction between

**152** The psychoanalytic phenomenon

virtual and actual, and the psychological belief in a lawfully functioning mind – propped up the analyst when the patient saw him differently than he saw himself.

Have these principles been challenged? Have they ever! Nothing is more characteristic of our age than the critique of objective reality. Personally, I find it ironic that just when mankind has learned to control the objective world, some of its sages have decided it isn't really there after all – there are only social constructs to be reconstructed. And if real, physical objects have disappeared from view, how much more unavailable are objective features of persons and minds. An analyst today who would protest that he isn't *really* behaving as the patient thinks would be laughed out of our enlightened conference rooms. The so-called positivistic analyst used to smile indulgently at transference "distortions." When the new analyst feels himself misunderstood, as he inevitably will, he can only squirm and subject himself to interminable self-inquiry. Nor can today's sophisticated analyst reassure himself that his patient's mental machinery will eventually vindicate him: we are told that there is no such structure to the mind. In short, the modern analyst has made himself much more vulnerable.

Indeed, if I may say so, the modern analyst positively prides himself on his humility, because doubts about objective reality are endorsed by our new social norms. The modern analyst is required by our respectful, anti-elitist mood to avoid manipulative, authoritarian – and even authoritative – posturing, and to *embrace* the vulnerability to which his relativistic philosophy, in any case, has already condemned him.[2]

Now, back to our loss of the concepts that used to make us comfortable working in the vineyards of virtuality. Today, interpretations are thought to be just like any other interpersonal action; they are thought to funnel into the patient not items of information, but the analyst's whole human perspective, including much that he's not aware of. And the patient is thought to react to interpretations roughly as he would to any other personal action on him. Without the possibility of a clean interpretation – *clean* as in nuclear weaponry – the analyst, along with his interpretations, has become helpless to control his self-image in the strobe light of the virtual images the patient plays over him.

So far, I don't think you'll disagree with me about the reasons for our new, cognitive vulnerability: There are no more mental objects and there are no more surgical interpretations. And you might also agree that their absence makes us more uncomfortable with what we used to think was a playful costume party of transference images. Now I'd like to further suggest two more debatable reasons for our growing disinclination to mix virtual and actual worlds.

I cannot escape the impression that one reason yesterday's analyst was comfortable being misrepresented was that, in the privacy of his own mind, he could imagine the possibility of a precise decoding of each virtual role and relationship that he appeared in, tying it to a specific aspect of the patient's childhood. There would be, at least theoretically, a concrete and specific historical actuality that corresponded to each of his virtual appearances. That made the virtual seem much more clearly defined. Even the bare possibility of making a one-to-one translation gave hope that the virtual reality of the analyst's appearance could be lifted up by its edges and delicately removed from his underlying actuality. Or, to mix the metaphor, it would be by shaving off the childhood reality that the virtual present would give way to the actual present. We recall that Freud (1904, p. 260) thought of psychoanalysis as sculpture *per via di levare*.[3] (Stereotypes were what was needed – stereotypes of loving, stereotypes of childhood relationships, traumas, and so on.)

I think analysts have lost confidence in the specific details of pathogenesis. Reconstruction has fallen into disfavor. The repression paradigm is no longer paramount (Anna Freud 1936, 1954). And so the analyst is less sure that virtual reality can be translated simply into a specific, earlier actuality, leaving the real present to be seen for what it is.

And I think there's been one more loss that has sapped the analyst's ability to tolerate the mixture of virtual and actual: I mean the vanishing of the transference neurosis. Maybe the older analysts could comfortably entice virtual images onto themselves because they supposed that those virtual images would coalesce into a sharply outlined transference neurosis, which could then be dissolved. In a comment that a book by Wallerstein (1995) drew to my attention, Anna Freud (1954) said:

> We see the patient enter into analysis with a reality attitude to the analyst; then the transference gains momentum until it reaches its peak in the full-blown transference neurosis which has to be worked off analytically until the figure of the analyst emerges again, reduced to its true status.
>
> *(p. 618)*

With their belief in childhood prototypes fading, and the transference neurosis as well, analysts may have lost their heart for playing out virtual roles. Let me summarize why analysts may now be disinclined to flirt with virtual reality while holding onto objective reality:

1. Analysts no longer believe in an objective reality that would offset their virtual appearance.
2. They have lost confidence that they can define what is merely virtual by reducing it to what is biographically actual.
3. They don't believe any more that amorphous virtuality gets sucked up into a neat transference neurosis that can then be discarded.

And when you add to these deficits the positive ethical commandment to judge not thy neighbor's accuracy, we may have the recipe for the current rebellion against the early Freudian paradigm.

And the results? What has it all led to? The logical possibilities are limited: Maybe everything is virtual. That is what Schafer (1992) says in his narratology. Since there is no actuality to contrast it with, the analyst need not flirt with a

**154** The psychoanalytic phenomenon

flickering virtuality. That also seems to me the implication of object relations theory – as, for example, in Fairbairn (1958). (Perhaps the Kleinians pioneered this option?)

Turning that around, if everything is virtual and objective reality is a myth – if there is no reality that can be misperceived – we may just as well say that everything is actual. That, I believe, is the tendency (if not the detail) of social constructivism and intersubjectivism. According to these accounts, images that used to be labeled as merely virtual turn out to be all the reality there is; the virtual has been made actual by the very perceptions and interactions of the two people involved. And if that is the case, then it makes no sense for the analyst to play a double game; he has no real self to hide away from the virtual images that play around him. He might as well, it is argued, be straightforward in his dealings with his patient, for the alternative – that is, trying to be mysterious – would simply establish another real (constructed) relationship, and in that case an unhelpful one. The analyst is thus relieved of the burden of encouraging virtuality to play out around himself.

You can see how I differ from Renik (1995, p. 476), who holds that analysts revel in idealization. I think they sweat under it.

I believe that there's comfort for all if the analyst is straightforward. Staying on one level is more respectable – it's literally "being on the level" – whether that level is a smooth, undiscriminating blur of an analyst who is both virtual and actual, or a plain, flatout actual investigator, or an analyst comprised entirely of virtual images with no reference to objective reality. Such consistency is far cleaner, more reliable, more collaborative than the shadowy, old dodge which seemed to say, "maybe what you see is virtual or maybe it's really me." Being honestly one thing or another rids the analyst of the onus of mystification. An unmysterious analyst has no secrets, and his reward is to be less alone in his work. Best of all, he is morally in the clear. The advantages are numerous; the relief is demonstrable.

Is there a downside? I warned you that I don't know the answer. Now as before, every analyst – even a perfectly straightforward one – will always be *interested* in the patient's virtual experiences. But if the interplay of truth and illusion sits less well with the analyst – if he goes out of his way to be unmysterious – it seems to me that patients may have less investment in their own flirtation with virtual realities. To speak bluntly, psychoanalysis may soon dangle less teasing bait. Nobody ever enjoyed saying, "Maybe I really am what you think I am," when he knows perfectly well that he's not. Nobody ever *liked* the teasing aspect of analysis. But analysts now have a new excuse for avoiding it: The new analyst doesn't think there is a "really." Or, if he does believe in reality, he doesn't feel it's right to fish for guesses by hiding his truth.

Patients might respond to the new, on-the-level analyst differently than to the old one who used to coax virtual worlds into tormented life by a notoriously coy stance – a stance that conveyed the following messages (and here I speak the old messages):

Flirting with virtual reality 155

- "Although I know who I am and I know how I want you to be with me, you may regard me any way you like; you may be right; you may be wrong; and you must take your chances."
- "I don't want to be spared any request or demand, so I will give you few hints of the shape and limits of our relationship; perhaps I have decided to rigidly limit my involvement, but you may hope that there are loopholes."
- "You may risk counting on me for all sorts of things, but I may content myself with passively witnessing your fortunes; you may rely on me for anything, but I may have already excused myself from fulfillment."
- "I don't want you to view me in any one way rather than any other, even though I may regard some ways as more correct."

In these attitudes, the analyst used to make it clear that he disdained to be pleased or protected, despite his natural craving for an agreed-upon working relationship and a recognized professional identity. He did not used to say, "We can investigate your virtual images of me, but please, while we're doing it, recognize that what I really am is just an investigator of those virtual images." Instead, the older analyst just toughed it out.

At this point, the new analysts among you might issue a strong objection. You can make a powerful argument that it doesn't matter what the analyst declares himself to be or not to be, to want or not to want, implicitly or explicitly. Even if he shouted it out loud, isn't it just pretense? Don't patients respond instead to the analyst's inner wishes? If, as Hoffman (1983, 1991) has cogently argued, patients know there's an ordinary person under the uniform, what's the point of trying to be mysterious?

That's a pressing, good question, and the profession will have to run through many practical and phenomenological considerations before we can say what patients know and what analysts are able to conceal. But here I want to mention only one consideration.

I believe it is not enough to think about what the analyst actually reveals (deliberately or inadvertently). We must also always consider what his *gestures* say, especially what they say about his deliberate *intentions*. For the older analyst, the gesture was his flirtatious mysteriousness (flirtation being defined by the possibility of dire error). By this gesture, the analyst announced an *intention* to provide (or maybe to enforce) dangerous freedom, dangerous because it was freedom within a field of possible error. The analyst did not suggest that he was with the patient wherever the patient was. He made it clear that he could tolerate – and would ask the patient to tolerate – misidentification and misplaced hopes. So even if the analyst's persona turns out to be all playacting and easily seen through by the patient, it remains to be said whether something might be gained by the analyst's *act of attempting* to hide his judgments.

Now, I take it as axiomatic that features of treatment are effective only when patients see them as opportunities. If patients don't see them as opportunities, they won't take advantage of them. Thus, the analyst's gesture of secret judgmentalness

**156** The psychoanalytic phenomenon

(his reserved judgment of actual versus virtual) will be useful if, and only if, it answers to some need of the patient. If patients *only* wanted to be secure, then the analyst's hidden judgmentalness would not only be arrogant and threatening, it would be *only* arrogant and threatening, and nothing good would come of it. A blank screen is useful only to the extent that it tempts some of the patient's wishes for blankness. Likewise, the analyst's flirtation with virtual identities and virtual relationships is effective *provided* that there is something in the patient that finds the offer irresistible – something that happily welcomes the mere *offer* of uncertainty by a mysterious partner, never mind how *actually* mysterious the analyst turns out to be.

Do patients, in fact, find that gesture useful? They certainly seem to. The same Hoffman who told us that patients always know how the analyst is really reacting also tells us that, despite that knowledge, patients insist on squinting a double vision of the analyst. They know full well that he is an ordinary person, but they go on attributing something virtual to him anyway. Despite the discomfort of that double vision, and despite the ordinariness that analysts betray at every turn, patients go on regularly and involuntarily accepting anything that passes for a virtual flirtation. That is the most banal fact of psychoanalysis. Maybe analysts should fuss less about their failure to achieve anonymity and ask themselves why the patient is so ready to pretend that the analyst has succeeded. Renik (1995) implies that they do it to please the analyst, but the magnitude of the effect suggests something more profound. Why should patients find satisfaction in an imperfect simulacrum of anonymity? Or, more precisely, what *sort* of satisfaction do patients get or even look for in such a situation? Heaven knows that patients, like everyone else, *mostly* want a *real* companion. In what part of their souls do they also want a deliberately teasing, mysterious analyst – not just an open-minded one, but a mysterious analyst?

For an answer, we can round up the usual suspects. The unconscious wants realization in the present and finds it especially easy to hang that on a flimsy, teasing framework (Freud 1912). People want to deny the passage of time and to re-create the past in the present (Klauber 1987). Patients want an opportunity to idealize a selfobject (Kohut 1977). There is a need for sheer exercise of certain capacities such as love (Ferenczi 1933; Klauber 1987; Lichtenberg 1992), and a teasing framework is an ideal gymnasium for the exercise.

Then there's a wish to obtain ownership of one's mind, to deliberately conjure up versions of social virtuality that intimidate one, and then to show oneself that they can be blown away. Many analysts have counted on those self-liberating motives implicitly, and some explicitly (Gray 1994). Patients would be motivated in these ways to utilize even make-believe mysteriousness for a kind of counterphobic or implosive therapy to test themselves and rid themselves of hobbling dependency. Add to that the human zest for invention of meanings, the wish to find more possibilities in the world, the exhilaration of writing and rewriting one's own inner novel, and you have accounted for an appetite for the analyst's teasing. Lichtenberg (1992) counts on that, as do the deconstructionists, and possibly Winnicott (1971) and Schafer (1992) as well. Come to think of it, even common sense says that patients might wish to be free of our interference as they explore their own imaginings; they may prefer to deal with ghosts that they can manipulate, and they might welcome mysteriousness for that reason.

Opportunities like these might be what the patient sees in the analyst's otherwise annoying flirtation with virtual reality; these objectives might exist quietly alongside the louder demands for a genuine relationship. Pulling toward autonomy, patients may accept the analyst's flagrant invitation to a flirtation so that they can finally dispose of the analyst (a Winnicottian notion, I suppose).

But when we rhapsodize about esthetic and autonomy motives, we've got to be sure we haven't lost psychoanalytic motives. We would be on safer ground if we also found some more earthy motives. After all, psychoanalysis is only partly a playful activity; patients aren't looking for wonderful, new experiences the way youths in the 1960s tried out LSD. Treatment starts from pain and proceeds through struggle. I mentioned Freud's discovery that treatment was not just a matter of perceptions; it turned out to be a wrestling with strivings. If gut wishes oppose change, wouldn't it take other gut wishes to promote change?

And yet, in the final reckoning, hermeneutics, creativity, playfulness – these are not unconnected with desire and lust. We don't need to suppose that we explore virtual worlds just for the adventure. We do it because we know – or we learn in treatment – that wishes connect with the world only when both the wishes and the world are elaborated in detail, along with their dangers. That's the origin of secondary process, isn't it? Even when we read a novel, we're not just vicariously living out somebody else's fantasy life; we are expanding the horizon of our own world to encompass a plausible scene in which our fantasies might become realities. And when we play with appearances in treatment, we don't just multiply virtual realities; we search for a larger reality – call it a better narrative, or a selfobject, a higher plane of integration, a more reliable vision, a more satisfiable self, a sense of integrity, or a less reproachful reality. In short, we look for a universe in which what is genuinely in us can be more at home. It has to be a real universe or it won't serve the purpose.

Love may be an illusion, but illusion is not what love is looking for. Autonomy is worthless without a sense of personal solidity and a negotiable environment. Winnicott's (1971) famous playfulness is actually designed to connect a true self to a true world. Waelder (1934) wisely said that realisticness requires more than mobile perspectives; it requires also libidinal rootedness. The two go together, and we don't have to separate motives of independence from motives of attachment, even if they often seem to pull in different directions.

The analyst speaks. The patient wonders: "What larger horizon does that comment emerge from?" Regardless of what the message *is*, if the patient can think of it as coming from a more objective world, its *origin* – that is, the perceived domain of ultimate truth – will by itself orient his own pursuit.

The analyst is attentive. The patient wonders, "How much does he like me?" It is the sense that the analyst might or might not *really* be attached to the patient that makes the question important. And that, in turn, would matter little if the analyst didn't seem somehow a bit extraordinary.

**158** The psychoanalytic phenomenon

That leads me to my next-to-last message, which is that a flirtation relies on the possibility of objective truth. Flirtation says, "What you imagine may be true (or it may not be)." Much as a golfer plants a flag in the next hole to guide his swing, patients plant their analyst in an imagined spot from which they suppose their true nature can be seen. That's why they feel so much is at stake. That's why they insist that the analyst be "the one who is supposed to know" (to misuse Lacan's phrase). The analyst represents the possibility of an ultimate truth, and with that, the possibility of being lovable despite the truth. Even when the analyst's limitations are blatant, even when he shrugs off the grandiose mantle, even when patients feel misunderstood, even when they recognize the analyst's humility, they persist in looking on him as a knower whose favor is worth cultivating. You may call it an infirmity, a human failing, a wish for magic, a quest for superdaddy. It might be related to the Kantian ideal of Reason. It may even be the sort of significance-generating mechanism that builds a notion of God. Of course, none of these meanings will delight an analyst.

But can't we also say that this idealizing is a way of constructing an image of achievement, like imagining a home run and then trying to hit one? I am not referring to the patient's imitation of the analyst's wonderful way of thinking – a self-image that we would be well advised to keep at a distance. By *image of achievement*, I mean that if a person can imagine the possibility of being truly known, he can steer himself toward knowing truly. (That is Loewald's [1960] message, in a nutshell.) We must remember that one of the reasons a parental transference has such power is that the truth of our nature once seemed to lie in our parents' perception of us. Patients set the analyst up to represent the possibility of a true judgment, even if eventually they actualize that possibility within themselves.

All of which is to say that without virtual reality wishes are stunted, but without objective reality wishes are worthless. That's why analysts have customarily invited wild imagining, but also hinted that they know about truth and falsity.

Am I, then, concluding with a shameless idealization of the analyst? That would be to ignore one main reason that we maintain virtuality – namely, to dodge parentalizing idealization. All of us here will agree that analysis is supposed to free people from the bondage of idealization. What I am doing is to connect that old truth with its old partner, the principle that analysts don't force autonomy by *refusing* the patient's attributions. Every analyst allows – indeed, wants – patients to flirt with virtual reality, including the analyst as a virtual superior knower and as a virtual lifetime partner.

Well, then, if *every* analyst wants patients to indulge their virtual worlds, to whom am I preaching at such painful length? Ah, now you have squeezed me into what I promise is my very last task. Let me answer this way: People naturally scout for the role or image their partner seems to prefer. They ask, "What is he trying to come across as?" I maintain that people won't *freely* burden an intimate partner with idealizations and awkward and uncomfortable expectations just because these are not prohibited. If it's virtual images he wants, the analyst has to make at least some subtle gestures of invitation. If an analyst doesn't in some small way exhibit *positive* readiness to be seen in various merely virtual guises, I think he will, in fact, be covertly asking to be seen in a more determinate way, a more "realistic" way – that is, he will subtly invite patients to see him for who he really is (or thinks he is).

I say *subtly*, for, as mentioned, no good analyst *blatantly* tries to deidealize himself, any more than he tries to idealize himself. But since analysts today rebel against the uncertain role they used to play, and since they are ashamed of the mystifying relationship they used to enforce, I believe they are now in danger of leaning away from – rather than into – psychoanalytic illusions. They chart a more straightforward course. They set their behavior in a clearer context. They picture their doings more simply. I cannot imagine that this will have no effect on treatment – though in all honesty, as I said at the start, I do not know how big an effect it will have, or what the cost/benefit ratio will be.

Now you have only to sit through my peroration and you will be free. Here it is: Patients use virtual reality as a radar screen for detecting their true wishes. One can give their exploration of virtual worlds either little support or much support. Projects that give virtuality the least support are called cognitive or behavioral therapy. There is no mystery about the cognitive therapist's image, his job description, or his relationship to the patient. These are all spelled out in bold print. It is an unambiguous social situation, where an interpretation of transference, for example, would be as inappropriate as in a dental office. If patients need more exploration of their virtual world, they must turn to psychoanalysis, which supports virtual worlds by the deliberate unclarity of its roles and relationships. But within psychoanalysis we now have a choice of *how much* to support virtuality. We make that choice by determining how vigorous an *invitation* to extend to the patient's ambiguity quest (Bird 1972).

That, in turn, depends on how much uncertainty we can tolerate in what it is that we seem to be promising our patients. Patients will use us as they must, no matter what. They can be relied on to flirt with virtual versions of us, more or less freely. But how about us? Are we willing to do a little flirting ourselves – for instance, by being noncommittal about our plans? We must ask ourselves: "Can I live with myself as an eternally undefined partner, refusing to be clear about what I'm up to, yet beckoning my partner to take his chances?"

There's no mistaking the cost. If we choose to be amorphous we will be more vulnerable to self-doubt and to our patient's reproach. We will have only our theories to justify us, since neither custom nor common sense will countenance such social misbehavior. Nowadays, we will suffer the additional curse of being out of step with our culture, which demands that caretakers lay their cards on the table.

We don't have to pay that price. In all kinds of ways, we can say, for instance, "I'm just an investigator, ma'am." And that will be fine. The fate of psychoanalysis does not hang in the balance. I have been dwelling on marginal differences among analysts.

Whether we lean a little this way or that, our universal trademark remains the willingness to let patients invest us with virtual identities and burden us with

**160** The psychoanalytic phenomenon

personal expectations that we did not ask for. That will continue to connect us with a powerful and progressive tide in patients – one that draws fuel from their every wish and moves ultimately to freedom. I content myself with this conclusion: After 100 years of psychoanalysis, it is not a simple or settled question how best to exploit the strange encounter with the virtual world.

Thank you.

## Notes

1 This paper is slightly modified from the Victor Calef Memorial Lecture presented to the San Francisco Psychoanalytic Institute pm February 8, 1998.
2 A side comment is called for here: I'm counting on you to appreciate that setting up mock battles between straw men is not a logical error; rather, it is the easiest rhetorical way to contrast general trends. If you're allergic to straw men, well, you may call my generalizations Ideal Types in the fashion of Max Weber, and let me get on with my talk. As to my occasional snide tone, please bear in mind that I personally share some of the views of these modern straw men.
3 Italian, "by means of lifting out".

## REFERENCES

Bird, B. (1972). Notes on transference: universal phenomenon and hardest part of analysis. *Journal of the American Psychoanalytical Association*, 20: 267–301.

Busch, F. (1996). Free association and technique. In: *Danger and Defense: The Technique of Close Process Attention*, ed. M. Goldberger. Northvale, NJ: Aronson, pp. 107–130.

Fairbairn, W. R. D. (1958). On the nature and aims of psycho-analytic treatment. *International Journal of Psycho-Analysis*, 39: 374–385.

Ferenczi, S. (1933/1955). Confusion of tongues between adults and the child. In: *Further Contributions to the Problems and Methods of Psycho-Analysis*. London: Hogarth, pp. 156–167.

Ferenczi, S. & Rank, O. (1925). *The Development of Psychoanalysis*, trans. C. Newton. New York, NY: Nervous & Mental Diseases Publishers.

Freud, A. (1936/1946). *The Ego and the Mechanisms of Defense*. New York, NY: International Universities Press.

Freud, A. (1954). The widening scope of indications for psychoanalysis: Discussion. *Journal of the American Psychoanalytical Association*, 2: 607–620.

Freud, S. (1904). *On Psychotherapy*. Standard Edition, 7.

Freud, S. (1912). The dynamics of transference. Standard Edition, 12.

Freud, S. (1912–1915). *Papers on Technique*. Standard Edition, 12.

Freud, S. (1914). Remembering, repeating and working-through. Standard Edition, 12.

Friedman, L. (1991). A reading of Freud's *Papers on Technique*. *Psychoanalytic Quarterly*, 60: 564–595.

Gitelson, M. (1962). The first phase of psycho-analysis. Symposium on the curative factors in psychoanalysis. *International Journal of Psycho-Analysis*, 43: 194–205.

Gray, P. (1994). *The Ego and Analysis of Defense*. Northvale, NJ: Aronson.

Hoffman, I. Z. (1983). The patient as interpreter of the analyst's experience. *Contemporary Psychoanalysis*, 19: 389–422.

Hoffman, I. Z. (1991). Discussion: Toward a social-constructivist view of the psychoanalytic situation. *Psychoanalytic Dialogues*, 1: 74–105.

Klauber, J. (1987). The role of illusion in the psychoanalytic cure. In: *Illusion and Spontaneity in Psychoanalysis*. London: Free Association Books.

Kohut, H. (1977). *The Restoration of the Self*. New York, NY: International Universities Press.

Lichtenberg, J. (1992). *Self and Motivational Systems*. Hillsdale, NJ: Analytic Press.

Loewald, H. (1960). On the therapeutic action of psycho-analysis. *International Journal of Psycho-Analysis*, 41: 16–33.

Racker, H. (1968). *Transference and Counter-Transference*. New York, NY: International Universities Press.

Renik, O. (1995). The ideal of the anonymous analyst and the problem of self-disclosure. *Psychoanalytic Quarterly*, 64: 466–495.

Schafer, R. (1992). *Retelling a Life: Narration and Dialogue in Psychoanalysis*. New York, NY: Basic Books.

Spillius, E. B. (1988). General introduction. In: *Melanie Klein Today: Developments in Theory and Practice*, Vol. 2. London: Routledge, pp. 5–16.

Stone, L. (1961). *The Psychoanalytic Situation: An Examination of Its Development and Essential Nature*. New York, NY: International Universities Press.

Tarachow, S. (1963). *An Introduction to Psychotherapy*. New York, NY: International Universities Press.

Waelder, R. (1934). The problem of freedom in psychoanalysis and the problem of reality testing. In: *Psychoanalysis: Observation, Theory, Application—Selected Papers of Robert Waelder*, ed. S. Guttman. New York, NY: International Universities Press, pp. 101–120.

Wallerstein, R. S. (1995). *The Talking Cures: The Psychoanalyses and the Psychotherapies*. New Haven, CT: Yale University: Press.

Winnicott, D. W. (1971). The location of cultural experience. In: *Playing and Reality*. Middlesex, UK: Penguin, pp. 112–121.

Zetzel, E. (1966). The analytic situation. In: *Psychoanalysis in the Americas: Original Contributions from the First Pan-American Congress for Psychoanalysis*, ed. R. Litman. New York, NY: International Universities Press, pp. 86–106.

# 10

## FERRUM, IGNIS, AND MEDICINA: RETURN TO THE CRUCIBLE

Anyone who visits a meeting of the American Psychoanalytic Association these days will be astonished at the breadth and vigor of its debates. We see intellectual ferment everywhere. But is that all we see? Is it just a variety of arguments – conflict vs. deficit, narrative vs. fact, etc.? Or is there an edifying story here – a story about a journey into our current issues and on to the goal of psychoanalysis in its second century?

Well, yes of course, there's a story ... and another story ... and, unfortunately, another story, each crafted to celebrate somebody's favorite outcome. In reality, there is no privileged history of anything. So the short answer to my last question is no. There is no road that led here. Psychoanalysis concerned itself with modern issues very early and with original issues again very lately. It has straggled into view over a wide field and it is still straggling. It wasn't a disciplined march. There is no triumphal entry. Sorry.

Now, that's not a very promising beginning; I should start over and be less circumspect. This time I'll weave together highly personal impressions and generalizations and indulge in grand and free confabulation. That's not so reprehensible, really. The art historian E. H. Gombrich tells us that if we want to achieve a likeness we have to begin by hacking out a rough image and then comparing it with reality. Only by match and mismatch do we reach a faithful representation. So we can't lose, you and I: I will tell you my fable and you will spot my mistakes and we will end up seeing things more clearly.

In order to help you take your position I'll forewarn you of my conclusion. My moral is that today's arguments are efforts to pull the secrets of human nature out of the very fabric of the treatment situation, treatment here regarded not merely as an instrument of discovery but as an isolated wet specimen to be examined.

How can mere arguments reveal facts of nature? Well, consider this: analytic treatment comes about, in the first place, because of the analyst's attitudes. There is nothing else to make treatment happen. If treatment does something unusual to people, then we can learn about people by picking out the attitudes that make treatment happen, and especially by watching how the attitudes sit together and squirm together to get the job done. And where better to observe treatment attitudes sitting and squirming than in our collective controversy over the course of our discipline's history. With psychoanalysis, the history of ideas is not a background study; analytic history literally assembles the tools of treatment, and it is history that paints subtle meaning onto our stock concepts. And history is even more important for our purpose this afternoon: When over the years analysts try, this way and that, to match their attitudes to the task of treatment, they are doing nothing less than palpating the human condition.

Intending no disrespect to other schools, I'll talk only of Anglo-American, Freudian analysis. And I'll pay no attention to the influence of momentary fashions, philosophical and otherwise, because I am discussing not ideas in general, but how attitudes are designed to serve the needs of an established treatment.

Now, it will not escape your notice that when I ask how ideas serve the needs of treatment I am presuming that there is a psychoanalytic treatment out there waiting to be served – I am supposing that psychoanalytic treatment is an enduring structure that can be lit up by turning on various ideas and attitudes, and, further, that we are so familiar with this treatment that we can hold up its physical likeness in one hand and its associated ideas in the other and tell which treatment postures go along with which ideas.

I am suggesting, you see, that Freud did not design a treatment; he discovered one. First he stumbled on the treasure while following his personal aims. Then he modified the personal motives and made them into a behavioral map by which others could find the treatment directly. The attitudes he recommended, having been reenacted over the years, in essence if not in detail, make Freud's discovery available in every consulting room where it can be repeatedly identified and empirically examined. We can spot psychoanalysis by its gross appearance, especially by the attitudes that produce it. I will try to catch the spirit of those attitudes by imagining their root form at the time of discovery and then noting what sort of tinkering was necessary to turn them into reliable producers of the treatment Freud had stumbled on. I want to trace Freud's attitudes of discovery as they are transformed into attitudes of technique. Then I will speculate on their subsequent fate.

If I am wrong in my assumption – if treatment is just the application to patients of whatever analytic theory happens to be knocking around at the moment – then my method is pointless. So if you doubt that psychoanalytic treatment has an enduring life and shape of its own, please suspend disbelief this afternoon, because I need two heroes for my story of how we got here. One hero is the collectivity of you and your predecessors – no problem there. But the other hero is psychoanalytic treatment itself, and to conjure that one up I must, as I go along, refer to its identifying physiognomy. And let me make it clear that when I say physiognomy I mean just that – the grossly observable features of the treatment situation. Please be prepared for a certain bluntness of language. Remember, it's attitudes that

**164** The psychoanalytic phenomenon

we're trying to get hold of – attitudes that turn treatment on. And to portray attitudes we must paint with a broad brush and use bold colors, because that's how attitudes are identified – certainly not by careful, technical phrases. Indeed, when practitioners insist on putting their attitudes into technical terms they are usually hiding elements of manipulativeness, and that is another, very useful attitude: that of innocent attitudelessness.

Come with me now back to 1895 and look at the experience reported in *Studies on Hysteria*. Everyone knows that psychoanalysis grew out of the search for memories, and that Freud's ambition was to make great discoveries. If the historical path to treatment is any clue to its nature, then curiosity must certainly lie at its heart. That needs no argument, so I shall proceed to the next attitude on my list.

So vivid is the image of Freud as Discoverer that we sometimes forget that a proud man here is a proud man there. As a self-proclaimed physician, Freud had pride in his practice and in his person. He hated to have his bluff called. He disliked having patients show him he was wrong when he told them they would go into a trance. He did not want his authority to be dependent on his patient's response (Freud 1917, p. 451). No wonder he welcomed Breuer's cathartic treatment, "a practice," he tells us, "which combined an automatic mode of operation with the satisfaction of scientific curiosity" (Freud 1914, p. 9). Breuer's treatment was automatic in that it was guaranteed by the patient's normal digestion of memories.

In fact, the new treatment followed the patient's own inclination so reliably that hypnosis proved superfluous. And going a step further, Freud discovered that he always got what he was after if he obeyed hints from patients like Frau Emmy v. N. (1895, p. 63), who wanted him to stop bird-dogging his objectives and listen to hers. Once again following the patient's wishes, Freud made inclinations such as Frau Emmy's into his own fundamental rule.

This new procedure put Freud in an entirely different position: No more praying for a trance. No more begging for simple memories. No more pleading for clues to symptoms. If the therapist has any question at all, it's a mild wondering about the mood of the moment. Now almost anything the patient says will satisfy Freud. Since he no longer hungers for atoms of significance, and since he is expecting only a vague network of thoughts with only a remote reference to his interests, he can't miss: his professional pride and intellectual confidence are no longer at risk. My point is that psychoanalysis, in addition to being a method of discovery, was Freud's way of immunizing his treatment authority. He writes: "It is of course of great importance for the progress of the analysis that one should always turn out to be in the right *vis-à-vis* the patient, otherwise one would always be dependent on what he chose to tell one ..." (1895, p. 281).

The trick was to endorse the patient's wishes. That's what made the treatment reliable. When he had formerly asked for a particular service, such as falling into a trance or reporting a memory, Freud was at the mercy of his patient, who might or might not grant his wish. The new treatment that Freud discovered required, instead of a particular service, a whole human relationship, and that is something

Ferrum, ignis, and medicina **165**

that people have a hard time withholding. Freud could count on it – provided he himself could muster a special interest.

Freud's unguarded description of this special interest reveals its raw nature, which later will be obscured by technical formulas. Freud's fresh, first impression is that the analyst's attitude is quite different from physicianly attention.

> I cannot imagine bringing myself to delve into the physical mechanisms of a hysteria in anyone who struck me as lowminded and repellent, and who, on closer acquaintance, would not be capable of arousing human sympathy; whereas I can keep the treatment of a tabetic or rheumatic patient apart from personal approval of this kind.
>
> *(1895, p. 265)*

What sort of attention is this? We can suppose that it involves a human endorsement and a personal (rather than just an ethical) wish to help. Carried forward, the analyst's human commitment and his curative intent remain for us today the most familiar – and certainly the proudest – of his treatment attitudes. And perhaps I would be wise to end my inventory of analytic attitudes right here, having mentioned curiosity, respectful sympathy, and a desire to help.

But I'll be reckless and ask, What did Freud's interest evoke in the *patient?* Although Freud later publicly pleaded that an analyst asks no more than the privilege of a gynecologist, he knew otherwise and said as much upon his first encounter with psychoanalysis. He recognized that he was doing something forbidden to physicians; he was deliberately courting a personal, affective intimacy. The patients "put themselves in the doctor's hands and place their confidence in him – a step which in other situations is only taken voluntarily and never at the doctor's request" (1895, p. 266).

And Freud was honest enough to recognize that the intimacy he wanted from his patient might be the sort of personal surrender that counts on a love relationship and must honorably be reciprocated with something more than cure:

> In not a few cases, especially with women and where it is a question of elucidating erotic trains of thought, the patient's co-operation becomes a personal sacrifice, which must be compensated for by some substitute for love. The trouble taken by the physician and his friendliness have to suffice for such a substitute.
>
> *(1895, p. 301)*

In this first glimpse of the situation, Freud remarks that, quite apart from individual transference, a patient will sometimes experience a dread of becoming

> too much accustomed to the physician personally, of losing her independence in relation to him, and even of perhaps becoming sexually dependent on

**166** The psychoanalytic phenomenon

him... . The determinants [of this situation] are less individual [than transferences]. *The cause of this obstacle lies in the special solicitude inherent in treatment.*

*(1895, p. 302; emphasis added)*

Let us be as bold as Freud. His effort to make great discoveries, and also conduct a confident cure, had unexpectedly put in his hands a peculiar power – the power of a psychological seduction. I shouldn't have to – but I've learned that I had better – add quickly that this seduction is unique, careful, modulated, responsible, therapeutically intended, unselfish, and nonabusive. I have no wish to be provocative. I know that many of you find the word *seduction* intolerable – and for very good reason. But since some elements of treatment exist for the very purpose of cushioning that discomfort, we will understand less about treatment if we hide the discomfort in a euphemism.

By seduction I mean an arrangement whereby the patient is led to expect love while the analyst, in Freud's words, plans to provide a substitute for it. Admittedly the love-substitute is something very special, with secrets we have yet to fathom, but it is not the love the patient is imagining. At that early moment in analytic history one of the conspicuous features of treatment was put in place, namely, the analyst's special interest, his constant, exclusive, selfless attentiveness – an attentiveness which I believe (though this is only implied by Freud) will inevitably spark a flickering apparition of the analyst's deep and lasting attachment to the patient. That illusion may be viewed skeptically, or rationalized out of awareness, or fended off, or kept in the background, or wondered about or feared, but it is always a nidus of uncertainty at the center of treatment, placed there deliberately by the psychoanalyst.

That's not the whole story, of course. The patient also rides the analyst's attention back into himself, where he finds a new respect for – and hopefulness in – the rich potential of his own distress. Even if you can't abide my bad language – my talking about illusion and seduction when every well-bred tongue knows how to pronounce "transference" and "regression" – I'm sure you will agree with me that Freud discovered a unique attitude, let us say, of expectant appreciation (an attitude that possesses perfectly extraordinary eliciting power), and you will agree that this attitude is a hallmark of psychoanalytic treatment.

And perhaps you will agree also that part of what makes the analyst's personal interest so unique is that it is allowed to remain ambiguous for years, while any straightforward declaration designed to clear up the ambiguity is deliberately avoided. Though he may question the patient's beliefs, the analyst never *says* what the extent and limits of his caring are. (I need not cite Freud's advice to neither encourage nor discourage transference love.)

Uncertainty about the analyst's attachment is a source of discomfort. But it is not just that; it is also a tactical problem inasmuch as the need for the patient's attachment gives evidence of the analyst's continued obligation to bargain. Freud learned soon enough that, left to themselves, patients would not aim at his target, and he was actually relieved to find, as he tells us, that "free association is not really free. The patient remains under the influence of the analytic situation" (1923, p. 40).

Thus, patients were still being subjected to suggestion, if not by Freud's words, then by his procedure. And, accordingly, Freud was still in the position of bargaining. For one thing, without hypnosis he would be the one who saw the hidden meanings, and he would have to persuade patients to believe what he saw (Freud 1904). But that was the least of his problems. The bigger problem was that, though he had coopted some of the patient's wishes to his own ends, in fact the only wish he ever really endorsed was the wish to remember; other wishes were always something to be tamed. And taming remained a problem. Patients could refuse to produce evidence. They could stop talking. They could demand an entirely different relationship. The method was not as dependably automatic as it had seemed.

Freud did not flinch from the larger implication. By 1912 he knew he was no longer in the modest business of retrieving memories. He was back in the persuading business. Even just to conduct the treatment he had to persuade patients to live differently, more courageously, more realistically, etc. (Freud 1912; Falzeder 1994). His wanting that from patients made him dependent on them again. Freud saw the trap more clearly than did Jung or Ferenczi, and he resolved to extricate himself. He would use his influence, but in a way that did not entangle him in compromises. Having already learned not to ask, he would now try to not even *want* any particular information. And he resolved to stop entreating patients to get well; he would make them come to him and solicit him. He wrote to Jung: "you still engage yourselves, give away a good deal of yourselves in order to demand a similar response... . [O]ne should rather remain unapproachable, and insist upon receiving" (Falzeder 1994, p. 314). But here's the problem: If the procedure has any point to it, the analyst has to go after *something*. If he is diffident about causes and he's not evangelical about health, what will he pursue?

Freud very early found an attitude that solved this practical dilemma, and successive generations have reproduced the handy attitude. How? By thinking in terms of resistance, which was Freud's behavioral map through this minefield.

The resistance was the something that Freud could be passionate about, struggle with, go after, and still remain a neutral conduit for what the patient ultimately wants and would naturally produce (were it not for the resistance). It was not just a rhetorical trick, *provided* there was something that both he and the patient could fight against. Freud thought there was such a thing: the enemy was a motivated *ignorance* of inner reality that limited the patient's autonomy. By fighting against the ignorance Freud was *freeing* the patient's decision making. In that way Freud could still count on the force of the patient's own wishes to serve the analyst's purpose. The analyst could press his own case without entreating the patient and without manipulating the patient because the patient's ultimate response was *guaranteed*, theoretically, by a third presence – objective truth, truth undistorted by the analyst's and patient's preconceptions and wishful thinking (Freud 1914). Objective truth serves two purposes: In the first place, it is a gratifyingly clear goal for a distressingly undefined partnership. In the second place, truth is a monitor that allows the analyst to exert influence without compromising his liberating purpose. Let me say just a few words about each of these two services.

**168** The psychoanalytic phenomenon

First, let us consider why it is so important to have a clear goal. Floating above both parties – usually silently – is the unanswerable question of what exactly the analyst's investment is in his patient. Any therapist will be less uneasy if he can point away from that uncertainty to a straightforwardly mutual task of investigation that goes on regardless of the relationship. In other words, a personal ambiguity is balanced by an objective work relationship. And that balance is fostered by the idea that whatever is or isn't real in the relationship, it is all for the purpose of bringing objective truth into sight. Thus, an attitude oriented to objective reality takes some of the vertigo out of the relationship.

Now, about the second way that objective reality serves the analyst – how does it lessen mutual dependency? Freud worked his way out of mutual dependency by balancing his affectionate interest, which led to personal entanglement, against an opposite, disentangling attitude – an attitude that can be fairly characterized as socially adversarial. I say, *socially* adversarial. Obviously Freud was not an adversary of his patient's welfare. That qualifier understood, I will now speak simply of adversarialness. Many have commented on Freud's bellicose treatment images. We are all familiar with his famous martial metaphors. From first to last Freud was in a struggle. If it's a matter of Freud's own writings, I hardly need to argue my case for adversarialness, and in fact, that very word has often been used in personal criticism. But my purpose here is to emphasize the universal service that this adversarial attitude renders to the treatment that Freud discovered.

Let us look back at the original adversarial attitude that led Freud to the treatment. Freud, as I have suggested, was impatient for great discoveries, and, as Schafer has noted, that made him an adversary to patients who barred the way. But let us ask: did Freud become less adversarial when he stopped fishing for memories and started nourishing a whole relationship with his patients? On the contrary, the adversarial attitude became even more essential at that point. For now it was not just the Conquistador who was fighting; it was also the adamant therapist. The researcher's impatience was being trimmed to a different service, a different ruthlessness – one that would sustain the newly discovered treatment. After all, free association was a way of paralyzing the patient's will, and that's a fairly adversarial thing to do. But it is just one example of a general attitude. Through each revision of treatment, Freud was reconfirming and deepening his first lesson, namely that wanting something from a patient defeats the purpose. As I have noted, Freud found that he lost leverage when he engaged patients too wholeheartedly. They would play out their neurosis on the instrument of his therapeutic desire. He had to retain autonomy not just to make discoveries but to keep himself free of the patient's manipulation, and the patient free of his.

By 1912 Freud saw that an allegiance to objective truth would solve the problem: addressing himself to objective truth, he could preserve his independence even while he was involved with the patient's wishes. The patient was wrestling with a transference figure, but Freud was wrestling with resistance to objective truth, and ultimately – I emphasize, ultimately – none of the patient's holds could succeed in making out of the search for truth a repetition of an unhappy old childhood routine. The patient finds that this, the most open intimacy of his life, paradoxically diverts him to objectivity.

And for his part, Freud could make a demand on the patient without offering a piece of himself in exchange (without losing his skin, as he put it). He would offer the truth rather than his own love or approval. The injunction to confront objective truth gave the patient an endless task by which he could endeavor to win the analyst's favor. You know that patients will scan every treatment for a sign of what is wanted of them. What they find in that search is what I will call the demand structure of the treatment. If you don't offer one demand, the patient will perceive another. Freud provided a demand: Let up on your yearnings and aim for objective truth!

And that, in turn, would free the patient. The patient could please Freud only by seeking the truth. And the truth would then make the patient free, because he would be putting himself into a position where he could *choose*, instead of being compelled automatically. The rule of abstinence is simply a corollary of these considerations.

And so from 1912 to 1914 Freud recommended to us the cardinal concepts of transference, resistance, and objective truth so that we might put ourselves into this useful, semi-adversarial frame of mind. We welcome what the patient is revealing, but we think he's revealing it in order to conceal something more important. Nothing is more characteristic of psychoanalysts than their inclination to *see through* everything. The adversarial attitude is so ingrained in analysts that it affects their collegial discourse. Just as a patient's cooperation is never innocent of resistance, so a reported treatment can't go well without a zealous observer suspecting an error of collusion. And, justified or not, the profession's response to Loewald and to Kohut was surely influenced by fear that they were diluting a fundamental, adversarial attitude.

I realize that none of you will recognize adversarialness as a feature of your treatment. You are more likely to see what I am pointing to if I ask you to reflect on the balance you keep between analytic credulity and analytic skepticism. Though analysts cannot miss Freud's adversarialness, accompanied as it is by drums and trumpets, their own adversarialness is usually manifested quietly, as analytic flexibility. What I call adversarialness, and what Freud described in similar idiom, refers to the way the analyst sets his face against appeals by the patient, denies bids for validation and reassurance, sternly summons what is most reluctant, rebuffs advances to "buy" any picture of the patient or his fate, waves away comforting roles, and says to everything, in effect, "No; something else." Adversarialness deconstructs the patient's presentation and frees the analyst's imagination. It eyes appearances skeptically and keeps looking for a reality beyond. It shuffles dramas and story lines and deflates lessons and moralizing.

The significance of this last point can hardly be exaggerated. Ordinarily we see people as dramatic figures. Schafer is right: narrative is the way we understand human action. And where our imagination is least constrained, there we make up the simplest and most persuasive stories. We "know" public figures more crisply than we know our spouse. It's more obvious what to do about the national economy than how to deal with the kids. Until we are assaulted by complexity,

**170** The psychoanalytic phenomenon

until we are entangled by love and responsibility, we see a simple, old-fashioned melodrama of good and evil, and when we don't have to act we moralize fiercely.

So we can't help seeing patients that way or they us. Analysts, despite themselves, often view process this way. Once in a while they slip and hear themselves say that their patient is trying to get away with a wicked treatment perversion, or flagrantly abusing the process in some fashion. But then they recapture Freud's adversarial attitude, which says that what's seen is in any case just surface, and they sober up on the objective truth of the mind with its perfectly neutral psychodynamics. A mental mechanism may malfunction, but it can't misbehave. One frequently sees Freud personally alternating this way: his letters express his moralized dramas while his published theory tends to neutralize them.

Moralizing keeps drifting into treatment, as indeed it must, but it is constantly swept out. Of course, the analyst must experience his own effort dramatically – no one perseveres in a tough project over years without some agonistic framework. So an official drama of treatment is available – but only one: the crusade against resistance. Yet fighting the resistance is probably the least confining, the least defining, drama that a therapist can act in, because resistance itself is so ill defined. (Compare, for example, the fight against a "false self," which is so much more dramatically specific.) Other than the single image of fighting resistance, no drama is finally accepted by the Freudian analyst. No sense of "what we're doing together" hardens into routine. No patient is finally pigeonholed. The adversarial attitude refuses them all.

The adversarial attitude and the hunt for objective truth – these characterize the whole of treatment. Every time an analyst sees an event as an instance of something larger, he is endorsing Freud's view of the mind as an object. Every time an analyst disengages himself from an ordinary social response, he is utilizing Freud's adversarialness to social offerings and is imitating Freud's reach toward a mental object behind appearances.

So here's my list of attitudes – the founding attitudes of psychoanalytic treatment. Do you recognize this picture? Endless curiosity; endorsement of the patient's thrust; an evocative sort of affection; a faithful intimacy; a nervous dance around any illusion of lasting attachment; a demand that the patient rise above his wishes and face the truth; constant skepticism about all appearances; a lightness about the patient's dramas and the drama of treatment; absence of role and judgment. And I might add, as I mentioned at the start, a studied disingenuousness, that is, an attitude of innocent observation.

Well, what do you say? You say: yes, the portrait does convey a faint likeness and it might look better in a dark corner of the attic. What a dull list of hateful attitudes! What about plain human affection? How about easing pain, defeating demons, mastering fate? Where is the playfulness and creativity, the enlargement of experience? Where is the excitement of surviving risky genuineness? Aren't *these* the daily rewards for which analysts rise in the morning and go to work? And I say, yes, you are right, analysts do go to work for those reasons. They can do that because the *workplace* is there, assured by their taken-for-granted, baseline attitudes.

My caricature is an underdrawing of the workplace – or the laboratory, as I shall presently describe it. But even as such, I confess, it lacks one identifying feature that has been the subject of ardent controversy. I must now add a note about what might be called the analyst's attitude of incubation.

We saw that Freud first achieved mastery by hitching his research wagon to the patient's memory machine. But even in 1912 he knew that patients weren't suffering just from retained memories; he knew they also had a general *interest* that is fastened onto their parents. For a while it was tempting to think that adult life is just too difficult for these patients, and that treatment is a halfway house to being a grown-up.

The idea that patients have to grow up in treatment took deeper root when theory expanded in the 1920s. After all, the superego appraises reality not in a factual but in an attitudinal way, and it might well need some growing out of. And that impression was reinforced when, in 1923, Freud allowed that there's a sense in which patients are not split-minded but wholeheartedly oppose their treatment and, indeed, throw their whole selves into every meeting with the world. With that, I think, Freud took his first steps down a dark path at the end of which he would find so few uncorrupted egos that human development came to seem an education in cowardice adapted to a projected world, itself built out of need and fear. (That's my hyperbolic inference from Freud 1937, p. 234ff.) Don't think for a moment that the theory of signal anxiety did away with the maturational image of treatment. It is true that in later theory infantile stubbornness was no longer the villain. Freud now acknowledged that people have self-protective, good reasons for lagging behind. But the same theory told him that the world we are taught to live in is a fearful world, and if we are to free ourselves from it we have to be brave as well as wise. The need for some sort of growing up in treatment was never absent from Freud's writings, from his first mention of the repetition compulsion to the late picture of a spoiled child who is unduly fearful because he has been overprotected.

This takes us into the realm of world building and world breaking. The constructivist implications of Freud's theory were understood by his coworkers. In the 1930s Hartmann was by no means alone in pointing out that significant reality is largely social reality, and its appreciation often a matter of having a realistic *attitude* or a realistic *perspective* and useful *reflexes*, or a composite *orientation* arranged by a *well-integrated* psychic apparatus. Being realistic involves experiencing "appropriate" *meanings*, some of them quite peremptory.

This was not the kind of mind Freud cared about; it would never be capable of free choice in a field of objective reality. But analysts with more mixed objectives were not so quickly discouraged. It did not displease them to think that psychoanalysis can help patients with their problem solving, even if the problem isn't a simple recognition of objective truth. It is largely this problem-solving paradigm that we know as ego psychology, a term that should include Melanie Klein's work.

The reality that these ego psychologists ended up with was an individualized grown-up-ness, though Anna Freud and the North Americans did not discard a factor of neutral perception.

**172** The psychoanalytic phenomenon

Analysts can't relax there. If treatment aims at an individualized maturity rather than truth, the analyst can no longer act impersonally when he makes his customary demand. The demand structure of psychoanalysis presupposed an objective reality that both parties could turn to and salute. Feeling respect for truth in his bones, the analyst was reassured that his body English would be disciplined, his role responses tentative, his personal influence erasable. If the maturational view took over, treatment might end up as a cloud of encouraging perspectives mixed with bundles of shaping influences. The sympathetic and seductive features of treatment might wash away the spice of challenge.

In this predicament practitioners on both sides of the Atlantic looked to the same principle for salvation: If disciplined analysts will confine themselves to non-manipulative interpretations, then by definition their personal attitude won't impinge on patients, and the structure of treatment will remain psychoanalytic. In other words, if an interpretation can be objective, then it doesn't matter how confused the notion of reality becomes. The call is to save interpretations and let reality fend for itself. That may seem an odd solution, but it is logical, and in many quarters during the 1950s and 1960s an idealized interpretation was fast becoming the sole repository for the threatened demand structure of analysis.

Therefore, it was a matter of analytic life or death that an interpretation should convey nothing but precisely what is hidden, so that it will not transmit the analyst's persuasive attitude.

Now, that is too heavy a burden for any human communication to bear. Thus, in the eyes of those who followed, this brave first effort to preserve the structure of treatment and thereby safeguard the patient's autonomy was seen, instead, as a priestly, rule-bound formalism, smug, authoritarian, and doctrinaire – perfect, in other words, to serve as a foil for rebellion by the next generation (our generation), which, as always in history, turns contemptuously from the Academy back to nature. In this case, nature is the crucible of live treatment.

Thus, after decades of taking the structure of treatment for granted, analysts today are poking at it to see how it's built. They are systematically varying treatment attitudes and watching the results.

Consider, for instance, the objective truth demand. What happens to the rest of treatment if you remove it? Objective reality was the bulwark of analytic skepticism. We were skeptical because reality was hiding behind appearances. Respect for reality buffered the analyst against the patient and the patient against manipulation. Now analysts are trying to think about patients in terms of story lines that are free of objective truth reference. Maybe that will make patients more responsible and creative. Maybe analysts can find a more flexible discipline to replace the old truth demand. For instance, it may suffice for the analyst to simply *decide* to read a psychoanalytic narrative into the patient's history and behavior. Maybe just being firm in that *decision* will anchor the analyst when he is being pulled by the patient's undertow. And maybe the analyst can limit such firm decisions to that one manipulation. We shall see.

That's one experiment. There are others. Analysts are also trying to be *more* objective – for instance, by using interventions that do more neutral pointing and less perspectival describing, pointing for instance to visible and categorical affects, muffled resentments, or shifts in direction.

Some investigators maximize adversarialness: They spare no island of taken-for-granted cooperation – everything is a compromise formation. Others reduce adversarialness: their experiments will tell us whether empathic affirmation reduces the patient's masochistic collusion while yet steering clear of a social relationship. Investigators are tinkering with the old analytic attitude of curiosity. They attend less to pathology and more to the process of preconscious emergence. Even the attitude of passive observation is being experimentally altered, as analysts remind themselves that they are partly making up what they see and partly producing it inadvertently. How will that affect their ability to maintain a level scrutiny?

Despite this widespread innovation, I think all of these controversies are experiments: they do not trash the laboratory. In my opinion, few psychoanalysts would be happy with a treatment that discarded the features I've mentioned, though we may not agree on their names, or the proper balance among them. If you look closely enough, I think you will see that we are all counting on trans-mitted reflexes and traditions to keep the main features of treatment in place while we experiment with shades and proportions.

And there, I think, lies the answer to that old, embarrassing question: Why did psychoanalysis wall itself up in institutes and reproduce by inbreeding? Freudian theory didn't need to do that. It could have survived nibbling and adulteration – has, in fact, survived that in popular culture and the academy. But the thing that Freud discovered, the thing we know as psychoanalytic *treatment* – that is quite ephemeral. It is solely the product of attitudes. It is that crucible that needed protection.

Treatment structure has no protection outside of tradition. Without special support it might have disappeared forever, exploding into a galaxy of assorted relationships, each one molded according to how it pleased the therapist to see himself. And if treatment is the crucible of psychoanalysis, its preservation was paramount. That is something to be kept in mind today, when the threat is pointedly aimed at the treatment.

Here is my peroration: Besides their other contributions, analysts do basic research. The standard treatment atmosphere is an imaging technique for mind: general features of mind are measured as the analyst notices the attitudes he must invoke to sustain the analytic atmosphere. It is a kind of echo-cardiography of the soul. Of course, it does not produce a readout in pixels. Is it then just a speculative enterprise? Not a bit. Attitudes and their impacts are features of the empirical world. As the analyst switches this attitude on and that one off, he records which combinations most brightly light up the unique analytic situation. It is the slight alterations in treatment attitudes that constitute experiments in this peculiar laboratory of the mind, the laboratory that is dedicated to research on the pathway of desire, the nuances of interaction, the limits of freedom, the relationship of cause and reason, the nature of meaning, the meaning of responsibility, and all the special paradoxes of humanness. I really cannot imagine what other form research on these issues could possibly take.

## 174 The psychoanalytic phenomenon

The supreme irony of today's psychoanalysis is that the gravest threat to its existence finds the profession in an unparalleled, efflorescent vigor – I would call it a renaissance. In that respect, at least, you must consider yourselves fortunate.

## REFERENCES

Falzeder, E. (1994). My grand-patient, my chief tormenter: A hitherto unnoticed case of Freud's and the consequences. *Psychoanalytic Quarterly*, 63:297–331.

Freud, S. (1895) *Studies on Hysteria*. Standard Edition, 2.

Freud, S. (1904). Freud's psycho-analytic procedure. Standard Edition, 7: 249–254.

Freud, S. (1912). The dynamics of transference. Standard Edition, 12: 99–108.

Freud, S. (1914). *On the History of the Psycho-analytic Movement*. Standard Edition, 14: 7–66.

Freud, S. (1917). *Introductory Lectures on Psycho-analysis*. Standard Edition, 16.

Freud, S. (1923). The ego and the id. Standard Edition, 19: 13–66.

Freud, S. (1937). Analysis terminable and interminable. Standard Edition, 23: 216–253.

# 11

# IS THERE A SPECIAL PSYCHOANALYTIC LOVE?

My title could refer to many different questions, most of which I will not take up. Some of them are simple: For example, one hardly need ask whether analysts are fond of many patients in various ways. Some related questions are complex – for instance, those concerning erotic love. We know that analysts sometimes experience erotic love for a patient and respond in various ways, a matter of great practical importance comprehensively discussed by Gabbard (1996).

In this chapter I ask a more elusive question: In the *ordinary* scope of their work, do all analysts (in principle) *regularly* develop any *particular* kind of feeling about *all* of their patients (alongside the individual feelings that happen to spring up from the match), and if they do, is there a respect in which it can it be considered *love*?

That may seem the sort of hopelessly ambiguous and even pointless question one hears only from the naive. And yet many of our most sophisticated psychoanalysts have asked it, usually to assure themselves that they do, indeed, love their patients.

That is especially striking, since analysts have every reason to avoid the question and could easily have dismissed it as futile. On grounds of common sense alone the safest bet would be that the only universal constant in the analyst's psychology is his professional apparatus, his mission, his experience, and his procedure, all else being an accident of his person and his patient. Isn't it most likely that two people working together on an analytic project experience just whatever those particular two people personally stir up in each other, and react to those feelings according to their respective roles as analyst and analysand? That is the simplest and most "hard-headed" diagram of the treatment relationship. No wonder many discussions of countertransference assume such a businesslike staging.

What is truly remarkable is that many analysts have not been content with this most down-to-earth and convenient paradigm and have instead searched for universal feelings that are regularly awakened in all analysts. I speculate below about

**176** The psychoanalytic phenomenon

why analysts haven't settled for the easier, individualized picture, and have sometimes gone so far as to include love in their standard picture. The aim of the chapter is to explore analytic thought about a baseline affection, not to weigh its validity. I am in no way concerned here with what an analyst *should* do or feel.

## DO ANALYSTS HAVE LOVING FEELINGS FOR PATIENTS?

It is especially impressive that analysts have been willing to contemplate general loving feelings, considering that the possibility of even random affective reactions made them squirm for many years, and a fortiori any sort of *constant* affective reactivity. The reason for the discomfort is obvious. The technical model of analysis is a paradox: the analyst is supposed to be an objective observer, but one whose inner responses are in important ways uncontrolled and freely *moved* by the patient's impact. Theory seems at once to forbid and require detachment. Analysts cannot say that their feelings are just those of a researcher investigating the patient's nature, since they are supposed to be *personally* reactive. Ferenczi (1928) wrote that the analyst's "cathexes oscillate between identification (analytic object love) on the one hand and selfcontrol or intellectual activity on the other" (p. 98).

If the theory of the analyst's feeling is paradoxical, clinical experience is even more confusing. Whereas comfortable theoretical euphemisms can always be found, clinical experience is less tractable. Early in their discussions, analysts began to reflect on the specific form of their affective registrations. How much was expressive of the analyst, how much the patient? Did his emotions just flash a private signal to the analyst, or did they reach out to the patient? Was the analyst, indeed, even aware of his feelings, and if so, at what stage in their development? Did they form an enduring attitude? What was their effect on the patient and on the treatment?

In the 1950s and 1960s, the controversies over countertransference were almost as bold as today. Balint (1949) had been arguing for a decade that the "analyst's relationship to his patient is libidinous in exactly the same way [as the patient's relationship to the analyst]" (p. 231). In 1942 Robert Fliess endeavored to render that psychoanalytic truism compatible with the above-it-ness that analysts aspired to by describing a temporary work ego that momentarily samples the patient's libido and restores it to the patient, uncontaminated by the analyst's own libidinal reaction. What analysts needed was theoretical assurance of their ability to partialize their reactions, so that they could distinguish their emotional liveliness in their offices from the sort they have at home.

## ARE THE ANALYST'S LOVING FEELINGS A STANDARD PART OF TREATMENT?

Another problem arises if it turns out that the analyst's affectionate feelings for the patient are actually helpful or even essential, as Tower (1956) suggested. How could a patient be sure he would evoke them in his analyst? It might be a matter of

Is there a special psychoanalytic love? **177**

chance. Tower's example illustrates that one of her patients succeeded in "winning" her by a remote, unconscious exchange. But another patient failed to elicit the same yieldingness. (Tower did, however, believe that her readiness to be "conquered" by the successful patient reflected a more characteristic feature of her attitude, which she put in maternal/child terms.)[1]

Tracking the debates about whether there are baseline feelings reliably evoked by all patients, the path becomes harder to follow, principally because writers do not always distinguish clearly between the *meaning to the patient* of the analyst's manner, which is safe to write about, and the true feelings revealed by the analyst, which is a touchy issue. Especially in the older literature, it is unusual for the reader to be shown, as Tower does, that even the basic treatment format includes elements of the analyst's own, very personal, passions (in the case of Tower, her susceptibility to personal wooing on an unconscious level). More typical of the literature is the ambiguity in Stone (1961) as to whether the mother of separation has to do only with the analyst's function or whether it also reflects the analyst's own sense of himself. The latter is where the question of love would come in. The ambiguity is not dispelled by Stone's assurance that a physicianly role captures all of the feeling on the analyst's side. That is even more ambiguous, because, although we may all have some notion of an idealized physician, we don't know which idea Stone had in mind or whether the analyst is supposed to share it with the patient. The ambiguity is expectable, since these authors were thinking more about the analyst's impact on the patient than about the analyst's experience of the patient. Nevertheless, as noted above, analysts have not taken the easy way out; they have again and again explored the possibility of universal feelings on the part of the analyst, often showing an inclination to accept the feeling of a parent toward a child (Spitz 1956; Money-Kyrle 1956).

## WHY DO ANALYSTS WANT TO THINK THEY LOVE THEIR PATIENTS?

It is important to ask why analysts have searched for any common element at all among the variety of feelings they have. One reason might be a subliminal theoretical syllogism: if the analytic atmosphere regularly induces an expectable affective experience in patients (connected to regression or transference, or closeness-in-distance, or self-understanding), it would be reasonable to suppose that the same atmosphere also induces an expectable experience in analysts, though one that is related to their different position in the dyad. This was noted by Money-Kyrle (1956).

But then why suppose that such a feeling is related to love? An obvious reason might be that analysts are not inclined to deny libidinal connections between people, and if the analyst's feeling of love is frequent, hard to survey and master, and especially if it is therapeutically effective, professionalism would seem to require that that emotion be evoked in all analysts by all patients, rather than being available only on occasion and by luck of the draw.

**178** The psychoanalytic phenomenon

In addition, however, I suspect another, nontheoretical reason that analysts would like to think they develop a regularly expectable affection. Analysts find themselves in a morally difficult position as the result of the implicit promise of loving that their procedure silently extends. And it is this promise that they wish to redeem. There is an early testimonial by Freud (Breuer & Freud 1895) to the analyst's sense of an affective quid pro quo owed the patient: "In not a few cases, especially with women and where it is a question of elucidating erotic trains of thought, the patient's cooperation becomes a personal sacrifice, which must be compensated for by some substitute for love" (p. 301 n. 2). And it is impossible to read Ferenczi's *Clinical Diary* (1988) without appreciating the burden on analysts of knowing that patients presume a love that is not there. I suspect that this sense of a secret betrayal helped to fuel Ferenczi's desperate experiments in radical, mutual honesty. His work was certainly not inspired by a grandiose illusion of his own, enormous capacity for love (see, e.g., Ferenczi 1988, p. 26.) The pain of his underfulfilment was evidently not anesthetized by the standard psychoanalytic anodyne, the equation of love with understanding (first formulated by Ferenczi himself in 1928).

It's not hard to see how this uncomfortable situation comes about. Analysts show a focused attention that patients naturally understand as a sign of ordinary love. Analysts exercise a degree of self-effacement that usually attests a loving devotion, a kind of nondefensive and nonparalyzing surrender discussed by Schafer (1983). Analysts often use the word *dedication* to describe this gesture (for it is a gesture, as well as a mental state). In analytic writing, these references, like all affectionate terms, constantly acquire the standard modifier of *sublimated*, or *alternating*, and are always carefully distinguished from masochism or "altruistic surrender."

Many analysts, of course, take the position that the patient's expectation of love is simply part of his transference baggage, and is not a procedurally evoked illusion. But I have found that analysts who do accept some responsibility for awakening an expectation of love protest that it is not an illusion, not an implicit false promise. They protest that analysts do provide "a kind of love," as Merton Gill put it at a meeting of the Rapaport-Klein Study Group (June 14, 1992).

## ANALYSTS WANT ANALYTIC LOVE TO BE DIFFERENT

But if analysts want to believe that there is some sort of resemblance between the love they seem to offer and what they are prepared to deliver, they are nevertheless reluctant to think of it as too close an approximation, for the very good reason that an identity of love imagined and love provided would render the relationship an ordinary social one and, moreover, one as limited in demography as in analytic usefulness.

Facing the challenge, some writers have tried to specify certain particular feelings that are universally present because they are called into being by the enterprise and not just by the personal vulnerabilities of patient and analyst. These authors looked for some constant lovelike feeling that an analyst always has and always radiates, that is helpful or at least not prejudicial to the treatment project. Gitelson (1952) referred to a "contact feeling" (p. 5) and later (1962), borrowing a term from Spitz, to a "diatrophic" attitude (p. 198). Loewald (1970) referred to the analyst as a cathector of the patient. Tower (1956) scolded the analytic community for what she stopped just short of calling dishonesty in refusing to acknowledge the inescapable transference-countertransference exchanges that are beyond the analyst's control. Not until Jacobs (1991) was her challenge fully met. Tower remarked on the frequent countertransference "structures" that are often unknowingly built and subsequently worked out. She advanced the courageous idea that unconscious negotiations and "winning" by the patient may be decisive for success. Although Myerson (1994) has explored a related theme, perhaps only Nacht (1962) has been as bold, saying that it is the analyst's unconscious love that is basically responsible for cure. He probably meant by that something like Kohut's empathy. By contrast, Stone (1961) charted his course between Scylla and Charybdis by describing a basic attitude of mother of separation, reassuring analysts (in opposition to Freud's initial feeling, cited above) that this attitude is no different from the ordinary role of physician. King (1962), however, did not think that even that definition gave a wide enough berth to libidinal hazards, and preferred to pare down the mother of separation idea to just plain separation.

Winnicott (1960) thought that a maternal function might be served, but added that with neurotic patients it did not require that analysts actually feel themselves into the role. He did not regard this mother–child relationship in analysis as a shared sense of the analytic relationship, but saw it rather as the patient's enjoyment of a newly created symbolic space. Sandler, Dare, and Holder (1973) also postulated a professional rather than a libidinal positioning of the analyst. Loewald (1960), Stone (1961), Gitelson (1962), and Tower (1956) felt that a parent/child constellation of feelings might be always involved, but whereas the first three identified this with the most abstract function of a caregiver, principally the meaning-giving act, Tower's clinical experience taught her that the analyst's side of the relationship can be much fuller and more libidinal than that, on a highly derivative, unconscious, and tacit level, of course.

Given their views of the analytic transaction, it is not surprising that Loewald (1960/1980), Stone (1961), Gitelson (1962), and Nacht (1962) in general terms, and Heimann (1950) and Tower (1956) more specifically, describe love of one sort or another as a regular feature in the analyst. What is noteworthy is that even Hanna Segal (1962), who had expressed grave doubts about Gitelson's diatrophic attitude and took strenuous exception to Nacht's statement (1962) that the analyst's love means something more substantial than the niceties of interpretation, nevertheless went on to say, quite offhandedly, that like Nacht she thought "that a good therapeutic setting must include unconscious love in the analyst for the patient … " (p. 232). This casual concession is, I think, what we often see even among those who emphasize the cognitive essence of treatment. What are we to make of that fact? In Segal's case, the answer is pointedly and urgently supplied in her very next words:

**180** The psychoanalytic phenomenon

> In that respect, the analytical situation does not differ from any other sub-limation, as in any successful sublimation, unconscious love must be stronger than destructiveness.... In every relationship there is an appropriate expression of love and hatred and the appropriate expression of love on the part of the analyst to the patient – not only an appropriate, but a specific expression of love in that situation – is understanding and correct interpretation.
>
> *(p. 232)*

One supposes that even King (1962), who identified the analyst as a provider of separation, would endorse *that* sort of love. And analysts across the board have most frequently tried to equate their love with their understanding (witness Loewald's love of truth, and love of the object of study). Even Nacht, who was so shockingly outspoken about love being more important than interpretive accuracy, replied to Segal that:

> that inner [interpretive] attitude [in the analyst] should be impregnated with love for his patient. Of course not the same kind of love he has, for instance, for his brother, his wife, or his close friend. No, it is a kind of love in which he is not personally concerned, although it *is* a deep feeling.
>
> *(p. 233)*

But just as Segal seemed to take back what she had given, so Nacht immediately put back what he seemed to have taken away:

> I suppose it is rather difficult to describe [this sort of love] in common lan-guage.... It is a kind of openness that one can understand only if he has already experienced it himself with his analytic patient in the analytic relationship.
>
> *(p. 232)*

We can sympathize with Nacht. If this love exists, it is surely not easy to describe. Neither he nor we can be satisfied with its description as *understanding*. Analysts may use the word to point to something like love, but the word *understanding* is by itself much too broadly applicable to convey anything interesting. One fears that its ambiguity is just what is being traded on when love is equated with understanding: it ensures a safe union of warmth with distance.

The comfortable thesis that, yes, analysts do provide love, but (never fear) it is nothing else than their understanding – this is the "hidden attractor" on which almost all definitions converge, as they progressively refine and sublimate and modify and control the more recognizable forms of love that are being mentioned. After various, specific *feelings* are discussed, author after author concludes that love is embodied in the analyst's understanding, which in turn is embodied in inter-pretations. (Tower is the startling exception.) A cynic would say that this is simply to walk away from the problem claiming victory. And no doubt the cynic would be partly right. If analysts are supposed to offer uncluttered understanding but find it awkward to disclaim love, the safest declaration will be that what they generically offer is exactly what is wanted by way of love. But a cynic would be ignoring the many experiences in the consulting room that honestly suggest this equivalence to analysts. One such experience is watching understanding being received by patients as though it were love. But that observation cuts both ways, since it might be argued that understanding is there being *misperceived* as love. More persuasive is the fact, evident to anybody but the cynic, that the analyst himself often experiences a certain kind of *feeling* that attends his understanding, and that analytic under-standing seems to describe a certain kind of interpersonal relationship. Vague as they may be, this feeling and this relationship indicate that there is an empirical something that analysts are trying to get at in their discussions of love, even while they may also be guilty of juggling and sanitizing terminology in order to have it both ways in regard to personal involvement with their patients. But the problem with the formula that equates love with understanding is that it simply moves the mystery of the analyst's not-ordinary love to the problem of the analyst's not-ordinary understanding.

That would seem to have been no problem for Loewald (1970) and Kohut (1977). They did not have to twist understanding into something that looks like love, since, in both of their accounts, a basic form of love already amounts to accurate understanding – an understanding that articulates a growth potential. But is empathy the sort of love that patients imagine? The act of empathy may indeed approximate to the analyst's feeling of love; that seems to me intrinsically plausible, and I will suggest something of the sort myself. But a consistent Kohutian might object that empathy is not ordinarily a reciprocal activity in psychoanalytic treat-ment, and the analyst is not supposed to find the same sustenance and structure in empathizing as the patient finds in being empathized with. For that reason, Loe-wald is inclined to identify the analyst's love with a passion that he can share with his patient – namely, dedication to the objective truth of the patient's individuality. (For all his antipathy to Freud's "truth morality," I think Kohut's position on that issue is basically the same as Loewald's.)

I conclude that analysts have been uncertain about how much strong feeling they regularly have for their patients, and to what extent the feelings that they do have are compatible with the objectivity they have claimed. Nevertheless, while debating the breadth and width of the analyst's feeling and its manageability, ana-lytic writers have often treated it as a foregone conclusion that something related to love is generally felt by analysts for their patients.

I turn now to six authors who have written explicitly about the analyst's regular loving feelings, and to another who may be indirectly discussing the issue.

## RACKER'S FRANK AFFECTION

Racker describes the analyst's affection most straightforwardly, allowing it personal rootedness in the analyst's childhood. This is a daring admission, because that is

**182** The psychoanalytic phenomenon

precisely the sense of love that analysts have shied away from, and from which they have hoped to shield themselves by equating love with understanding. What analysts wanted to avoid in their professional self-description is the love, based on a childhood stereotype, that is described in analytic theory. Such love seems illicit in an analyst, available only for some patients, and prejudicial to treatment. But Racker implies that love objects are fungible, so the analyst can use his own objects to repair patients' relationships with theirs.

Racker (1968) argues that any detailed, empathic understanding of another person requires a libidinal motivation, and he is comfortable calling it positive countertransference. This was accepted in principle by others (e.g., Heimann 1950; Reich 1951), but Racker goes further in maintaining, along with Nacht (1962), that the analyst's love is needed not just to inform the analyst, but also to motivate the patient:

> In this context Freud speaks of the 'boiling heat *(Siedehitze)* of the transference,' and, according to my experience, such temperatures can only be achieved if the analyst also contributes sufficient heat, sufficient positive countertransference made real through his work, to the analytic situation... . The positive intention of not showing more than the indispensable of one's own person does not have to be carried as far as to deny (or even inhibit), in front of the patient, the analyst's interest and affection towards him. For only Eros can originate Eros... The analyst's relation to his patient *is* a libidinal one, and is a constant emotional experience ...
>
> *(pp. 30–31)*

In Racker's theory, the matching of one's own early relationships to the patient's internalized objects *joins* the two persons, and that is his definition of Eros. Whereas other analysts will say that the giving of interpretations is *taken* as love, perhaps as a feeding, Racker implies that accurate interpretation simply *indicates* that love has happened. And it should be noted that Racker believes it can happen regularly only if the analyst is able to keep the kind of distance that allows him to picture his transference role.[2]

But then is this really love? Is there any *particular* form of the analyst's Eros that is both palpable (as erotic love would be) and acceptable (as erotic love is not)? In what way does the analyst feel love when he identifies with elements of the patient's conflict? Like most analysts who push the inquiry far enough to risk something specific about love, Racker's picture ultimately shapes up as parental love, purged, one assumes, of the passionate ingredients that Freudian psychology usually finds in such love. (See Gitelson 1962; Stone 1961; Money-Kyrle 1956; Berman 1949; Spitz 1956.)

Racker allows the analyst to love the patient as a father loves a child, and he does not shrink from the consequence that the analyst will want the patient's love in return, as a loving father would want his child's love. Indeed, Racker believes that the analyst who cannot allow himself a parental wish cannot analyze, since he

Is there a special psychoanalytic love? **183**

will lack the determination and entitlement necessary to *push* the project as needed: "The masochistic analyst tends to renounce parenthood, leaving the direction of the analysis overmuch to the patient" (p. 178). But Racker also recognizes the danger this entails: "The patient is the chief object of direct desires in the analyst, who wishes to be accepted and loved by him" (p. 165). Such a wish may seek to bind the patient to the analyst. The analyst's love must be somehow detachable and more fluctuant than a parent's.

> For as long as we repress, for instance, our wish to dominate the analysand neurotically (and we do wish this in one part of our personality), we cannot free him from his neurotic dependence, and as long as we repress our neurotic dependence upon him (and we do in part depend on him), we cannot free him from the need to dominate us neurotically ...
>
> *(p. 132 n)*

What works toward mutual freedom is that "the analyst has some capacity to observe this countertransference, to 'get out of it,' to stand outside and regard it objectively ... " (p. 159).

But if Racker is right that analysts react in a variety of identifications, and often step outside all of them, where will we find a steady, *specific* love in the analyst? It seems to me that Racker is pointing to a particular feeling induced by a constant *direction of movement*. Presumably the analyst feels a movement that represents the movement of Eros, a quest for union or wholeness. "The intention to understand creates a certain predisposition, a predisposition to identify oneself with the analysand, which is the basis of comprehension" (p. 134). It is that *intention* that draws the analyst into all those specific forms of love, hate, and detachment. What is stable in love is the *movement* prompted by that intention; any more *specific* love is intrinsically unstable; it is either a momentary concordant countertransference (empathy) that will be overturned in the next moment, or a complementary countertransference (as in an enactment) that will be frustrated at best and paralyze treatment at worst. (It is axiomatic for Racker that no complementary countertransference can be stable.) Analytic loving is a movement toward the patient, and it is exactly the same movement as the effort to understand in a psychoanalytic fashion.

Can we match this up with a subjective feeling of love? When Racker insists that nobody will keep trying to feel his way into someone else's world unless motivated by libido, I think he has in mind the way a deliberate reaching out can turn into an attachment that is no longer deliberate. He sees that movement as a natural source of love. It is one answer to our question, in the tradition of Balint, who, as mentioned, held the analytic relationship to be mutually libidinous.

## LOEWALD'S PERCEPTION OF ESSENCE

In considerations of analyst love, Loewald has been influential in two ways: (1) He writes that the analyst perceives the patient's potential through a higher gradient of

**184** The psychoanalytic phenomenon

articulateness and integration (Loewald 1960), and that is a picture of an especially appreciative understanding, which reminds us of love. But on the face of it this feature more readily explains the patient's belief in the analyst's love than it does the truth of that belief. We think that one who gazes favorably on us may love us, and we often suppose that those who endorse our development do so out of love. (2) Loewald (1970) has emphasized the genuine love that invests the intense study of any truth. That, however, cuts both ways. I am reminded of a news report that, during a heating crisis at the New York Museum of Natural History, the curator responsible for a particularly important and very large cockroach took it home to her warm bed in order to preserve its life. Even if we grant that the passion of an ardent student is often underestimated, still, interpersonal love has usually meant something more than that. And the something more that is meant by love is exactly the opposite of the analyst's desire for intermittency of contact (including vacations), his readiness to terminate, and his unwillingness to proceed without payment.

But there is another clue, in Loewald's later writings (1988), where he suggests that intent human perception ultimately involves a creative search for the kind of meaningfulness initially instilled in our primal, holistic experience. Perception and thinking are efforts to superimpose a differentiated sense of the world on the original unitary experience of infancy, which is the source of this meaningfulness. Seen in this light, an effort at understanding as prolonged and intense as a psychoanalyst's might constitute a primary love, so to speak – some sense of "at last I have it." In generalized terms, it might be equivalent to Racker's merger of the analyst's and the patient's objects. It also suggests that love for the patient is something like love for a work of art.

Loewald thus offers a way of conceiving understanding as a genuinely interpersonal movement.

## SCHAFER'S APPRECIATION

In some respects, Schafer's appreciative attitude (1983) combines features of both Racker's and Loewald's approaches.

> By appreciation I refer to a family or spectrum of terms that range from the analyst's being mildly admiring to experiencing wonder that may border on awe. No doubt, appreciation may be a manifestation of, a screen for, or simply colored by disruptive value-laden identification in the countertransference. Being appreciative of the analysand may also amount to the analyst's adopting a defensive stance against consciously envying and derogating the analysand. But then any of the other constituents listed above (respect, empathy, etc.) may also involve transferential and resistant actions on the analyst's part, and it is generally accepted that the mere possibility of such involvement is no argument against the analytic usefulness of one or another constituent. Appreciation, a mode of engagement frequently expressed or implied in

## Is there a special psychoanalytic love? **185**

informal clinical discussion as well as published case reports, is not usually taken necessarily to imply any lapse from the analytic attitude.

*(pp. 58–59)*

(Note that Racker would say that even the use of an affirmative attitude to defend against hostile feelings toward the patient is not just reasonable, but a paradigmatic analytic effort.) This affirmative empathic attitude includes seeing the analysand's action as potentially coherent, designed to cope impressively with foreseen catastrophes, and as carrying the seeds of growth and development (pp. 45–46). The appreciative attitude is expressed in a creative configuring of the analysand's analytic persona (p. 56).

Schafer suggests that this attitude is an aspect of a special mind-set the analyst falls into when working. He calls it the analyst's "second self." Analyst and analysand, each acting as a second self, develop a relationship that is "fictive" in the sense of being a specialized construction (in contrast to the ordinary fictiveness of social relations).

What loving affects are experienced by the analyst's "second self"? Schafer suggests that empathizing can *generate* "liking," which in turn feeds "empathizing" in a "benign circle" (p. 39).

That is relevant to our inquiry, since liking and loving are related, and at the end of *The Analytic Attitude* Schafer (1983) ventures to relate them:

> On this basis a special kind of empathic intimacy, strength, appreciation, and love can develop in relation to an analysand which it would be a mistake to identify with disruptive countertransference. Admittedly, the distinction between this kind of closeness and disruptive countertransference is not always an easy one to draw, and it is not absolute, but I think that it is a distinction that can be made; indeed it must be made in the interest of developing and maintaining the analytic attitude… It is within this mutual construction [of second selves of analyst and analysand] that personal experience can become possible that will at times transcend in richness and intensity what is ordinarily possible even in the most intimate of daily relationships.
>
> *(pp. 291–292)*

Schafer here isolates just what we are looking for, namely, a baseline feeling of love independent of the particular feelings evoked in particular analysts by particular patients. And we note that it is conditioned by the analyst's own affirmative, generative, creative "construction" of the analysand as the latter presents himself within a constructed reality of the analytic relationship. Like Racker, Schafer believes that the analyst's efforts at understanding in themselves tend to awaken a lovelike feeling. And, in line with his narrational view of human reality, he believes that a lovelike feeling is due partly to a quality of wholeness and esthetic "rightness" that crowns the analyst's efforts (as well as the patient's).

## STEINGART'S APPERCEPTIVE CAPTURING

Steingart (1995) is one of the few authors to elaborate at length on the relationship between the psychoanalyst's understanding and love. Like Loewald, Steingart emphasizes the real love that is evoked by any object of intense and devoted study. Like Schafer, he believes that the analyst's specific functioning brings out in him a more reliably appreciative, loving attitude. One might say that the analyst tends to assume a more ideally altruistic, sensitive, and universally humane persona. But besides describing the analyst's altruistic ideals, Loewald, Schafer, and Steingart all emphasize the analyst's apperceptive *activity*. In characterizing that activity, Schafer stresses its creative component, while Steingart argues that it is a hunt for objective truth. The object of fascination, says Steingart, is the patient's in-and-of-itself psychic reality, so the analyst's studious, noninterfering, all-accepting, nontendentious activity can be compared with "wrapping" his mental state around the analysand's associations.

Though both Schafer and Steingart agree with Loewald that devoted study is already a form of love, they do not wish to leave it at that. In Schafer's picture we can imagine the personal affect that analytic understanding might generate in an analyst's more ideal "second self." That feeling might exceed qualitatively if not quantitatively the love of a natural scientist for his object, especially when it is augmented by the analyst's own creative exercise in making coherent sense out of his perceptions. Steingart approaches the matter of passion slightly differently. Taking issue with Schafer's theory of the analyst's creative constructivism, he defines the analyst as ideally intruding no wish or goal into his perception of the patient, and he denies that the analyst at work assumes a fictive and higher "second self." Where, then, does Steingart find the analyst's extra affection that goes beyond the scholar's ordinary passion? He finds it in the *way* that analytic understanding is gained and, in particular, in the experience of "the immediately felt transference or (possible) countertransference, or an experience of some sort of empathic realization" (p.111). In this connection he quotes Loewald (1979): "It is a curious fact that unless the patient feels understood we feel we have not fully understood him" (pp. 381–382). Here and elsewhere Steingart makes it clear that the understanding he is equating with love includes – and is not just derived from – the personal impact of patient and analyst on each other, and some degree of meshing of their movements. One gets the impression that the analyst's loving understanding, although it includes conceptual abstraction as found in an interpretation, is something more than that – something like a "feel" for the patient. In Bertrand Russell's terms, we might say that it is an (exponentially heightened) knowledge by acquaintance; it might even be the most intense knowledge possible of a singular existence. And that is certainly the impression we get also from Loewald and Schafer.

In these three accounts, there remains some ambiguity about the object of the analyst's love. We might say that Loewald's analyst loves the patient's mind (and its potential for development), Schafer's the patient's person, and Steingart's the patient's psychic reality, or mind. There may be significant differences in these terminologies; certainly, patients would think so.

## THE NOVICKS' WORKING PARTNERSHIP LOVE

In a careful, technically usable exposition, Novick and Novick (2000) have accepted the transference status of the analyst's love and its ordinary libidinal nature. Accepting those "dangerous" characterizations, they use their frankness to caution against what they consider sadomasochistic perversions of love, which is their description of overidealizing relationships that gratify fantasies of power and dependency (in either party, or alternating between them). Like Schafer, the Novicks endorse an appreciation that is to be distinguished from idealization. They issue the customary general caution against the analyst's unsublimated love, but they also identify specific danger signs to help him avoid it. In general, it seems to me, they suppose that proper analytic love emerges under conditions of social rolelessness. Respecting the essential meaning of analytic neutrality, the Novicks specify that proper analytic love fits into none of the ordinary dramas of social life. That is consistent with the analytic principle of seeking no particular attitude from the patient. But the Novicks do not imagine that love arises in a totally ungratified analyst. I think they picture the sort of affection that a hard worker usually feels for a coworker who fosters his project and affirms his competence. Providing heuristic categories as they do, the Novicks tend to portray a perfectly freeing and undemanding relationship as a norm rather than as an asymptote to be approached.

But though they do not think of it as the universal background to analysis, the Novicks recognize that some patients push for what they call a closed relationship; they know that some patients want more than a working project, and the authors hope the analyst will be informed by this but not seduced.

So we might say that the Novicks' formula for the analyst's love is a combination of positive and negative features. They seem to recognize loving fantasies in the properly functioning analyst, but only the sort of fantasies that accompany this peculiar work project – a project characterized by the effort to take social distance from someone who is seeking social closeness. Of course, satisfactions from work and competence do identify ordinary social roles. And, in fact, according to the Novicks, it is precisely because they are not achievable without the patient's cooperation that love for the patient can arise in their fulfillment. It seems that the analyst can have his affection stirred by being "allowed" the successful exercise of his competence in the analytic quest, with the patient reaping the reward for his inexplicit mediation, as well as for his visible cooperation.

## INGREDIENTS IN THE ANALYST'S LOVE

Among the clues to the nature of the analyst's love that we have found in Racker, Schafer, and Steingart are the following: (1) The analyst's love may be induced by the analyst's own activity. (2) The analyst's love may be compared with the

188   The psychoanalytic phenomenon

appreciation of art and literature, as well as to the study of a natural object. (3) Love may be generated by intimate acquaintance arising from the impact of transference passion (and its interplay with countertransference).

## LOVE AND UNDERSTANDING

In line with Freud's comment that the analyst manifests a particular affection, "a substitute for love" (Breuer & Freud 1895), analysts have vaguely assumed that they offer something besides their own transference and countertransference (as strictly defined). Since what analysts offer, apart from transference and countertransference, is understanding, understanding was bound to be what analysts would identify as the love substitute. (Reassuringly, "understanding" sounds like the "attention and concern" that Freud originally identified as the love substitute.) Nevertheless, understanding seems a rather bloodless sort of love, and, as we have seen, analysts have now and then bravely ventured to put some juice in it.

They are helped by a deeper understanding of understanding. Early analysts tended to picture their understandings as simple registrations of the patient's unconscious, supplemented by a recognition of universal symbolism. In our new view, understanding includes the analyst's unconscious *reactions* (wishes and fears) and *personal* associations. In general, a fuller psychology of the analyst at work has been developed (see, e.g., Brenner 1976; Jacobs 1991). If the analyst's understanding involves this fuller libidinal, cognitive, and autobiographical response, it would seem to be more available as a carrier of his love.

But that poses problems. In the first place, this love would seem to be a little too much like ordinary love to allow the patient the freedom (and frustration) that analysis requires. Second, as we have seen, if understanding requires an emotionally positive response by the analyst, it would seem too chancy and not universally available (though this was challenged by Nacht, Racker, and Tower.)

The first worry is usually allayed by supposing that the analyst's emotional responses are scaled down and fed into cognitive machinery that bleaches them of their libidinal aim, leaving only their informational content. Unfortunately, that proviso sends understanding back to a state of bloodlessness that doesn't mesh with what people mean by "love."

But we have noted other possibilities in the literature. For one thing, though understanding might be bloodless, the *effort* to understand is a *striving*. We have seen Racker deliberately *try* to rid himself of negative feeling, and restore familiar positive ones, and we have watched Schafer start a circular reaction of affection beginning with a deliberate act of empathy. Klauber (1981) wrote that analysts funnel their frustrated libidinal feelings and need for recognition into interpretations, which are thus emissaries of love. These are all personal strivings that are nevertheless thought to be characteristic of the entire profession. The striving, moreover, must push past obstacles both of the patient's making and of the analyst's discipline. Racker observed that nobody struggles without libidinal fuel, but it may be just as true that this reaching for a patient *generates* a libidinal charge. Since these strivings are initiated at the behest of both personal and professional motives, they might stimulate feelings common to all analysts with all patients. Such feelings might conceivably include something like love. Schafer (1983) suggests that the analyst is actually a better person in the consulting room than in the rest of his life, and that if a patient is the stimulus for the analyst's feeling himself a better person, the analyst may find the patient lovable on that account. The patient earns affection for bringing out the analyst's sense of his goodness that Schafer describes. Klauber (1989) adds that even the illusion of loving is a liberation, and we may presume that the analyst may develop real gratitude for this liberation-by-illusion within himself.

Moreover, it is not just the analyst who tries to understand; the patient joins in the effort. Coworkers often bond affectionately, especially over a long stretch of time, and especially when they have survived harrowing trials together. Further, the patient over time affirms the analyst's effectance, and that feedback may generate affectionate feelings.

Thus, we might say that analysts do offer patients a kind of love, inasmuch as a kind of love is produced by the act and effort of trying to understand patients, and the experience of working alongside them through many trials. The trouble is that the same thing might be said of any investigative psychotherapy, and I think that analysts have wanted to identify the love they feel with something more particularly psychoanalytic. For instance, we have noted that analysts are inclined to identify their love with powerful and fundamental growth endorsement, and that is where child-rearing metaphors come in. But it is also where the growth endorsements and child-rearing metaphors go out, since analysts are not supposed to infantilize patients. Indeed, one can imagine many nonpsychoanalytic therapies that oblige the therapist to assume a much more blatantly parental attitude. Is there no special love-equivalent generated by what is specifically psychoanalytic in psychoanalytic understanding?

## PSYCHOANALYTIC APPERCEPTION AND LOVE

Love is not stirred by even the most complete psychoanalytic case report, which proves that ordinary understanding is not the love we are looking for. The presumably loving understanding we are looking for is related to the personal "take" that occurs in a live encounter and, more especially, to the faithful, comprehensive, detailed, and highly individualized personal take that is the peculiarity of a psychoanalytic understanding. That is the aspect of the encounter that Steingart (1995) describes so evocatively.

But that does not mean that an ordinary "reading" type of understanding is irrelevant to love. The kind of understanding stimulated by reading a novel, for example, may yet offer some important pointers for our inquiry (see Schafer 1983).

It is the nature of the psychoanalytic inquiry to lay out a whole life before the eyes of both participants. As Schafer (1983, 1992) demonstrates, a patient's life presents a passage organized in terms of purposeful strivings and disappointments.

**190** The psychoanalytic phenomenon

In other words, patients see themselves, and are seen by us, in a narrative context. Witnessing a whole life in those terms is to be engaged with the equivalent of a work of narrative art. (Another example might be the sad, esthetic recall of a loved one who has just died, when the impact of the person's life as a completed whole forces itself on the mourners.) Narratives synthesize actions, character, and plot with the exigencies of fortune. Contemporary hermeneutic philosophers, such as Ricoeur (1984–1988), say that the coherence of the plot exhibits more than what is given in its details – indeed, more than we can possibly spell out – because the overall story projects a whole, special world. Regarded this way, what the patient's life course illustrates is not just the operation of universal psychological laws, such as informs our understanding of a case history. If a causal theory of the mind entirely absorbed the analyst's awareness, there would be no room for any sort of love except the love of scientific truth.

Further, as Ricoeur observes of readers, the analyst's own preexisting world and his sense of himself always contain meaning not yet worked out. The analyst's "horizon" (as the hermemeuticists like to call it) acquires new vistas as it overlaps with the patient's world. Analysts have frequently remarked on the self-healing or self-improvement that accrues from their activity.

Thus, we should not be too quick to give up the comparison between the analyst's love for the patient and a reader's "love" for someone in a novel or play. No doubt, specific fantasies make up the bulk of both loves. But there may be a universal remainder: both patients and fictional characters may represent, in their very individuality, an illumination of the universal moral field. Indeed, Loewald's procedure of reading a future actualization into the patient's as yet unformulated potential is a kind of *reading* love of the patient. And, of course, it fits with Schafer's view (1992).

Even if there is some cogency in these reflections, analysts will recognize in them a serious danger of sentimentality (leading, for example, to infantilization or idealization of the patient). For that reason, analysts rely on a neutral picture of lawfully related mental objects to offset their appreciation of social/human/mean-ingful/dramatic/ethical/valuational "objects" (and remind them of their treatment obligations). Ideally, the analyst reacts on all these levels, and ultimately uses a sober vision of mental objects to balance his ethical and dramatic responses to the patient. If he just "read" and appreciated the drama of the patient's life, he would end up an actor inside it. But, by the same token, were he restricted to a theoretical view alone, he could not establish the necessary human bond or blend general information and particular circumstance into an understanding of the individual.

## LOVE ARISING FROM NONRESPONSIVENESS

Were we to tell a patient that his analyst's love is something like a "reading" love he would likely recoil, imagining his analyst to be entertaining himself in amused detachment. This image is far from the taxing reality of practice. Although the loving understanding that analysts have been trying to pin down bears some resemblance to the understanding involved in reading, it is surely not the same thing. The analyst's understanding is more responsible, personal, alive, and unsettled. An analyst who is compared to the reader of a novel will feel accused of more voyeurism than is warranted.

And yet, it seems to me, if there is a specifically psychoanalytic feeling of a loving sort it may partly arise from the very nonresponsiveness and noninvolvement that is the hallmark of our trade. Indeed, if nonresponsiveness and non-involvement acted only as restraints and did not help to generate loving feelings, we would probably have to conclude that psychoanalysts do not offer any especially psychoanalytic kind of love.

How might the analyst's detachment combine with intense involvement to generate a loving feeling? What makes analytic listening different from reading, and from several other types of psychotherapy, is the fact that analysts feel themselves personally addressed by their patients, both in speech and in silence. They feel addressed – always by way of indirect, and often by direct, appeal. As Steingart has emphasized, the analyst's understanding does not consist of some final conclusion; it includes the experience of the arduous journey that led to the conclusion, especially the road through transference and countertransference.

Being personally addressed while being largely nonreactive is a little like being addressed while in disguise. The analyst sees the patient's gaze upon him, but imagines that it is not really he who is seen. (Please note that I am describing an aspect of the *analyst's* experience, not the patient's. I am not referring to Freud's "mirror," which is meant to describe the *patient's* experience. The debate about how much of the real analyst the patient sees is irrelevant to our inquiry.) The experience is not the same as watching a person (or a character in a novel) who takes no action toward one. It is a closer and more powerful experience than that. Of course the analyst is not actually in disguise. He is more personally addressed than that. Yet he does not feel the appeal to have been fully earned – it seems in some respect misaddressed.

The analyst, although standing in the crosshairs of the patient's sights, is aware of being not fully the person intended. Being squarely in the focus, the analyst cannot help but react, and his reactive feelings (colored by his personal proclivities) help to identify what it is that the patient desires. Perhaps there is no other way that a personal appeal can be experienced so purely. To follow my thought, the reader is invited to consider the analyst's mid-position between two more familiar types of relationship. First, look at an ordinary social partner, who feels genuinely and fully intended when addressed. He will perceive the appeal for a response in the light of its possible outcomes for himself, filtered through his own hopes, fears, and capacities. He feels the interaction most acutely; one might say he appreciates it most specifically. (It is "knowledge by acquaintance.") But his vision is heavily skewed by his own interest. Next consider an uninvolved, third-party witness (as the analyst often is when the patient is recounting events in daily life). This bystander's vision has a little more "purity" or "innocence" because he can appreciate the appeal more "disinterestedly" (and voyeuristically). He is protected by a mode of

## 192 The psychoanalytic phenomenon

discourse that does not directly involve him. But as a third party he pays for that advantage, forfeiting the full thrust and true meaning of the appeal, which is something that can be weighed up only inside the partner to whom it is delivered. Further, if someone tells us about a scene in his life, our imagination of the narrator's authorial intent is overlaid with our guesses about his intention as an actor within the scene he is describing, and is further interlaced with our own way of construing the narrated situation. We must work hard to disentangle all this in our analytic listening. (That is one reason we are sometimes advised to confine our attention to the concealed appeal that motivates the telling of the story.) But now look at the psychoanalyst's position, or rather that aspect that is unique to him as an analyst. When the psychoanalyst feels the direct brunt of the appeal (by which I mean the request or desire that is implicit in every communication to another person), and simultaneously manages to disidentify with its proper object, that appeal is appreciated in its full intensity while yet being relatively untainted by the analyst's own aims and capacities. The place of the interpersonal appeal in the life of the patient is alone on the scene.

It can only add poignancy to this loving "reading" that, in order for it to come about, the analyst must struggle to disengage from the thrust of the patient's appeal. (That can involve taking distance from a transference bid, or even just resisting the focus of attention that the patient is guiding the analyst toward.) That very struggle acquaints the analyst with the essence of the patient's striving. (Many analysts believe that they register important appeals by a delayed recognition of their own unwitting collusion.) On one level, analysts always respond in an ordinary fashion, weaving the patient's appeal into their own skein of memories and fantasies. But, as Jacobs (1991) illustrates, they then endeavor to objectify this effect and the features of the patient that produced it, thus furthering their detachment. This sort of detachment tends to decrease erotic love but it may increase a reading "love." Ricoeur (1981, 1984–1988) describes a similar rhythm of immersion and objectification in understanding a text. He writes that the appreciator must first separate what he is looking at from his own view of it – it must be objectified. Only then can the appreciator try to feel a way *into* it. Having first tried to see the work on its *own* terms, he can then grasp both the strangeness and the familiarity of the universe that is opened up to him by the story. Analogously, we may say that the analyst detaches himself from the patient's view in order to see its organic unity.

So perhaps we can describe the analyst's experience of analytic love this way: It is the personal, first-hand experience of the patient's appeal solely in terms of its value for the patient and its place in the patient's drama. Since such an appreciation is likely to further the ultimate interests of the patient, it would also have the "promoting" quality that common sense accords to love, and would contribute also to the patient's feeling loved. Among all the many false clues in the psychoanalytic situation that seem to signal that the analyst loves his patient (encouragement of transference, the analyst's self-effacing attention, etc.), here we may have one clue that is not illusory.

We might therefore suppose that an actual, loving feeling is generated by the union of the two special analytic features – the taking of distance, and immersion in the patient's experience – that cause the analyst to be affected in a unique fashion by the drama of a patient's striving. This might be the phenomenological counterpart to the abstract formula that love equals the analyst's understanding. I remind the reader again of the evident fact that, should there be such an affect as I have described, it would merely add to the enormous variety of ordinary, much more powerful feelings and forms of attachment that individual analysts develop toward their different partners, as occasioned by the match.

I offer this not as the definitive candidate for the analyst's special love, or even as a candidate for it at all, but only as one possible aspect of one of the many ingredients of it that have been suggested over the years. The loving feeling I refer to might accompany Racker's continuous transformation of complementary into concordant transferences, and Kohut's experience of being the sort of selfobject that does not use the patient as a selfobject. My way of framing the possibility differs only slightly, and only in emphasis, from such authors as Loewald, Schafer, and Steingart.

## STERN'S MATERNAL PLAY

Although I have not tried to be comprehensive in my survey, I must at least mention a more recent relevant discourse, though it is not labeled as a discussion of love. Observations of mother–infant interaction have led some theorists, such as Stern (1998), to suggest that the analyst shares with the patient a kind of interpersonal joy in spontaneous discovery that previously had been an ingredient in maternal love. *This* analytic understanding is not conceptual. It is an intuitive, creative, existential recognition, and if we accept it as a form of love, it is a kind that is supposedly unrelated to the old libidinal satisfaction. A formula like that allows the analyst's display of understanding to be regarded as an affective exchange without hazard of lustful fixation. It is different from Loewald's recognition of the patient's potential, in that it is not a translation into a higher order of articulation, but rather a momentary recognition of an immediately available new development. If we ask what exactly the analyst is loving when he loves a patient, Loewald's answer would be that the analyst loves the patient's essence – the creative source of the person's life developments. In contrast, Stern's more existential theory would suggest that the analyst's love is an inclination to join the patient in creating novel relationships, and to enjoy the resulting pleasure in the emergence of novelty. One can see the tendency in current thinking to make analytic love more acceptable by breaking mother love down into behavioral elements, such as mentalization, playful interaction, and the like (Fonagy et al. 2002), thus legitimizing the analyst's parental self-image in a time of egalitarianism.

## CONCLUSION

I have drawn out and emphasized one thread – the ordinary impact on the analyst of the "un-reception" of the patient's appeal, which is felt but not accepted. I am

## 194 The psychoanalytic phenomenon

referring to a peculiar intimacy that can be experienced only by someone who is in many respects a merely virtual partner. I suggest that the poignancy of this particular kind of one-sided intimacy is capable of generating particular affects in the analyst on a thoroughly real basis, apart from the playful or fictive elements in treatment that are described by Schafer. This visceral impact would supplement the "reading" love that inspires awe of the patient's agonistic coping (Schafer; Steingart). The elementary feeling I have described might help to explain Steingart's principle that the *way* the analyst achieves understanding is part of the loving understanding he achieves. That principle needs some elaboration. Why, after all, isn't the route to knowledge registered simply as accumulated evidence rather than as an affective state? The answer implied by Steingart (and previously proposed by Heimann and by Tower) is that when it comes to human beings, in contrast to other studied objects, the personal appeal by the object of study has to be felt to be known. I suggest that the peculiar way it is felt may create an affect all by itself, in addition to supplying the matter to be known.

## Notes

1 Her solution to the problem of individual match vs. general effectiveness bears some resemblance to Boesky's idea (1997) that patients resolve their intrapsychic problem by working out one or another of its manifestations in a relationship problem that matches the analyst's. There is also a kinship with the thesis of Bird (1972).
2 Lear (1990) has discussed the role of Eros in treatment in a particularly interesting fashion.

## REFERENCES

Balint, M. (1949/1953). Changing therapeutic aims and techniques in psychoanalysis. In: *Primary Love and Psycho-Analytic Technique*. New York: Liveright, pp. 221–235.

Berman, L. (1949). Countertransferences and attitudes of the analyst in the therapeutic process. *Psychiatry*, 2: 59–166.

Bird, B. (1972). Notes on transference: Universal phenomenon and hardest part of analysis. *Journal of the American Psychoanalytic Association*, 20: 267–301.

Boesky, D. (1997). The art and craft of psychoanalysis. Paper presented to the American Psychoanalytic Association, December 20, 1997, New York.

Brenner, C. (1976). *Psychoanalytic Technique and Psychic Conflict*. New York, NY: International Universities Press.

Breuer, J. & Freud, S. (1895). *Studies on Hysteria*. Standard Edition, 2.

Ferenczi, S. (1928/1955). The elasticity of psycho-analytic technique. In: *Final Contributions to the Problems and Methods of Psycho-Analysis*. London: Hogarth Press, pp. 87–102.

Ferenczi, S. (1988). *The Clinical Diary of Sandor Ferenczi*, ed. J. Dupont. Cambridge, MA: Harvard University Press.

Fliess, R. (1942). The metapsychology of the analyst. *Psychoanalytic Quarterly*, 11: 211–227.

Fonagy, P., Gergely, G., Jurist, E. L. & Target, M. (2002). *Affect Regulation, Mentalization, and the Development of the Self*. New York, NY: Other Press.

Freud, S. (1906/1988). Letter #8F to Jung. In: *The Freud/Jung Letters*, ed. W. McGuire. Cambridge, MA: Harvard University Press, pp. 11–13.

Gabbard, G. (1996). *Love and Hate in the Analytic Setting*. Northvale, NJ: Aronson.

Gitelson, M. (1952). The emotional position of the analyst in the psychoanalytic situation. *International Journal of Psychoanalysis*, 33: 1–10.

Gitelson, M. (1962). Contribution to symposium on the curative factors in psychoanalysis. *International Journal of Psychoanalysis*, 43:194–205.

Heimann, P. (1950). On counter-transference. *International Journal of Psychoanalysis*, 31: 81–84.

Jacobs, T. (1991). *The Use of the Self: Countertransference and Communication in the Analytic Situation*. New York, NY: International Universities Press.

King, P. (1962). Contribution to symposium on the curative factors in psychoanalysis. *International Journal of Psychoanalysis*, 43: 194–234.

Klauber, J. (1981). *Difficulties in the Psychoanalytic Encounter*. New York, NY: Aronson.

Klauber, J. (1989). The role of illusion in the psychoanalytic cure. In: *Dimensions of Psychoanalysis*, ed. J. Sandler. London: Karnac Books, pp. 165–175.

Kohut, H. (1977). *The Restoration of the Self*. New York, NY: International Universities Press.

Lear, J. (1990). *Love and Its Place in Nature: A Philosophical Interpretation of Freudian Psychoanalysis*. New Haven, CT: Yale University Press.

Loewald, H. (1960). On the therapeutic action of psycho-analysis. *International Journal of Psychoanalysis*, 41:16–33.

Loewald, H. (1960/1980). The therapeutic action of psychoanalysis. In: *Papers on Psychoanalysis*. New Haven, CT: Yale University Press, pp. 221–256.

Loewald, H. (1970/1980). Psychoanalytic theory and the psychoanalytic process. In: *Papers on Psychoanalysis*. New Haven, CT: Yale University Press, pp. 277–301.

Loewald, H. (1979). Reflections on the psychoanalytic process and its therapeutic potential. In: *Papers on Psychoanalysis*. New Haven, CT: Yale University Press, pp. 372–383.

Loewald, H. (1988). *Sublimation: Inquiries into Theoretical Psychoanalysis*. New Haven, CT: Yale University Press.

Money-Kyrle, R. E. (1956). Normal counter-transference and some of its deviations. *International Journal of Psychoanalysis*, 37: 360–366.

Myerson, P. (1994). Expressions of countertransference and the curative process. *Contemporary Psychoanalysis*, 30: 213–235.

Nacht, S. (1962). Contribution to symposium on the curative factors in psycho-analysis. *International Journal of Psychoanalysis*, 43: 194–234.

Novick, J. & Novick, K. (2000). Love in the therapeutic alliance. *Journal of the American Psychoanalytic Association*, 48: 189–218.

Racker, H. (1968). *Transference and Countertransference*. New York, NY: International Universities Press.

Reich, A. (1951). On counter-transference. *International Journal of Psychoanalysis*, 32: 25–31.

Ricoeur, P. (1981). *Hermeneutics and the Human Sciences: Essays on Language, Action and Interpretation*, ed. J. Thompson. Cambridge: Cambridge University Press.

Ricoeur, P. (1984–1988). *Time and Narrative*. 3 vols. Chicago, IL: University of Chicago Press.

Sandler, J., Dare, C. & Holder, A. (1973). *The Patient and the Analyst: The Basis of the Psychoanalytic Process*. New York, NY: International Universities Press.

Schafer, R. (1983). *The Analytic Attitude*. New York, NY: Basic Books.

Schafer, R. (1992). *Retelling a Life: Narration and Dialogue in Psychoanalysis*. New York, NY: Basic Books.

Segal, H. (1962). Contribution to symposium on the curative factors in psycho-analysis. *International Journal of Psychoanalysis*, 43: 194–234.

Spitz, R. (1956). Countertransference: Comments on its varying role in the analytic situation. *International Journal of Psychoanalysis*, 4: 256–265.

## 196 The psychoanalytic phenomenon

Steingart, I. (1995). *A Thing Apart: Love and Reality in the Therapeutic Relationship*. Northvale, NJ: Aronson.

Stern, D. (1998). Non-interpretive mechanisms in psychoanalytic therapy. The "something more" than interpretation. *International Journal of Psychoanalysis, 79*: 903–921.

Stone, L. (1961). *The Psychoanalytic Situation*. New York, NY: International Universities Press.

Tower, L. (1956). Countertransference. *Journal of the American Psychoanalytic Association*, 4: 224–265.

Winnicott, D.W. (1960/1965). Counter-transference. In: *The Maturational Processes and the Facilitating Environment*. New York, NY: International Universities Press, pp. 158–165.

# 12

# WHAT IS PSYCHOANALYSIS?[1]

Good evening, friends! How do I know you're my friends? Look at my title. In the year 2004, who but friends would come to a talk entitled "What Is Psychoanalysis?" You might as well have signed up for "Is There Life After Death?" What is psychoanalysis – indeed! A tired, old, useless question is what it is, right? We don't fuss like that any more. You thought, "Have you no sense of decency, Larry, at long last? Have you left no sense of decency?" "This is psychoanalysis!" "That's not psychoanalysis!" Oh, not once again, after a century of yapping dogfights.

Who cares what's psychoanalysis? What difference does it make? The patent expired long ago, and the label doesn't sell anyway. What counts for each of us is what we like and value in what we're doing. We say: "I like the intimate contact," "I like helping people understand themselves and expand their meanings," "I like seeing people achieve their goals," "I like discovering unconscious fantasies," "I like radical honesty, or empathy, or finding how the brain secretes a mind," "I like philosophizing about the human condition." For each of our likes, there's an interesting theoretical elaboration these days, and that's what psychoanalysis is for each of us. No more ancestor worship. We try to stay compatible with science as it moves forward, and for the rest, we do what we find value in doing. End of subject.

And yet ... and yet ... what a shame if something special, strange, and unnatural, something weird and different from other human doings, just disappeared before we fathomed what it meant and what it could do.

So, while many of our colleagues are remodeling treatment from the ground up – reasoning it out, or doing what works, or putting it together from pieces of neurobiology and infant observation – all of them worthwhile, and indeed necessary, projects – I propose we ferret out what was special in the old psychoanalysis, what was strange, weird, unique, and ask not "How can we make it more reasonable?," but "What sensible idea can we wring from its original weirdness?"

## 198 The psychoanalytic phenomenon

To view the full freakishness of psychoanalysis, I suggest we look backward in time – watch the unnatural monster stir the tranquil tarn of reasonable procedure, watch it rise up and twist itself into bizarre rules. And then watch its torque relax, watch its unnatural shape unwind, and see the monster sink reassuringly back into the peaceful, green foam of common sense.

What I'll narrate is, in effect, four amateur monster movies. They are four extremely out-of-focus camera angles on psychoanalytic treatment as it first lurched into its famous eccentricity. They share a common plot, of course; it's just one monster. You must prepare yourself for loads of redundancy, as the various snapshots capture the same features over and over again. And above all, please don't confuse monsters with demons. Monsters should be approached with tenderness and fond appreciation.

A monster is the solitary representative of an endangered species. Listening to what follows, you might occasionally think of the shy, beloved Nessie in her deep Loch Ness.

You will notice that I mostly avoid technical terms. The whole purpose of analytic terms was to dress the scaly monster in a business suit. Unusual terms make the monster look (professionally) normal. Conversely; normal terms show how unnatural the monster is, and that is my purpose. Mind you, I'm not one of Strachey's ungrateful detractors. My aim is not to reclaim Freud for common sense, but, on the contrary, to light up the early unnaturalness of psychoanalytic treatment and its subsequent normalization.

## I

My first story is about a venerable medical triad.

Psychoanalysis emerged from an age-old, three-stage, medical procedure that you're all familiar with. The protoanalyst of *Studies on Hysteria* (Breuer & Freud 1893–1895) first examined his patient, then diagnosed her illness, and then treated her. You know what I mean: The patient was interrogated, a traumatic memory was discovered, and a treatment manipulation was carried out that might consist of inserting the memory into the patient's awareness. Nothing strange about that, no sneaky twists or turns, no funny posturing; the physician was a physician and looked like one.

Now watch what happened as psychoanalysis took on its special shape: These three procedures all morphed into one single thing – one odd, nearly indescribable new thing. The examination, the diagnosis, and the treatment, now almost indistinguishable, were tightly fused together for an indefinite term. No formal examination was conducted. The examining collapsed into the diagnosing (by which I mean that the disorder might be defined as the sum of the treatment reactions). And, apart from a few gross categories, the diagnosing, in turn, was totally identified with the treatment, since all the treatment amounted to was a leisurely tracing of causes and connections.

And what, you may ask, had become of the treatment manipulation? Ah, that! That was not even to be mentioned any more. Something strange had happened to it. Where the physician's manipulation used to be, there we find, instead, references to the patient's transference and regression. These diagnostic labels neatly concealed the analyst's own seductive procedure, including the tempting freedom he allows, and his continuous, selfless attention, which, to primates like us, effectively signals love.

Insofar as responsibility for this seductive effect was acknowledged at all, it was studiously attributed to the background setup (which got credit for "permitting" "regression"). An analyst would not be an analyst if he actually *intended* that manipulative effect; the treatment specifically depends on his *not* intending it. The old medical manipulation had escaped from the analyst's now-innocent hands and fluttered up into the office draperies, so to speak. Indeed, manipulation was so thoroughly cloaked in the examination that even you modern free thinkers listening to this are shocked to hear me talk about manipulation and seduction. Although a few writers knew better (including Freud, in some places [1925, pp. 4041], and Macalpine [1950]), analysts were asked to think that the only proper manipulation was the patient's own action on himself.

As a result, analysts were required to be professionally responsible for something they didn't think they were doing. They had been hired to cure, but had somehow packed their treatment tools into what looked like a diagnostic test. "I only analyze," they would say complacently. And, ideally, that was, indeed, supposed to be their sole interest. Things were beginning to seem a lot queerer than they used to. The ordinary man would say, "Well, now that I know what's wrong with me, how does that help? When does the treatment begin?" (Indeed, general psychotherapists actually hear that question more often than they'd like.) It's a tribute to the power of cultural custom that this weird, apparently nontreatment treatment came to seem halfway normal in the twentieth century. And it is no surprise that it started coming apart almost at once, freeing each cramped ingredient to pursue its own renormalization.

The first element to break out of the amalgam was the manipulation (guided by a measure of diagnosis). No longer content to hide, manipulation came out of the closet in the straightforward form of after-parenting, or after-education – a term unwisely made available by Freud himself (1916, p. 312), and pursued first by Carl Jung (1930, p. 33), and then by three great Hungarians and a lovable Englishman.[2]

Another early proponent was the much maligned Franz Alexander, who first suggested a superego–ectomy (Alexander 1925, pp. 25ff.), but later (in effect) settled for a small transplant (Alexander 1956). (By this figure of speech, I do not mean to perpetuate the misunderstanding that Alexander advocated coddling patients.) In a harsher fashion, Herman Nunberg (1928) thought implicit threats (of withdrawal of the analyst's interest) were necessary, while more recently, John Gedo (1979) has been frank enough to open the package in broad daylight and select appropriate manipulation for certain conditions. David Raphling (1996, 2002) valued the subtle directiveness of all analytic treatments, and Irwin Hoffman (1998) turned unapologetically to intermittent manipulation.

Psychoanalysis has understandably shunned studies of manipulation, but in view of the fact that human interaction is intrinsically manipulative, this innocence

## 200 The psychoanalytic phenomenon

comes at a price. Of course, the historical and essential thrust of psychoanalysis has been to minimize manipulation, but the very effort to block normal, interactive manipulation has got to involve a manipulation of its own. Indeed, just because it is so essentially preoccupied with manipulation (in a negative sort of way), psychoanalysis is in the best position to deepen our understanding of manipulation beyond the simple, dramatic schematisms of common sense. But that project would have to bypass fearful debates about whether manipulation is evil, and whether analysis is free of it. The challenge should be neither avoided nor abbreviated, but exploited, as it was by Ferenczi in his 1912 analysis of suggestion, much appreciated by Freud.

Non-Freudian psychotherapists, such as the ingenious Leston Havens (1986), Milton Erickson,[3] and many clever family therapists, have experimented fruitfully with manipulation. Within our own circles, you are all familiar with forms of afterparenting inspired by new infant observation and legitimized by the neurophysiology of implicit memory and procedural knowledge. And, at our extreme fringe, professional extractors of abuse memories enjoy the simplicity of honest (i.e., direct) work. Whatever you may think of these procedures, they are procedures, and that's what a person normally expects from a treater.

Next to peel away from the amalgam was the diagnosing. Diagnosing today is liberated to run its own treatment, as the pure act of understanding. Diagnosing – that is, figuring things out – was always the most conspicuous element of the amalgam. It was the package wrapping, to mix my metaphor. Being a mutual activity, the pure act of understanding reduces the inequality between analyst and patient that is so onerous for modern practitioners. And the work of understanding is always welcomed by both parties as a declarable, matter-of-fact activity to counterbalance the uncomfortable fogginess of what is going on – the is-it-offered-or-is-itnot uncertainty about the is-it-personal-or-is-it-professional relationship (which was the manipulation that had been stuffed into the psychoanalytic package).

The natural and most welcome path to normalcy, therefore, is to let diagnosing shake off those appendages – the examination and manipulation – and reclaim its ordinary purity as the plain and simple act of understanding, unadorned by technical constraint. Psychoanalytic theories may sport some pretty fancy concepts, but there is nothing at all strange about trying hard to understand someone by whatever means, and many analysts today have isolated that one normal element (understanding) from the unnatural amalgam. So normal is this element that even some traditional analysts who engage in a more specialized pursuit, declining to use just any old means to understand patients, still can't bring themselves to say flat out that there's something else going on besides understanding. Trying to hold their own against those who recommend self-disclosure or a frank exchange that facilitates the patient's understanding, they may say something like, "The reason you can't do just *anything* to facilitate understanding is that psychoanalysis is only interested in certain kinds of understanding (including, for example, understanding a negative transference)." Thus, even these old-fashioned types may feel obliged to go along with the commonsense view that trying hard to understand someone is what it's all about.

What is psychoanalysis? **201**

This relapse into normalcy is itself a thoroughly normal phenomenon. Quirkiness is hard to sustain, especially when it carries a hint of deviousness. To hobble the sensible, praiseworthy, egalitarian – and, above all, straightforward – pursuit of understanding with those old technical taboos and restraints seems utterly senseless to today's more normal practitioner. Why would an understander ever let arbitrary injunctions stand in the way of *any* good-faith effort to understand a patient? The old rules needlessly mystify a perfectly clear task; they bar many ways of examining the patient; they fuss up the cooperative work of diagnosis, and they clog it with a lot of pretentious hocus-pocus. We all yearn for normalcy. What psychoanalyst isn't happiest saying, "I don't believe in technique: I just try to understand my patients"?

So now we have scrutinized the bizarre monster's lumpy fusion of *examination, diagnosis,* and *treatment,* and we have observed its subsequent devolution into normal parts.

And I turn to my second monster sighting.

## II

While the psychoanalytic monster was doing something strange to the triad of examination, diagnosis, and treatment, something strange was also happening to the analyst's vision. He had begun with a perfectly ordinary image of the bits and pieces that make up the mind. He could see that some of those pieces gave trouble. A noxious memory was stuck in the mind and couldn't be regurgitated. It would be located and extracted by straight-thinking catharsis technicians who had a sharp eye for foreign bodies. But then, as psychoanalysis took its wild turn, the analyst's vision began to waver; it blurred and jumped around vertiginously. Now he thought he saw bits and pieces of mind that weren't bits and pieces. Somehow it was the whole mind itself – a person, not something stuck in a person – and yet also – how could it be? – still bits and pieces.

For example, there was the bit called resistance. It was a distinct bit, active against other bits, but it was also the patient's unsavory, little ways, and all his desperate wanting; it was the whole patient in a particular act – the act, alas, of fighting the analyst (Freud 1912, p. 108). Or consider the ego. A pretty important bit, you'll agree. But Freud (1937, pp. 240–241), at least, never forgot that it was just a way of considering a whole person; it was a person in his aspect of adaptation, and elaborators of Freud's theory, such as Waelder, Hartmann, and Loewald, made that clear.[4]

The analyst sees a whole patient, whose acts are meaningful and intentional, but he also continues to see a blind organism whose objective parts interact with deterministic, causal force. The rest of the world, in contrast, sees things just one way or the other: the bench scientist sees a human organism; friends and neighbors see a scheming person. Psychoanalysts see both at once, and that makes them very, very weird indeed.

And, as I said, weird is hard to sustain. It tires and yields to normalcy. Vision clears. Vertigo steadies. Nowadays, some analysts look straight at persons – who,

## 202 The psychoanalytic phenomenon

being, after all, not things but persons – are plainly creating unlimited, new meanings in everything they do. We call those analysts hermeneuticists or inter-subjectivists, or perhaps narrativists. Others take the alternative route to normal vision: They look objectively at patients and see amygdalized procedural memories heedlessly repeated, subcortical pathways mindlessly registering danger, left frontal lobes spinning confabulations, and sometimes a random, chaotic, spontaneous novelty generated out of cell membrane potentials. Those are integrative neuropsychoanalysts, and no-nonsense empirical developmentalists, and their work is among the most fascinating of our time.

Either way, whether by taking a consistently hermeneutic or a consistently natural-science view, some analysts have shaken off the clumsy double vision that afflicted psychoanalysis in its odd season. As a bonus, they can also shed the burden of Freud's hybrid theory of mind. Psychoanalytic theory of the mind is too mechanistic for hermeneuticists and too "unscientific" – too philosophical – for observational scientists. As Paul Ricoeur (1970) declared, Freud's theory is what it is precisely because it yokes together heterogeneous terms of force and meaning, cause and motive. Since that odd coupling is no longer necessary for a straight look either at a person or at an organism, psychoanalytic theory of the mind, with its baroque metapsychology, is gratefully abandoned.

I don't suggest that all psychoanalysts have ceased to struggle with the overlap of cause and meaning, any more than they have finally separated diagnosis (understanding) from treatment (technique). Far from it. But in each case, we can see how roads that initially came together in a singularity have tended to diverge again toward normalcy. Now for my third sighting.

## III

In my first sighting, I talked about psychoanalysis in terms of acts – acts of examining, diagnosing, and treating. In my second, I talked about analysis in terms of pictures – pictures of cause-and-effect parts and pictures of meaning-making souls. Now I ask you to consider psychoanalysis in terms of roles – defined roles and ambiguous roles.

Before psychoanalysis took off into strangeness, the protopsychoanalyst was unmistakably a physician, a neurologist, a hypnotist, and a suggestionist. And he was happy to be seen as such, because those socially identifiable roles were part of the treatment. But as he took his peculiar turn, he deliberately shed those recognizable roles and refused to replace them with anything else. Despite the usefulness Freud had previously found in his physicianly image (and would continue to exploit and recommend), he now announced that everything that could possibly characterize a physician must be forfeited. The nature of the relationship was to remain in doubt. The patient was supposed to see him in as many ways as inclined.

For instance, an analyst would not handle a declaration of love the way a physician would and should, nor as behooves any respectable member of society. More significantly, the analyst was not to disclose any special interest, such as the research interest a physician might have, or even the wish for a dream to help him help his patient. He shouldn't even want to figure out the patient while treating her. He was not to confirm that he wanted anything in particular; he let it be known that anything at all would do. In short, the analyst was to be a thoroughly ambiguous figure.

Here is surely a first-class weirdness. As Freud noted and illustrated throughout his *Papers on Technique* (1911–1915), there is no model for this ambiguity in society. Nobody likes it; nobody wants it. And it was bound to wear thin over the years.

And not so many years, at that. Those Hungarians I mentioned quickly settled into identifiable, nurturing postures. Winnicottians and Bionians described themselves as containers. Leo Stone (1961) imagined two mothers, one of closeness and the other of separation. The eternal temptation for analysts to imagine themselves as parents has often been noted. New knowledge gleaned from infant observation has reinforced this temptation.[5]

Few analysts, as I mentioned, see any point in mystifying the simple role of a kindly person trying to understand a partner. It is true that, despite the popularity of the role of understander, many analysts are still reluctant to share confidences with patients, as understanders customarily do in order to show safety and encourage reciprocation. But even anonymous analysts may defend their old ways by saying simply that self-disclosure distracts attention from the patient. In other words, they offer a perfectly normal excuse for their unsociable reticence, saying, "It's supposed to be about the patient and not about me." Fewer and fewer defend the old ambiguity for ambiguity's sake, designed to keep the uncomfortable patient groping and the uncomfortable analyst awkwardly evasive and deceptive. The outlandishness of not declaring what you are up to was bound to be eventually rejected by patient, by analyst, and by society – which, I am afraid, now considers it frankly illegal ("no informed consent").

## IV

My fourth and last monster sighting is harder to document because of the peculiarity of the landscape. Seen close up, the apparently tranquil tarn of common sense was already a little spooky even before psychoanalysis disturbed it. One could detect a mysterious miasma over its surface, causing time to stand still, without past or present. Time, if I may put it this way, is the abnormal part of normal human experience.

So, in our fourth monster sighting, the waters aren't so placid to begin with: the monster in that setting looks a little like a lake fish, and it's harder for me to show you how it could disturb such an already-disturbed scene. But it's a matter of degree. Even against that background, psychoanalysis is still plenty strange. We would see its strangeness best through eyes that are as yet unjaded by analytic training and unhabituated by popular culture. Where can we find such innocent eyes? In one man only. Please join me in a longish and familiar detour through Freud's *Papers on Technique* of 1911 to 1915, where he describes, as I would put it, the discovery of psychoanalytic treatment.

**204** The psychoanalytic phenomenon

Let me remind you that Freud begins *Papers on Technique* by obsessing (and that is the only way to describe it) about why the transference is the main instrument of the resistance. I have two questions about Freud's question: First, why was he surprised that patients wanted something from him, rather than wanting to remember something for themselves? And second, after finally acknowledging that this is exactly what you'd expect from people, why did he nevertheless insist on thinking of patients' actions on him as remembering?

The naive reader who follows the torment that Freud frankly records – his hesitation, disconnections, repeated starts, false conclusions – will imagine that Freud had not yet developed a theory that could explain what he was finding. That naive reader would be wrong. The theory wasn't complete, it's true. But Freud never did finish his theory, and that's because he asked all the relevant questions rather than dodging them for convenience. But his questions outlined what a complete theory would be. He raised these questions as soon as gaps appeared in his answers, so most later developments were foreshadowed early on. Though emphases shifted with selective elaborations, it's hard to find a feature of his later theorizing that isn't present in some form even before the fruitful 1920s.

In particular, Freud had done all kinds of thinking about the relationship between passion and memory, much more than I can allude to in my allotted time here. I will simply cite two suggestive indicators:

a    Already in 1897, Freud wrote to Fliess: "A second important piece of insight tells me that the psychic structures which, in hysteria, are affected by repression are not in reality memories – since no one indulges in memory activity without a motive – but *impulses* that derive from primal scenes" (p. 239, italics in original). (I think Rapaport somewhere pointed to Freud's vacillation as to whether memory or passion was the etiologic agent.)

b    And then again, by 1912 at the latest, Freud recognized that what we loosely call an unconscious memory isn't really a memory at all. He didn't wait for the sophisticated critic to come along, but asked himself, in effect, "How can I call something a memory if it's timeless?"

So we want to take Freud by the collar and say: "Look! You said that objects are fungible. And you said that what's in the unconscious is wishes and wish-fantasies, and you said that wishes latch onto any convenient reality, and you said that, being timeless, unconscious memories aren't experienced as memories. Why – *why* – do you find it so infinitely puzzling that patients are trying to get you to love them in their old way, rather than dutifully calling up scenes of their childhood?"

Many answers come to mind: Freud's habits from hypnotherapy, his preference for rationality, his impatience to make genetic discoveries, and his need to retain a professional distance by locating the patient's demands in another reality. And we should note another stated reason: like the rest of us, Freud found it daunting to carve particular items out of continuous process without the objective justification provided by individual frames, such as separate dreams and reported memories.

But all that doesn't seem to explain the desperation with which Freud clung to the memory retrieval paradigm, or his sense of a rude force that was already hammering at that model, even as he was claiming victory for it in the first of the *Papers on Technique*, "The dynamics of transference" (1912). Suddenly, on the very last page of that essay, with his argument already completed, he throws up his hands, puts his elaborate memory theory aside, and without pretending that it follows from his reasoning, says simply: "In all these reflections, however, we have hitherto dealt only with one side of the phenomenon of transference ... . We must turn our attention to another aspect of the same situation" (p. 107).

You might take that as an announcement that Freud was about to slice the phenomenon from a different theoretical angle. Nothing of the sort. "Another aspect," the "other side," is not another explanation of the phenomenon – it is not an explanation at all. Instead, what follows is a frankly melodramatic – and heartbreakingly realistic – portrayal of the agonistic grappling, and heated, personal struggle of the analyst with his patient.

Freud's just plain awe before that phenomenon pierced the clouds of all the preceding, soothing explanations, and reproached him for leaving his students with exactly no idea at all of what they were in for. It's as though he were warning, "Never mind what I just said about patients hiding; what you have to worry about – and I mean *worry* about – is their seeking." (If you think I'm making this up, go back and read again the disconnected last two pages tacked on to "The dynamics of transference.")

And that leads to our second question: why, after Freud thus boldly acknowledged that patients weren't using him to find memories – weren't even (as he had just assured us) making use of his person just to hide memories – why, after Freud confessed that patients weren't at all interested in memories but were openly seeking him out for satisfaction, why, even then, did he insist that the patient's strivings should nonetheless be thought of as remembering (Freud 1914, p. 150)?

Mind you, when he tells us, now, to consider the transference as remembering, he is not talking about unmasking an eidetic memory. At this point in psychoanalysis, we are no longer dealing with a disguised event that would normally have discharged its affect as a conscious memory. On the contrary: despite Freud's wish to see the process of remembering as a natural activity like breathing, and despite his effort to see transference as conjured up only for the purpose of befogging memory, bitter experience made it clear that these allegedly interfering, current passions are actually the real, natural form of that which he had been calling memory. So – why keep calling them remembering?

I answer both questions this way: Freud had tracked the monster to its ancestral home, the deep tarn of human time. By human time, I mean the way we are, at every moment, at least vaguely aware of our whole life at once, the past alive within us and the future dangling before us. We are at all times made up of an original, enfolding union and a final, absolute extinction, and everything in between. If we lived only in clock time – the physically real moment – transference would either be just the error, or slippage, that Freud had described in *Studies*

**206** The psychoanalytic phenomenon

*on Hysteria* (Breuer & Freud 1893–1895), or else it would be a mere defensive ruse to avoid a presently existing memory, as Freud was regarding it until the last page of "The dynamics of transference" (1912).

All Freud's patients – the Rat Man, for instance – were telling him otherwise. And of the many evidences that patients did not live in the present or in the past, but in both at once, the most glaring was the phenomenon of transference love. In the example of love, and the awkward position it put him in as a therapist, Freud first recognized the inescapable paradox of human time, not to be conjured away by words like fixation. Freud had to now – very, very reluctantly – accept the monster as it was: he was observing a mind and a relationship that was neither past nor present. Freud had tried to remain a therapist of the present. (That's what an abreaction specialist is.) As a practitioner, he knew that patients were somehow stuck in the past, but it took him a while to figure out exactly what that stuckness had to do with the present. Patients eventually made it painfully clear in the transference. When he finally recognized, not just in theory but in the agonizingly real moment, that the past was not really past, and when he realized that this aspect of treatment was its crucial fulcrum, Freud found himself in a never-never land with his patient.

There is a quick and easy way out of that never-never land, and most theorists would have taken it. One could declare this kind of love a charade, like sleep-walking or posthypnotic suggestion. Freud was too honest and thorough a theorist to take that bait. Transference love is as real – and unreal – as any other love. And yet the analyst feels it to be virtual, and he is required to hold that love at a distance without, however, dispersing it. Disrupted intermittently by interpretations, the enchantment of the transference flickers against its mere virtuality, and most analysts have found that flickering to be the hallmark of their craft (see Friedman 2005). Freud's "Observations on transference-love" (1915) – which concludes his *Papers on Technique* – is the diary of a man painfully feeling his way into a role that had no model: he was an actor inside and outside of a passionate, but nevertheless merely virtual, drama.

But what does it mean to say it's a virtual drama? Freud himself asked that question (in his own words, of course). He had bravely declared that all love is virtual (1912, pp. 99–100). In principle, all social reality is transference, as we now realize. So if we need to see the psychoanalytic drama as merely virtual, it can't be because it is make-believe. What renders the psychoanalytic drama virtual, I think, is this: that it boldly exposes the paradox of the past inside the present. The paradox itself is nothing new; it's part of our everyday reality. It's the *exposure* that makes it virtual. Ordinarily, the paradox of the past inside the present is disguised by social responsiveness. When people talk to one another, their responses constantly reassure each other that "yes … it's just me you're talking to, and, of course, it's right now that you're talking." That is precisely what analysts don't say; in fact, not saying it is half their job. That cruel stepping back exposes the non-contemporaneousness of the patient. And it is the unaccustomed spot-light on the person's noncontemporaneousness – his not-all-here-and-not-all-thereness – that makes the contemporary drama feel only virtual.

## What is psychoanalysis? 207

And now, thanks to your patience in accompanying me on this detour through Freud's laboratory, I can report my fourth and last sighting of the monster's rise and fall.

Historically, psychoanalysis emerges out of a perfectly normal activity: a joint effort by two people to recover a memory. There's a mechanics of memory. Both parties work the mechanism. Memory clues emerge, one by one, through a defile of consciousness. That's protopsychoanalysis, circa *Studies on Hysteria* (Breuer & Freud 1893–1895). But as Freud continues to stare at it, the treatment takes a funny turn, and we find him asking his patient *not* to try to remember – in fact, not to try for anything. Even weirder, the analyst is told not to try for anything, even cognitively. This is by any measure the most bizarre twist in the history of psychotherapy, an activity utterly unknown to man, a monster activity if there ever was one: a project purged of purpose.

Regard this well: the analyst is not a contemporary target because he makes no identifiable request. His indifference makes him featureless among one's daily companions. You can't place him in the social order because he wants nothing. The patient's unsolicited responses hurl themselves into a timeless void, revealing timeless purposes. Those purposes are framed in a free-floating, evenly hovering world, and find situations and persons wherever they can. The patient's efforts are no longer seen as firmly set in past or present, and they do not gel in either context. (Lacan described this vividly.)[6] Those efforts are torn from exclusive bondage to the past – an act of mourning. The same process makes those efforts flexible in the present.

It is the active interference with purposes – interference with wishes, efforts, and intentions – that distinguishes analysis from other psychotherapies. And yet like many other therapies, it proceeds as though it were an inquiry rather than an assault – a nifty trick, if I may say so. (If it works, it must have found a welcome. We should ask ourselves what human motive is satisfied – rather than being simply frustrated – by psychoanalytic interference. Is it a drive for mastery, or for play or freedom?) In any event, the term psychoanalysis would henceforth have two different connotations: it would be an analysis in the chemical sense of the word, forcing elements to precipitate out of their compounds, and an analysis in the logician's sense of reflecting on meaning.

Both of these actions – the breaking-down sort of analysis and the contemplative sort of analysis – focus on live, seeking desire. And one chief cleaver is the confusion of time. (I hope you understand that I use terms like desiring and wanting as shorthand for everything involved in a person's strivings, including associated fear, guilt, and punishment. I assume it is a psychoanalytic axiom that these all go together, and are, in turn, accompanied by shades of the patient's perceptions.)

My point here is that this peculiar machine for fracturing intentions, wishes, desires, and perceptions is a humanly unrecognizable activity, dealing with someone as present and past, with time rolled up into each moment of awareness. It is not only unrecognizable – it is painful for both parties. The analyst can react to the patient's approach neither as an illusion from the past, nor as a contemporary

## 208 The psychoanalytic phenomenon

gesture, and so he has no straightforward way to meet it. Consequently, over the decades, analysts have sought out a more normal tense – one that is more normal than the flickering reality of the past in the present.

We note that normalizing tendency already in the 1930s. I've mentioned the Hungarians with their reparenting techniques. Many distinguished traditions, such as Winnicott's (1960), have subsequently endorsed what Balint (1932, 1968) called a new beginning.

There is nothing odd about giving the patient a second chance. It imitates and often improves the long line of someone's life. What it doesn't do is collapse that line in a double vision and double willing of past and present effort and responsibility, since the analyst accepts the parental role, even if he points out that he is replaying the patient's past.

Reparenting is not the only road back to a normal time sense, of course. A didactic analyst can use memories to help a patient see how old patterns shape his current worldview, and by this clear, causal diagram, spare him the perplexing double vision of a self-aware transference reenactment. Some hermeneuticists and narratologists eliminate the past altogether by treating it as an invention of the present. These are all ways of remaining on a consistent level of contemporary reality.

Analysts can also regain normalcy in the opposite way, that is, by regarding everything (including their own behavior) as, essentially, *just* the past, with nothing else to flicker against. Object relations theory is tempting in that respect. And Kleinian theory allows an analyst to stay on a single level of pastness, though that may be more a matter of story line than clinical work, where the distinction between the paranoid-schizoid and depressive positions resembles the flickering contrast of past-in-the-present reality.

How about current models of implicit memory and procedural memory? These are impeccably normal. Nobody has trouble picturing a habit or a reflex. Neurophysiology cuts the Gordian knot of time: everything is present in the tissues right now. You can find a current brain state for every mind state, and it is all in the present. True, organisms have a past – but they exist in the present. It is only the *person* that is not solely in the now. What made Freudian treatment weird was not its viewing action as imprinted by the past; its weirdness lay in imagining that what is alive in the present *is* the past effort itself, not just the effects of that old effort. Once the Freudian monster had arisen, therapists were no longer working on a left-over remnant from childhood; they worked on a whole person stretched out in time. In the monstrous Freudian model, responsibility isn't something long ago, impacting on the present patient; rather, responsibility lies with the patient's continuous, meaningful, intentional authorship that he feels both backward and forward.

Today, by contrast, we talk in a more natural fashion about ways of being with another. Engaging, spontaneous here-and-now treatments aim for novelty, and they powerfully evoke our patients' inherent creativity. By heeding new biological knowledge, we acquire manipulative expertise with adults of the sort that T. Berry Brazelton had with infants. (Brazelton [1978] offers an extremely brief glimpse of how this sort of knowledge can be used, but his counseling techniques were best demonstrated in live practice.) When psychoanalysts dedicate themselves to straightforward understanding and explaining, they take their honorable seat beside the great, traditional, humanistic enterprises of art, music, literature, culture, and the general fellowship of human society. Such newer treatment is all about what human life is always about. When we speak to those issues, even our fond, technical jargon does not estrange us from common sense. Indeed, weird terms like *coconstructed reality* and *intersubjectivity* were actually invented for the express purpose of reassuring us that the lake surface is unruffled and the Freudian monster gone forever. In place of the unnatural Freudian paradoxes, these popular terms bring us back to natural practices common to *all* human socialization and *all* communication.

The sign of today's normalcy is that the old rules – the rules of the *Papers on Technique* – seem to be just that: rules. Rules and regulations. They make no sense. In default of any natural function, such undeniably bizarre rules can only be attributed to the narcissistic or sadistic preference of the old analysts. Unfortunately, people being what they are, historical evidence for that default hypothesis can easily be found.

## CONCLUSION

Now, clearly, anyone who talks about monsters isn't talking history. Psychoanalysis wasn't just one thing at its beginning, and it didn't move forward along straight lines. What I've been projecting is what the sociologist Max Weber called Ideal Types. And about those types I've told you nothing you didn't already know. Everyone knows that analysis was originally nondirective, yet designed for effect; that analysts believed in causality but also in responsibility and free will; that analysts were healers, but weren't supposed to settle into any social role; and that analysts intermixed present with past. And long before me, Sidney Tarachow (1963) and many others observed that analytic procedure has a persistent tendency to drift into an ordinary social relationship. Many writers, like Lipton (1977), have noted that Freud himself was pretty relaxed about it all.

Indeed, you will probably complain that I've ignored what you consider to be Freud's own major change in the treatment model after the structural 1920s. And it's certainly not news that the old features have been blurred over the years and are increasingly challenged.

In fact, I have not only oversimplified the history; I have also oversimplified the subject matter. There's a big difference between theoretical models and clinical procedures. Most self-disclosing analysts disclose precious little and generally follow orthodox protocols. In practice, hermeneutic analysts use a causal, folk psychology if only in order to communicate. By and large, the common, general format of the psychoanalytic procedure is taken for granted as a kind of *basso ostinato*, while the analyst's picture is tailored to fashion, slightly favoring one aspect over another. Perhaps the Freudian model is useful mainly as a reference diagram to keep clear what is being modified and what is sacrificed during necessary innovation.

## 210 The psychoanalytic phenomenon

That said, I would defend my caricatures on two grounds: The first is that what analysts actually do is by no means the whole story. What analysts are seen to be *trying* to do is also terribly important, since it shows patients the plan and purpose of treatment. If you see how I really feel about you, that certainly has an effect; if you see me leaning over backward trying not to let my stifled reaction influence you, that is no less important. I think this is not sufficiently recognized in debates like the one about self-disclosure. Striving for an unreachable ideal is one of the most powerful messages we can transmit. My second excuse for exaggerating the theoretical differences in our field is that, in our mixed treatments, the *proportion* of the ingredients is crucial. While it is certainly true, for example, that no analyst works entirely with procedural memories, to the extent that I set about manipulating a procedural memory, I am not only meeting the person differently; I am also forfeiting the older kind of manipulation, which required me to be nontendentious, disinterested, and respectful of free will. How much of that nondirective type of manipulation is sacrificed will make a big difference in treatment.

If a Freud Lecturer faced audience questions, you would pose two additional challenges: You would complain that I made it seem that the only reason for change in analytic models was the strain the old weirdness imposes on the analyst or the embarrassing position it puts him in. If Owen Renik (2001) were here, he would suggest another incentive, namely, that analysts switch procedures when they find more successful ones. I'd say: "Thank you, Owen – it's a good point."

But surely a program's success must be measured against its objectives. What was it that the Freudian rules were designed to accomplish? And can it be accomplished otherwise? There are doubtless many ways to reconfigure people's worlds. How do those ways compare with the Freudian way? These are open questions, and I'm sure you have your own guesses. As for me, if I hadn't known the Freudian setup, I could only think of treatment as akin to persuading an introspective person to read a good novel. To be sure, that is an experience that changes our world somewhat, and it does, I suppose, have something in common with the talking cure. Well, then, how about that? Let's try it on and see if it fits: analyst and patient create new visions by making new readings of the patient's experience, based on all the scientific knowledge one can acquire about human beings, including the shape of the transference. I know some very smart analysts who think that answers the question.

How about you? Isn't it a bit too anemic to capture your analytic experience?

I think most of you will agree with me that the Freudian monster shows us a more feisty activity. It is the painful but liberating splitting of desire as well as vision. In Freudian analysis, we see desires being muscled into relentless recategorization. We see live wishes and momentary reachings caught in real time and disrupted, like a tennis ball hitting a net and bouncing back into the server's court. Ultimately, the setup is nothing less than a weirdly distorted sociality, designed to disrupt a continuum of will and perception and the illusion of presentness.

What is psychoanalysis? **211**

I think that's what most of us have had in mind by psychoanalytic treatment. It's a very ambitious undertaking. It may not be achievable in more commonsense ways. The monster may rise again.

Thank you for your patience.

## Notes

1 This paper was presented as the Freud Lecture at the Psychoanalytic Association of New York, May 17, 2004.
2 The Hungarians I refer to are Imre Hermann, Sándor Ferenczi, and Michael Balint. A short account of the remarkable Hungarian tradition and how it differed from contemporary Vienna-Berlin and English psychoanalysis is provided by Balint (1937), who also offers a rare glimpse of Hermann's ethologically oriented psychoanalytic theorizing. The Hungarians thought that infants exhibit a primary need for attachment and non-erotic object craving (as discussed in Ferenczi 1933), an idea later picked up by John Bowlby (1969) and carried forward by current attachment theorists. The lovable Englishman I mention is, of course, Donald W. Winnicott, whose work is widely familiar today (for example, Winnicott 1954, 1960). The practical outcome of this tradition was to encourage therapeutic efforts to re-grow patients in a favorable analytic environment, a rationale cautiously introduced by Ferenczi and Rank (1925), and less cautiously elaborated by Ferenczi (1988) in his brave and honest experiments. (It is interesting to observe how analysts, whatever their approach, always address themselves to the local, respectability-conferring theory. Thus, Winnicott talks to, with, and against the reigning Kleinians, but seems to have engaged only in parallel play with his blood brother, Michael Balint. I do not attribute this solely to a wish for originality.)
3 Milton Erickson was a fascinating figure in the history of psychotherapy. I know his later work chiefly through its influence on a school of manipulative family therapists, of whom Jay Haley (1963) is a good representative. Haley offers a cynical but highly profitable scrutiny of the manipulative elements in psychoanalysis. Erickson's videotapes demonstrate a subtle, nondirective and intriguing form of "hypnotism" (which Erickson redefined in terms of interactive motivations and suggestions). As in all such masterful demonstrations, Erickson's effectiveness is enhanced by his persona – in this case, even by physical handicaps that included, as I recall, a barely audible speaking voice that subjects had to strain to hear. (For a brief biographical note on Erickson, see Gorton [2005].)
4 These three theorists picked up the "whole-mind" (person) thread of psychoanalytic theory – an original thread that had been relatively neglected while mental parts (the mechanistic aspects of mind) were elaborated. One sees this holistic project in the overall shape and direction of these theorists' oeuvre; representative examples might be Waelder (1930), Hartmann (1939, 1958), and Loewald (1960). Some contemporary analysts regard this theoretical direction as – to put it politely – a radical revision of Freudian theory. (Loewald has been accused of shamefully concealing his apostasy.) Such a misunderstanding of these authors simultaneously distorts early Freudian theory by ignoring its whole-mind aspects (see Friedman 1988, pp. 197–221), and glorifies new, inadequate theories that picture a mind without mechanisms. Treatment guided by such a new, one-sided picture will tend toward the inspirational.
5 But that trend may not be what it seems: one reason it is now more acceptable for analysts to imagine themselves acting like mothers is that mothers are understood to be acting like analysts in certain essential ways. That makes for a different sort of role than previous images of analyst-mothering, as we see in Spitz (1956), Gitelson (1962), Loewald (1960), Kohut (1984), Winnicott (1954, 1960), Bion (see O'Shaughnessy 1981), and Fonagy (2001; Fonagy et al. 2002).

6 Obscurity makes Lacan both hazardous and safe to cite. I will be told by a Lacanian that I completely misunderstand Lacan, and I will call another Lacanian to testify that the first has not the faintest idea of what Lacan is about. So I am emboldened to say that Lacan, like the famous Zen master, asks us to understand that a patient's desire is co-constructed with a partner he will never meet. I think Lacan has captured an aspect of truth in his picture of a lifelong search for an undefined satisfaction that is represented solely by the sheer continuity of the quest, and by a borrowed string of shifting and inadequate images of desire. That vector of personhood, neither past nor present, is what I find relevant to this part of my argument. Some passages that suggest this to me (if not to a Lacanian) are elaborated in Lacan (1977a), especially pp. 47–48, and Lacan (1977b).

## REFERENCES

Alexander, F. (1925). A metapsychological description of the process of cure. *International Journal of Psycho-Analysis*, 6: 13–34.

Alexander, F. (1956). *Psychoanalysis and Psychotherapy*. New York, NY: Norton.

Balint, M. (1932/1953). Character analysis and new beginning. In: *Primary Love and Psycho-Analytic Technique*. New York, NY: Liveright, pp. 159–173.

Balint, M. (1937/1953). Early developmental states of the ego. Primary object love. In: *Primary Love and Psycho-Analytic Technique*. New York, NY: Liveright, pp. 90–108.

Balint, M. (1968). *The Basic Fault. Therapeutic Aspects of Regression*. London: Tavistock.

Bowlby, J. (1969). *Attachment. Vol. 1 of Attachment and Loss*. New York, NY: Basic Books.

Brazelton, T. B. (1978). Forward. In: *Social Responsiveness of Infants: A Round Table*, eds. E. B. Thoman & S. Cotter. Skillman, NJ: Johnson & Johnson Baby Products Co., pp. xiii–xvi.

Breuer, J. & Freud, S. (1893–1895). *Studies on Hysteria*. Standard Edition, 2.

Ferenczi, S. (1912/1926). Suggestion and psycho-analysis. In: *Further Contributions to the Theory and Technique of Psycho-Analysis*. London: Hogarth, pp. 55–68.

Ferenczi, S. (1933/1955). Confusion of tongues between adults and the child. In: *Final Contributions to the Problems and Methods of Psycho-Analysis*, ed. M. Balint. London: Hogarth, pp. 156–167.

Ferenczi, S. (1988). *The Clinical Diary of Sándor Ferenczi*, ed. J. Dupont. Cambridge, MA: Harvard University Press.

Ferenczi, S. & Rank, O. (1925). *The Development of Psycho-Analysis*, trans. C. Newton. New York, NY: Nervous & Mental Disease Monographs.

Fonagy, P. (2001). *Attachment Theory and Psychoanalysis*. New York, NY: Other Press.

Fonagy, P., Gergely, G., Jurist, E. L. & Target, M. (2002). *Affect Regulation, Mentalization, and the Development of the Self*. New York, NY: Other Press.

Freud, S. (1897/1985). Letter to Fliess, May 2, 1897. In: *The Complete Letters of Sigmund Freud to Wilhelm Fliess, 1887–1904*, ed. J. Masson. Cambridge, MA: Harvard University Press, pp. 238–240.

Freud, S. (1911–1915). *Papers on Technique*. Standard Edition, 12.

Freud, S. (1912). The dynamics of transference. Standard Edition, 12.

Freud, S. (1914). Remembering, repeating and working-through. Standard Edition, 12.

Freud, S. (1915). Observations on transference-love. Standard Edition, 12.

Freud, S. (1916). Some character types met with in psycho-analytic work. Standard Edition, 14.

Freud, S. (1925). *An Autobiographical Study*. Standard Edition, 20.

Freud, S. (1937). Analysis terminable and interminable. Standard Edition, 23.

Friedman, L. (1988). *The Anatomy of Psychotherapy*. Hillsdale, NJ: Analytic Press.

Friedman, L. (2005). Flirting with virtual reality. *Psychoanalytic Quarterly*, 74: 639–660.

Gedo, J. (1979). *Beyond Interpretation: Towards a Revised Theory for Psychoanalysis*. New York, NY: International Universities Press.

Gitelson, M. (1962). The first phase of psychoanalysis. Symposium on the curative factors in psycho-analysis. *International Journal of Psycho-Analysis*, 43: 194–205.

Gorton, G. (2005). Milton Hyland Erickson, 1901–1980. *American Journal of Psychiatry*, 162 (7): 1255.

Haley, J. (1963). *Strategies of Psychotherapy*. New York, NY: Grune & Stratton.

Hartmann, H. (1939/1951). *Ego Psychology and the Problem of Adaptation*. New York, NY: International Universities Press.

Hartmann, H. (1958/1964). Technical implications of ego psychology. In: *Essays on Ego Psychology: Selected Problems in Psychoanalytic Theory*. New York, NY: International Universities Press, pp. 142–154.

Havens, L. (1986). *Making Contact*. Cambridge, MA: Harvard University Press.

Hoffman, I. (1998). *Ritual and Spontaneity in the Psychoanalytic Process: A Dialectical-Constructivist View*. Hillsdale, NJ: Analytic Press.

Jung, C. (1930/1954). Some aspects of modern psychotherapy. In: *The Practice of Psychotherapy. Essays on the Psychology of the Transference and Other Subjects*. New York, NY: Pantheon, pp. 29–35.

Kohut, H. (1984). *How Does Analysis Cure?*, eds. A. Goldberg & P. Stepansky. Chicago, IL: University of Chicago Press.

Lacan, J. (1977a). *Ecrits: A Selection*, trans. A. Sheridan. New York, NY: Norton.

Lacan, J. (1977b). *The Four Fundamental Concepts of Psycho-Analysis*, ed. J. A. Miller. London: Hogarth.

Lipton, S. (1977). The advantages of Freud's technique as shown in his analysis of the Rat Man. *International Journal of Psycho-Analysis*, 58: 255–273.

Loewald, H. (1960). On the therapeutic action of psychoanalysis. *International Journal of Psycho-Analysis*, 41: 16–33.

Macalpine, I. (1950). The development of transference. *Psychoanalytic Quarterly*, 19: 501–539.

Nunberg, H. (1928/1948). Problems in therapy. In: *Practice and Theory of Psychoanalysis*. New York, NY: Nervous & Mental Disease Monographs, pp. 105–119.

O'Shaughnessy, E. (1981/1988). W. R. Bion's theory of thinking and new techniques in child analysis. In: *Melanie Klein Today: Developments in Theory and Practice, Vol. 2, Mainly Practice*, ed. E. Spillius. London: Routledge, pp. 177–190.

Raphling, D. (1996). Interpretation and expectation: the anxiety of influence. *Journal of the American Psychoanalytical Association*, 43: 95–111.

Raphling, D. (2002). Psychic change in analysis: Its relation to analyst's and patient's goals. *Journal of the American Psychoanalytical Association*, 50: 765–777.

Renik, O. (2001). The patient's experience of therapeutic benefit. *Psychoanalytic Quarterly*, 70: 231–241.

Ricoeur, P. (1970). *Freud and Philosophy*, trans. D. Savage. New Haven, CT: Yale University Press.

Spitz, R. (1956). Transference: the analytical setting and its prototype. *International Journal of Psycho-Analysis*, 37: 380–385.

Stone, L. (1961). *The Psychoanalytic Situation*. New York, NY: International Universities Press.

Tarachow, S. (1963). *An Introduction to Psychotherapy*. New York, NY: International Universities Press.

Waelder, R. (1930/1976). The principle of multiple function: Observations on overdetermination. In: *Observation, Theory, Application: Selected Papers of Robert Waelder*, ed. S. Guttman. New York, NY: International Universities Press.

Winnicott, D. (1954/1975). Metapsychological and clinical aspects of regression within the psychoanalytic set-up. In: *Through Paediatrics to Psycho-Analysis*. New York, NY: Basic Books, pp. 278–294.

Winnicott, D. (1960/1965). Ego distortion in terms of true and false self. In: *The Maturational Process and the Facilitating Environment; Studies in the Theory of Emotional Development*. New York, NY: International Universities Press, pp. 140–152.

# PART FOUR

# Freud's own views and the future

## INTRODUCTION TO PART FOUR

Where did *Papers on Technique* fit into Freud's own practice? Where does it stand in contemporary practice? Will it influence the future of the profession? Should it be taught in our institutes? The following chapters address some of these questions.

# 13

## ONE FREUD OR TWO?

In my Introduction, I cited the many paths to the common opinion that *Papers on Technique* was casual of purpose and quickly outdated. I threw in Freud's own retrospective belittling comments as though they were just some of the many. The reader might have wanted to stop me there, and say: "How can you casually dismiss the author's own dismissal? Who would know better than the author whether he was laying a foundation for analytic treatment or merely patching up a trivial misunderstanding of the moment?"

In fact, I don't think Freud's scornful comments played a big role in the historical trivialization of *Papers,* though his reported sayings have recently been recruited to that purpose. More influential lately is the example of Freud's own informality at work, glimpsed, for instance, in his privately noted "herring parameter" (in the case of the Ratman), and in patients' memoirs. Evidently Freud was not encumbered by the "rules" that burdened his most devoted followers.[1]

But since Freud is the author of *Papers,* and since he is quoted as minimizing its significance, I am obliged to suggest what might have made his retrospective description seemingly bare of the riches I claim to find there.

Two issues are entwined here. One is Freud's practice; the other is his recall, and not just the recall of his initial purpose but his memory of the experience of writing the book. So it would not save my reading of *Papers* to argue that Freud's actual behavior is, as it is for all practitioners, only indirect evidence of his beliefs, since everyone must triage many concerns in even the most orthodox practice. The question is what Freud's beliefs were while he was writing the book.

Freud regretted writing *Papers*; of that there can be no doubt. But as far as I know he never disowned its content. And that is worth noting, since the easiest and most acceptable way of "moving on" would be to say, as others have, that *Papers* was outdated by the later structural theory. Instead, what Freud regretted was one thing and one thing alone, namely the use of his principles as absolute,

**218** Freud's own views and the future

context-free rules. In a letter to Ferenczi, Freud (1928) explained how his intention came to be misunderstood. As he recalled, he was trying to post a few simplified pointers for students who were intimidated by the intangible responsibility, which seemed to require mystical gifts. To reassure students that there was something definite that could be learned, Freud said he selected a few simple instructions to sustain them while acquiring the necessary experience which alone provides the subtle clues for action. He wrote:

> For my recommendations on technique which I gave back then I considered the most important thing to emphasize what one should not do, to demonstrate the temptations that work against analysis. Almost everything that is positive that one should do I left to "tact" [a term] which has been introduced by you. But what I achieved in so doing is that the obedient ones didn't take notice of the elasticity of these dissuasions and subjected themselves to them as if they were taboos. That had to be revised at some time, without, of course, revoking the obligations …

He continued:

> What we undertake, in reality, is a weighing out which remains mostly preconscious, of the various reactions that we expect from our interventions, in the processes of which it is first and foremost a matter of the quantitative assessment of the dynamic factors in the situation. Rules for the measurements can naturally not be made; the analyst's experience and normality will have to be the decisive factors. But one should thus divest "tact" of the mystical character for beginners.
>
> *(p.332)*

This letter is often read correctly as repudiating a therapy that amounts to following rules and/or considering rules as absolute injunctions. The letter is also read, incorrectly, as disowning *Papers on Technique*. On the contrary, we are given the following implicit advertisements of the book: 1. The book sets down the most important attitudes for therapists to adopt in order to conduct a psychoanalysis. 2. These attitudes are the most important because without them the analysis will not move forward. 3. These analyst attitudes that move analysis forward are the opposite of a person's inclinations ("temptations"). 4. These principles will need to be adapted to the circumstances of the individual patient at the moment, as part of the analyst's overall, preconscious assessment of the patient's operating mental dynamics. 5. But the principles behind these negatives ("the obligations") can never be disregarded.

This is Freud's view of *Papers*, and it is the one I have presented here.

And we should note that Freud is responding here somewhat defensively to Ferenczi's calling attention to the "plasticity" of technique. Freud regards it as obvious but he has to admit that his own *Papers on Technique* is what makes a

One Freud or two? **219**

reminder necessary. And elsewhere in the same letter, he still cannot conceal the suspicion that even though technique of course must employ "plasticity" and "tact," these terms can legitimize the analyst's indulgence in personal inclination and undefined empathy. I imagine Freud muttering under his breath, "Yes, Sandor, you've got me there. Unsophisticated analysts have been using my technique book unthinkingly; we'll need a new one. But when I imagine where you will take 'plasticity of technique' and 'tact,' I cannot fault myself for implying in *Papers on Technique* that the beginner must first learn the defining discipline."

But even if Freud did not repudiate *Papers*, neither did he celebrate it, least of all the way I have, as a book. We must, of course, make allowance for the context of his references. Controversy has swirled around "adherence" to "the rules," and if Freud is asked about that aspect of the book he can't be expected to discourse on its overall significance. Nevertheless, he doesn't seem to have been interested in changing the subject to that larger significance, either. I claim that *Papers* reveals itself plainly to be the record of an unasked for and often unwelcome *discovery*. But Freud did not seem to remember making anything like a discovery. All he remembered was his original *intent*, namely, to post a few reassuringly down-to-earth examples of how an analyst thinks. He seems to have forgotten the surprising experiences that had baffled him when he got into the writing; he forgot the mind-boggling conceptual and technical challenges that were thrust upon him; he forgot the dogged hunt for elusive answers. He forgot how, in quick succession, his elementary teachings were exploded by his solutions even while he was writing them.

That is some extraordinary forgetting! And in a span of less than 20 years. Is it plausible? I ask doubters to look at the text. The disparity between the announced intention and the complex actualization stares out at us from page to page: The declared aim of the book is simple and modest – so glaringly modest, in fact, that it obliges Freud to apologize for publishing elementary truths in a journal of new research. Moreover, and consistent with the initial intent, one finds housekeeping hints here and there and guild guidance, sometimes as though from a collegial big brother. And yet all of that miscellany is distributed in and around the spine of *Papers on Technique*, which is one long-line dramatic inquiry that constitutes its major content and continuity. You can track its dense, back-and-forth exploration of single puzzles, its repeated jabs at alternative conclusions; its revolutionary twisting of old concepts in search of the levers that switch on the newly emerging analytic experience or turn it off. All the old orienting practice shibboleths and concepts are turned upside down to capture the newly discovered phenomenon. In those central passages Freud makes not the slightest attempt to disguise the immediate novelty of his ideas. He openly reveals how hard even he finds it to work them out, and how strange the stance is that evokes the new phenomenon. In that on-going research he is just too deeply at work to care that he has let go the role of school-teacher and has been talking to himself in the laboratory.

Freud cannot be the only writer who learns his subject while "explaining" it to the youth. What is unusual, especially for Freud, is that he leaves it for publication in a transitional state, and, for all intents and purposes, never comes back (despite

## 220 Freud's own views and the future

his later promise to set things straight). Why is that? We can only guess. But I realize that my reading of the book implies that an error in Freud's memory accounts for his patronizing dismissal of it. How could I account for that?

In fact, I think there are many plausible reasons for Freud to have edited his memory. Many of them are the same as the reasons for the profession's general neglect of his book. For example, psychoanalysts have always had good reason to avoid thinking about therapeutic action lest it interfere with their necessary passivity. (See Friedman 2007.) On a more personal level, Freud frankly admitted that he had far more interest in the Unconscious than in the process of healing, and the indifference seems to have increased with age. Furthermore, anyone whose only treatment experience was a self-analysis might well expect patients to approach analysis as an adventure of discovery. In a self-analyzed analyst, the complexity of resistance would trigger less life-long curiosity. Whatever curiosity he did have could later be soothed by his new theory of the Ego – that Jack-of-all-trades who disposes of any and all process tasks without disclosing detailed trade secrets. Many of the agonizing dilemmas in *Papers* could be circumvented by assigning them to separate functions of the ego.

More specifically, I imagine that it didn't take long for Freud to realize that in writing *Papers* he had opened a Pandora's Box, and that after a brief but extremely conscientious encounter he was happy to leave the problems of technique forever behind him. After all, technique and therapy in general were never part of his original research program. In fact, one of the reasons the public neglects *Papers* is the sheer incongruity of its style and content sitting within Freud's oeuvre. In many ways it is a different Freud who is probing these issues in *Papers on Technique*, and that's just a fact. I urge readers to accept it to begin with if they wish to be faithful to the book, rather than forcibly making it sound like the Master's more familiar public voice, homogeneous with the rest of Freud's writing. If they don't take *Papers on Technique* on its own term they will find themselves simply skimming for phrases and losing the plot-line. Readers who insist on visualizing their own well-known Freud are mistaking Freud's unsystematic fumbling to be his usual expository strategies and rhetorical devices, unaware that what they are reading is not at all an artfully organized presentation, but a straightforward series of interim reports. The conclusions are not in view at the start; writing the earlier papers, he had still to digest these problems for himself. There was no leisure for a lecturer's tricks. Within the span of a few pages, aided only by a few old terms loosened from their moorings, Freud was taking the measure of no less a monster than a hall-of-mirrors hermeneutics of passion that could be fitted to a program of personal autonomy. He had to contend with the logic and epistemology of action. He was swept into character analysis, into object relations, interpersonal psychology, even ethics. The work stands apart from Freud's other writing in its condensed, self-contained innovation, barely reaching back to previous publications or to future grand theory.

To sympathize with Freud's early exhaustion, we need only attend to his outright confession that he would not have had the courage to tackle the complex psychology of analytic interaction without prior – and still tightly held – over-simplified models, which, however, left him bewildered when the familiar mechanics of those (hypnotic) models failed to explain the analytic phenomenon.

In my view, Freud deserves both sympathy and credit for a job that, while brief, begrudged and unfinished, has not been surpassed by any later enthusiast endowed with unlimited leisure. To me, the wonder is not that he later forgot the journey, but that he had refused to back out of it before he had done his usual meticulous mapping.

When late in life Freud (1937), as I see it, refused to apologize for the sobering results of treatment, scolded disappointed followers for taking his ideal structures literally, and claimed he had never promised them a real-life unaltered ego ally, we can see how far he had drifted from his very early, very brief interest in the psychology of the therapeutic interaction. We can imagine how alien the long-ago puzzles would be to the old man. Who can blame him for forgetting in those later years how he had stumbled onto a topic of infinite complexity which he was compelled by his scientific conscience to pursue while caught in the "laboratory" of *Papers on Technique*.

## Note

1 The implication is that Freud's behavior defines psychoanalysis (making allowance, of course, for a few peccadillos). I have never understood the persuasiveness of the argument from example, as though Freud set himself up as a dancing master, and never said *"Quod licit Jovis non licit bovis."* Maybe there is also a bit of *noblesse oblige* in the argument: "If it was good enough for Freud, why isn't it good enough for you? Do you claim to be more skilled than Freud?"

## REFERENCES

Freud, S. (1928/2000). Letter to Ferenczi, January 4, 1928. In: *The Correspondence of Sigmund Freud and Sandor Ferenczi, Volume 3, 1920–1933*, eds. E. Falzeder & E. Brabant. Cambridge, MA: Harvard University Press, pp. 331–332.

Freud, S. (1937/1964). Analysis terminable and interminable. Standard Edition, 23: 209–253.

Friedman, L. (2007). Who needs theory of therapeutic action? *Psychoanalytic Quarterly*, 76S (Supplement): 1635–1662.

# 14

# THE "FRAME" AND THE FUTURE

Analysts today are proud of recovering their essential humanity, and eager to denounce the starchy, old "tool and method pride" identified with *Papers on Technique*. (An earnest colleague at my institute, puzzled that I was teaching *Papers on Technique*, asked to be reassured that I taught it as pre-history.) Along with Freud, analysts are far more interested in the discovery aspect of psychoanalysis than in its technique. And rightly so: exploring and discovering constitute the interest, value, and visible activity of analytic therapy.

But the principles of *Papers on Technique* are not currently ignored. In the United States they are frequently honored in the form of a general, taken-for-granted sense of professional propriety, articulated in terms of "The Frame," outside of which lies "Enactment." The old interest in the technical aspect of treatment sneaks back as frame theory. (I have discussed this in Chapter 5, and again in Chapter 8.) Today we hear few sour exchanges about "the rules," but much collegial agreement about enactment. These latter terms are less fraught, partly because "the frame" sounds less pretentious, less judgmental, and less abstract. (For example, analysts are permitted to take various stances toward an enactment, ranging from disapproval to amusement.) Because it seems theoretically neutral, the notion of frame and enactment may turn out to be the last common way-station on diverging roads to the future. If you want to conserve the tradition, you can think of frame and enactment as short-hand for the whole of *Papers on Technique*. If you wish to reject *Papers*, you can connect frame and enactment to quite opposite ideas.

However, even when it is used as an "acceptable" way to teach the substance of *Papers on Technique*, it does not do so literally. It is more free-wheeling. Sometimes the job of the frame is to keep an analyst from "going off the rails." He can do what seems wise, necessary, creative, etc., but when he bumps into the frame, he is cautioned to move back. In the same spirit, a patient may be reminded that he is "acting out," that is, acting outside the frame, contrary to mutual agreement. The frame can be thought of as useful backdrop for high-lighting enactments, just as the "blank screen" was thought to provide visibility for transference, while unlike the blank screen the frame, is safe from sophisticated debunking. The frame's down-right, rough-hewn, split-rail image is too disarmingly unmysterious to court debate. In other words, the frame captures something of the Freudian discipline without overt commitment to its rationale. Newish meanings gather around it, simultaneously muffling and protecting the older principles.

If that's what can happen even in a traditional milieu, one can understand that other schools of analysis may respect "the" frame for many sensible services other than its original mission. It can be advertised as providing all kinds of safety. It can represent the ethical restraint on frankly exploitive – and even illegal – behavior. It can easily pass as a synonym for the playground of the transference. And for those who want to move as far as possible away from the old idea, the frame can be retained as a pragmatic, starkly neutral, self-imposed, conventional discipline, like the 50-minute hour, or monthly bills: "There have to be some limits." "This is part of what makes our discussion a psychoanalysis."

Understood either way, conservatively or innovatively, one detects in frame theory a common departure from at least one key feature of *Papers on Technique*, namely, a focus on cross-purposes between analyst and patient – the adversarial aspect of treatment that Freud discovered, resulting from the ambiguity of the analyst's role. The image of "The Frame" has a comforting quality of sociability – even a kind of hospitality. It can be explicitly recommended to patients as insurance for their safety (though it really guarantees risk). Patients can be asked to voluntarily accept the frame from the outset, whereas no sane analyst would hand *Papers on Technique* to a prospective patient as a contract. This theoretical trend is clear: The unwanted discovery in *Papers* that the patient is not wholly or even primarily a partner is still unwelcome. One might predict that where it can be muffled, it will be, and when it can be forgotten, it will be forgotten.

Nobody loves the adversarial aspect of analysis. Not only that; it is in principle alien to the working analyst's mind-set. He dare not see himself in such a relationship, or he will feel and act, at best, as a manipulator and, at worst, a bully. And it clashes with the analyst's more familiar endorsing and facilitating activities.

To be sure, a conscious acceptance of cross-purposes is sometimes useful in empathizing with patients. It can keep an analyst from unrealistic expectations, mollify his impatience and soften his demand. But generally speaking, it simply doesn't matter that cross-purposes are forgotten since no explicit rationales are pasted on the eyeglasses of the seasoned analyst at work. It is a different matter when it comes to examining the nature of psychoanalytic treatment.

It is in training and clinical critique that a shift will occur if we lose sight of the adversarial edge that provides the rationale for a Freudian frame.

## 224 Freud's own views and the future

## THE "WHY" OF THE FRAME IS ANSWERED IN *PAPERS ON TECHNIQUE*

What, then, is the rationale for the discipline illustrated in Freud's little book? What, after all, are the famous "rules" taught there, what is the "frame" they are translated into, if it is a translation? *They are the analyst's anticipations of how the patient will respond to his behavior.* Those trained anticipations modify the practitioner's natural responsiveness. Of course they don't dictate his responses. It need hardly be said that the analyst's responsiveness is distilled from all of his life experience, as well as from previous patients, his reading, and his personality. But that much of his responsiveness that corresponds to technique – that which follows "the rules," or heeds "the frame," or constitutes whatever is "not an enactment" – that responsiveness amounts to a tacit sense of what promotes and what reverses the analytic experience.

These are specialist anticipations that don't (and shouldn't) intrude into the personal life of even the most empathic layman. And, of course, the working analyst is free, despite those anticipations, to choose any good path to his momentary treatment goal. But while he is at work he is always more or less subtly influenced by a background awareness of the specifically psychoanalytic consequences of his approach. In the back of his mind, that specialized awareness functions just as invisibly as his invisible human savvy attunes him to the significance of people's words in everyday life, and just as automatically as he screens his own speech and behavior in society at large.

Since these principles of technique are "if-then" anticipations, they are a body of knowledge, not a list of commands. To repeat, what is being referred to as The Rules, or The Frame, or Principles of Technique, is an awareness of certain kinds of consequences, relevant to the creation and sustenance of an analytic experience. *Papers on Technique* is fundamentally a report of those consequences.

I think that bears repeating: In the universe of *Papers on Technique, "the frame" is not a restraint or a chaperone. It is an awareness that certain ordinary attitudes discourage a psychoanalytic experience.* It bears repeating that most of those anti-analytic attitudes (the "don'ts") that *Papers* cautions against are normal social attitudes. It is the task of training to make what is perfectly normal feel inappropriate to analysts while they are at work. For that radical conversion it may be useful to project the difference onto a picturable "frame," and hang on it warning signs from the professional police admonishing both analyst and patient to stay clear of the guard posts. In reality, of course, the rules and frame don't lie outside the analyst. He imposes them. And he does it without noticing. In mature analysts the alertness has become part of his or her working sensorium. It has become a new, "common sense," no longer consciously referenced. (That sometimes leads to the illusion that technique is irrelevant or is even alien to the spirit of the work, whence the proud declaration: "I don't fuss with technique; I just analyze").

But when factions debate or a case is critiqued in terms of frame or enactment the implicit frame becomes explicit. At that moment, "The frame" has the job of representing technique in general, and it must answer the ultimate question on which the future shape of psychoanalysis depends: "Why practice this way, after all?" Is *Papers on Technique* our answer? Or is it a matter of taste and personality, humane vs. inhumane values, institutional politics?

## WHAT OF THE FUTURE?

The future of psychoanalysis is more contested than ever. But the old discipline is still very much alive in most Freudian groups that do not shun the hard strangeness of *Papers on Technique*. Some influential schools honor the adversarial aspect of analysis even more single-mindedly than Freud did in *Papers on Technique*. In Freud's book, analysts nudge patients toward a freer experience, hoping that it will provide avenues for investigation and narration. But Lacanian technique goes even further. It celebrates the psychoanalytic experience in itself, and not just as a medium for exploration. I believe that is also the case with branches of the Melanie Klein tradition.

But analysts have an unquenchable wish to feel as kindly in technique as they are in their aim. Hence there will always be efforts to replace the analyst's ambiguity and adversarial stance with a more comradely vision. For example, a current movement aims to burst the bounds of individuality. Its goal is the same as in *Papers*, that is to free patients from an analyst's imposed or suggested meanings. But they do not plan to do it by blunting the analyst's influence, as in *Papers*. Instead they hope to draw the seeking of both patient and analyst into an emergent sector of mutual identity, or even something like a shared sensorium. (Though an oxymoron, that's my understanding of the Third, the Field, Intersubjectivity, and Moments of Meeting.) The boldness of this movement testifies to the intensity of the desire for harmony in the analytic chamber. It will never go away and will forever challenge the spirit of *Papers on Technique*.

# 15

# AUTHOR INTERVIEWS HIMSELF

It goes without saying that my perspective pervades this whole book, but in the following imaginary interview I will express my own opinions more directly and informally.

READER: If an analyst pretends he's an objective observer, denies that he is making any covert demand or request, and is consequently immune to interpersonal influence, isn't he simply lying? Isn't he replacing analytic truthfulness with grandiose mystification?

L.F.: Yes indeed, if he believes he has actually achieved such an inconceivable state. In that case, he's fooling himself both about his reality and how he's coming across to his patient. He would be blind to the very nature of human communication and false to analytic theory. That's not all: He would be doing something worse. He would be implicitly asking his patient to "idealize" him (in the psychoanalytic sense of that word), and the pretense would contradict its own claim. The worst part of asking to be idealized is not the idealizing. It's the asking. Wanting to be seen in any particular way is exactly the sort of thing that turns off the analytic phenomenon. That is probably the central point of *Papers on Technique*.

READER: Doesn't that mean analytic ideals are absurd and even nefarious?

L.F.: Not at all. Ideals define every action. We always need an image of attainment in order to act and, in the real world, such an image is always an unrealizable ideal. An aim is always abstract compared to the achievement. In the real world, we accept approximate thermostats because they make us comfortable. We seek testimony under oath because it is best to add an incentive for truth to the many temptations to lie. We don't expect patients to tell the truth, or ourselves to be a blank screen, but we hope we will both strive for these unrealizable ideals. … More or less… . In most situations… . Or in many of them … Or …, well …, perhaps in a few exemplary instances.

Author interviews himself **227**

But forget the fancy arguments and consult common sense: The driver attends to the road. (He is ignoring his cell phone?) The mother loves her baby. (Ask Winnicott about that!) We respect our fellow man. (Provided he doesn't compete.) We appreciate our daily blessings. (When prompted by Schadenfreude.) Why ridicule the disciplined analyst for his unrealizable ideals?

READER: What's all that got to do with *Papers on Technique*?

L.F.: Unrealizable ideals are not peculiar to *Papers on Technique*. What is peculiar is the visible restraint they encourage in the analyst. And wouldn't you expect to be aiming impossibly high if you were trying to move in a non-directive direction?! Only a fool would think he could get anywhere close to such a self-contradictory position. But with the right intention, and still short of the ideal, the restraint it encourages has plenty of real consequences. See for yourself by following Freud's experiment in *Papers on Technique*: Grossly violate the (unattainable) analytic ideals by doing what comes naturally and watch the (modest degree of) non-directiveness of your treatment go up in smoke.

READER: But how is it possible for such an admittedly "futile" gesture to achieve anything useful?

L.F.: In addition to the measure of actual restraint, patients respond to the direction of the analyst's aim, as in all human communication. As Paul Gray taught, patients catch the analyst's drift and can appreciate it as an offer to share his ideal. By his action and inaction, the analyst is saying: "Imagine yourself really not caring what I think of you. ... Well, maybe that doesn't feel so good, but at least you can see that I'm not discouraging you from trying out a bold experiment." Of course, if the analyst's character is too much at odds with his professional aim, it may eclipse the image he's straining to model. But the more common problem is that the analyst doesn't understand the central reason for his professional stance. If the analyst thinks he is obeying rules, or playing a game, or protecting both parties with a frame, he hasn't really visualized the underlying ideal toward which his odd and inconsistent behaviors are supposed to converge. In that case how could a patient be expected to "get it?" Instead, a patient will simply see someone "acting like an analyst."

READER: You seem to have forgotten about the "analysis" in "psychoanalysis." You go on about Freud's discovery of a new phenomenon as though it doesn't matter how it's used or what comes out of it. What about Insight? Truths? Change? What about the creativity of the Unconscious? You're fascinated by the austere form of interpretation, yet you pass right over its rich content. What about the analyst's human appreciation and wisdom? What about his help in mental integration, his shuffling of old certainties, his rousing of defeated hopes? Doesn't the analyst's projection of new perspectives add just a little to the outcome? Are all these dramatic happenings just amusements compared to the bare austerities of technique? Would anybody go into this work after reading your book?

L.F.: I might cop a plea: A book on technique is a book on technique; you can look for the rest elsewhere. But that would be a dodge. I am celebrating

**228** Freud's own views and the future

Freud's book, and that book isn't just an occasion for that topic. It makes technique central to practice. Granted that it is not at all what Freud wanted to be remembered for. (In a sense he didn't remember it himself.) It's not what we see in Freud's own treatments. It is not what he writes about elsewhere. But the unequivocal message of *Papers on Technique* is that its subject is nothing less than the mastery of psychoanalytic treatment. Learn this, Freud says, and the rest is a snap. Only by totally ignoring *Papers* can one agree with Lipton (1977) that the very idea of technique is a late, un-Freudian distortion of what was originally a free, humane conversation. At this one point in his life, Freud made no bones about it: The art of interpretation is easily acquired compared with the real and painful work of handling transference. Like it or not, for the author of *Papers*, technique is where the action is.

READER: You are evading my question. Patients don't sign up for a dance. While your analyst is carefully comporting himself technically, is your patient learning something or other? Can't you spare one or two words about the relationship between the analyst's technique and the patient's insight?

L.F.: As a matter of fact, Freud did just that. He could hardly do otherwise, being the rare, committed theorist who never dodges the "next" question. He had discovered how to evoke the analytic phenomenon, and the "next" question is What does that have to do with insight and interpretation? Freud's answer is an abbreviated theory of therapeutic action. I will sketch it here schematically in my own, somewhat tedious words (supplemented by some inferences from the text):

Freud described two vectors pointing toward "cure." One is the analyst's targeted guidance to areas of conflict. The other vector is the patient's unsatisfied attachment to the analyst. As to the first, the analyst spots inhibitions in free-association and suggests unconscious reasons for them. Because of the second factor (attachment) the patient becomes willing to give the analyst the benefit of the doubt, imagine him as benevolent, and stare at those uncomfortable parts of himself. Since the analyst has dodged familiar characterizations, any of the patient's temptations and fears that would have automatically edited his behavior for social consumption have been cleared away. That leaves only himself and his analyst to fear or please (technique has seen to that), so he now recoils repeatedly mostly from his own judgments, and in the vortex of that push-and-pull (and encouraged by what remains of his wish to please his analyst) he gradually comes to feel the hidden passion that had caused his hesitation (resistance). Phenomenologically, that means the patient actually feels the good reason for hiding his wish from himself and allows himself to actually feel the pain of giving up self-protection. (The pain is the warrant of its accuracy). He experiences the vivid pain of conflict rather than a crippled flow of thought. He has thereby forfeited the comfort of restricted consciousness but gained in return undeniable access to mental resources and a speakable form for his quandary. He can finally make the integrations and accommodations that articulation allows.

Then, working with the patient's old and new memories, the two parties will create life narratives that make integrated sense out of the discoveries. Here the analyst's knowledge of unconscious constellations and typical developmental experiences, together with his expertise in tracing long-line dramas ("fantasies"), help the patient link together the new information he experienced internally. Needless to say, spoken interpretations will be proportionately more conspicuous than the crucial, silent self-confrontations that technique has made possible, so psychoanalysis will have every right to bill itself as interpretive and informative in its overall shape. And all those other features you asked about – and many more – will find their place in this schema of therapeutic action.

(By the way, I'm not sure I agree with you that patients don't come to us for a dance.)

READER: Are you claiming that Freud regarded insight as the patient's private emotional experience rather than information from interpretation?

L.F.: He is quite explicit about that. I have tried to explain why Freud's declaration to that effect has been brushed aside (see Chapter 3). Of course, the patient's private transformative experience, is a very particular kind of experience. (It resembles Ferenczi's original experiments more than his later ones.) It is the actual experience of conflict- not simply its acknowledgement, or persuasion from being shown behavioral evidence of its existence. (It makes me think of Jimmy Durante's theme song: "Did you ever have the feeling that you wanted to go, and yet you had the feeling that you wanted to stay?") But the remodeling of the patient's psyche to accommodate the newly discovered experiential fragments is a long, interactive process, so the analyst's knowledge and insights are vital to treatment, as also is his general and special hermeneutics. But as to the material used in rebuilding, that is not imparted by the analyst; it is actually found by the patient, and it is particular, individual and subjective. Technique conjures a world of freedom but what is found in that world is a private experience. That, I think, is how technique figures in the theory of action (in *Papers on Technique*).

READER: I'm sorry I asked. Outlines are useful, but yours, for all its verbiage, was outrageously oversimplified, don't you think?

L.F.: It certainly was. For instance, conversation about what is uncovered by the patient is no less an "experience" than the unspoken processes of self-recognitions, and the very distinction between understanding and experiencing is misleading. What one takes away from an analysis are bundles of meanings from innumerable perspectives in innumerable visions and voices. The analyst's image of the patient is not the least of them, as Loewald told us.

More to the point, the nature of the analyst's famous "closeness-in-distance," which appears most vividly in *Papers*, is too subtle for any outline to capture. A patient's bond to the analyst is intimate, trusting and promising enough to encourage "playing his game," but yet indeterminate enough to minimize the profit or loss from evoking a particular reaction – not an easy formula to follow.

**230** Freud's own views and the future

I have left out two features of Freud's theory of action, one explicit and the other implicit. Freud explicitly counts on unfulfilled longings in the transference to keep patients working at the task. We may wince at the idea, but I believe what Freud had in mind is the same thing that Thomas French (1958) regarded as the engine of change, namely, a revival of discouraged hopes. That new hope calls out frozen conflicts into the open again for normal experiment and reintegration. But because of the nature of conflict, it will only expose such conflicts if the analyst resists the appeal. Implicitly, the grand purpose of *Papers on Technique* is to strengthen the analyst's resistance to the patient's appeal for a social response. It is only by running toward an expected partner and being held off, that patients can feel what's at stake in their efforts (the emotional source of their inhibition), and the good reason for their conflict. As portrayed in *Papers on Technique* the term, "resistance" best describes the analyst's constant behavior. The patient is behaving normally; the analyst is stubbornly bizarre.

READER: If that painful experience of self-confrontation requires attachment to the analyst as a stimulus, what can we say about Freud's self-analysis?

L.F.: Good question. Leaving aside other grounds of critique, and unless we consider his friendship with Fliess to be part of his treatment, we might conclude that Freud's self-analysis was not an analysis as described in *Papers on Technique*. That may be part of the reason for his later disinterest in that book.

On the other hand, Freud's own view of analysis leaned heavily on courageous introspection and psychoanalytic clues. He would probably have given himself credit for an unaltered ego, and an abundance of epistemophilia. And he seems to have thought that others who were as mature and determined to get to the bottom of things would need less technique, so to speak. That would account for the comradely clinical behavior noted by Lohser and Newton (1996).

READER: Does Freud's own free-form practice show that *Papers on Technique* can be useful even if isn't taken as dictating a single technique?

L.F.: We can think of the book either in parts or as a whole. Only as a whole does it reveal a revolutionary way of mobilizing the mind. But its separate experiments are also useful. They show how specific social behaviors interfere with analytic freedom. Thus one can use each of Freud's separate observations as a specific reminder of how a patient is likely to respond to a "natural" behavior of the analyst (which Freud would call "unanlytic"), even if the analyst has good reason to choose it over the default procedure because of special circumstance or an altogether different treatment philosophy. These principles are neutral findings – not rules – so they can stand by themselves as rough predictions: "When you do X, you should expect Y." You are perfectly free to say, "Fine; I'll expect Y." *Papers on Technique* records an experiment on human nature, and anybody working programmatically with another person cannot fail to profit from reading it.

READER: In that case, can we build different treatment frames with individual planks taken from *Papers on Technique*? For example, combining anonymity with a behavioral approach?

L.F.: I am uneasy about that. We can lose track of our rationale if the terms are separated from their underlying purpose and joined to other therapeutic programs. For example, most analytic therapies encourage some degree of privacy for the analyst. That serves a programmatic purpose when linked to other principles in Freud's model (such as indifference to patients' views of the analyst). In other contexts, however, the analyst's privilege of privacy may pick up another meaning by serving a different purpose, for instance, to shield the analyst's sensitivities, or to project an image of authority, or to claim an allegedly blank screen for the patient's transference. In those cases, I suppose you might say that this principle is being used with a different treatment program. But is it still the same "anonymity?" The meaning of the concepts in *Papers* does not lie in its buzz-words, taken individually. Their meaning is the same as in *Papers* only if they conspire to say: "Although you will feel my unusually intense interest in you, I will want nothing from you. You should take advantage of this absolutely unique combination."

READER: Well, which is it? You say that we can grasp each individual principle in *Papers on Technique* by watching what happens when we heed it or defy it. But then you go back to your fanatical chant: the principles in *Papers* must be taken in one gulp to understand what their point is.

L.F.: You have caught me. I can only say that these terms – anonymity, abstinence, neutrality, and the like, have double significance. Individually they represent particular experimental findings. Together they have the common tendency of creating a psychoanalytic experience. They can be taken at either level. In point of fact, the principles of *Papers on Technique* have mostly been observed as individual admonitions ("rules") where, I admit, they have been extremely useful even when analysts haven't caught on to the central tendency. That is a significant though small use, but ultimately, I fear, fatal to the Freudian enterprise, which will either be defended by a central rationale (as a boost to human freedom), or else worn away (as a dated and self-serving guild identity). Whence my inconsistency. And, I suppose, my fanaticism.

READER: Does *Papers on Technique* speak to current ferment in treatment theory?

L.F.: Many analysts today are troubled by problems that are secondary in *Papers*. For one thing, as we all know, today's public has a pervasive sensitivity to anything that smacks of authoritarian oppression. So analysts try to avoid imposing meaning on their patients. It's true that Freud was always sensitive to the charge of hypnotic influence because it challenged the validity of his discoveries. But in the matter of treatment, hypnotic suggestion, and even authoritarianism and paternalism were, if anything, even more respectable than the new psychoanalysis itself. No, the author of *Papers on Technique* was not worried that he might dominate or bully his patients beyond the deep concern that it would impeach his findings.

**232** Freud's own views and the future

But Freud did worry about the imposition of meaning for the opposite reason: He discovered that it was infernally difficult to prevent patients from imposing their meanings on him. His authority was not the problem; the patient's authority was the problem. Not imposing the analyst's meaning but deconstructing the patient's old meaning was the formidable task. *Papers on Technique* records Freud's discovery that it is far more difficult than anyone had thought to impose anything at all on a patient. (Transference, as newly understood, is universal, and in a sense, unscrubbable.) Getting out from under the domination of his patient required radical discipline. At his most dogmatic, the analyst is not nearly as much in command as he had thought in the early days. That is one way of saying what *Papers on Technique* "is all about."

READER: Can you be a little less aphoristic?

L.F.: Actually, I thought that was long-winded and pretty obvious. But if you want something more detailed, try this: Analysts are always trying to solve Freud's epistemological problem. And how could they not? Like everyone else, analyst and patient are constantly interpreting each other. But whereas ordinary decoding is socially and physiologically governed, analysts claim to make their own principled decisions about how to interpret (even if the principle is to respond "from their unconscious,"), so they must ceaselessly ask themselves what principles they're using. How should they make sense of their patient? What response will boost the patient's new meaning-making? They can never stop worrying about it. They naturally seek comfort in dogma. (That's why they are always arguing with each other.)

In *Papers on Technique* Freud makes a brave effort to solve this problem. In earlier years, it was as though the patient had asked Freud to help unlock traumatic memories (by overcoming "the resistance.") The memories seemed to be "written" by the patient and, when unblocked, they were delivered to the analyst for help with integration. But then Freud made the devastating discovery that patients were not asking for any such thing. It turns out that they were not collaborating. And the "blockage" was none other than the patient herself. All the pieces of the puzzle had fallen apart, and had to be reassembled in a different pattern, which is done in *Papers on Technique*. From that point on, it's no longer clear what it is that patients are offering in their associations or their appearance. The primary matter of psychoanalysis is now very vague. It certainly isn't the pre-packaged items of memory, though Freud cannot orient himself without thinking of it that way. He knows now that the primary matter for analysis is really a display of appetitive striving. In other words, *Freud found himself dealing with persons as persons, not as reporters.* Persons want things, and they go after what they want. In their speech, patients act, and they act *on their analyst.* How to make professional sense of all this is up for grabs at that point.

That's the discovery in *Papers*. As a therapist, the psychoanalyst has a pre-set purpose, so he has to carve his own meanings. Where are the joints? What are the relevant items – the "it's" – that the analyst should gather together? If anything and everything about the patient is significant, how will the analyst pick out a something to look at and talk about? And if the dream report is a doing to the analyst and yet also a dream, how should that combination be coded in the story of the session? If there's no report without a purpose, how does the analyst single out one purpose among many, and how can one treat it both as a demand and as an implicit perception (of the relationship)? (Every action implies a relevant world.) How should an analyst picture a memory that is at the same time a plea? How do you translate action or desire into words? How are you gratifying or frustrating a desire in the way you describe it? And how should both parties make a speakable story, or an outlined pattern, or a definite Gestalt out of a trend of wishes and pushes? Freud didn't ask the question these ways, but he made it clear that this sort of problem would have felt insoluble if he had started out with it.

Freud must now find his own psychoanalytic way to make a composite of the patient's ordinary speech, plus the push and pull on himself of personal wishes, and then transform it all into an imagined "vision" of articulated inner meanings and specific manipulations. The solution Freud comes up with is to retain the earlier, simpler image of dreams and memories oriented to childhood, that can be individually tracked along paths of mental functioning, while simultaneously draping over that machinery a new image of a whole, undivided person who is wrestling with him mano-a-mano at the moment. The plan is to count all of that as relevant meaning.

As he tries to work that out, Freud makes his historic treatment discovery: There will be no arbitrary meaning-making. The patient will make his own primary meanings out of his private experience. *And that will happen if and only if the analyst fades away, effaces himself as a wishing human being, refrains from offering lures and warnings, divests himself of all preference for any particular way the meaning may emerge. The analyst is intently interested in his patient, but ideally wants nothing at all from him, and the patient can consult only himself.* He has discovered that being closely connected with someone (a patient) while staying out of the way of his meaning-making creates a certain ambience that is unattainable – and even unimaginable – in any other interaction. I refer to it as "ambiguity" of role coupled with intense personal interest.

There is a paradoxical twist here: The road to this autonomy runs through the analytic relationship. The analyst must be libidinally important to the patient at least enough to make talking to him a problem. There has to seem some desired effect on the analyst, or one cannot learn how to brave the imagined loss. Without a problem, conflicted purposes would not be felt. But there can't be too much to lose (respect, forms of affection) or the patient won't feel safe enough to explore freely. There are also other reasons for requiring some kind of personal bond to the analyst. For instance, the attachment must be strong enough to induce the patient to endure discomfort, as well as to examine it, and the analyst's response must feel positive enough to suggest that what she calls attention to will be something useful and ultimately

**234** Freud's own views and the future

"pro-patient." Ideally, however, all of that is designed to clear the patient's way to a fuller subjective recognition of his passions and purposes.

Of course the patient is not left completely on his own. Analysis is not a purely non-directive treatment; it is also interpretive. Many have observed that psychoanalysis is both deconstructive and reconstructive. The two processes accompany each other throughout the treatment, as the analyst helps to organize or reorganize the data that the patient has discovered within himself. In Freud's view, the patient has made the initial factual discovery: he is his own authority.

"Technique" has to do mostly with the deconstructive side because deconstruction directly frustrates desires, making them declare themselves. And Freud is emphatic that this is much the harder part of treatment.

Freud placed the analyst's avoidance of role responsiveness at the very heart of psychoanalysis long before our day. Resistance is the defining term in any program of treatment, and, as I have said, it is implicit in the technique book that *resistance belongs to the analyst* – i.e., *resistance to social evocation*. Freud may have thought little about it in his practice over the years, but he studied it fiercely when the problem was before him in writing *Papers on Technique*.

But *Papers on Technique* is not prominent as a book in analytic history. (See my Introduction.) And its point has been still less recognized. Its famous derivatives are widely caricatured as rigid rules of an encrusted orthodoxy. To be sure, the task of social deconstruction is still recognized by most theorists (often under the heading of "regression"). But contemporary theorists worry most about reconstructive (i.e., defining) authority because it rings warning bells of domination, presumption, inequality and authoritarianism. How complacent are analysts in telling patients what's what with them? Who's right about the patient's motives – or the analyst's for that matter? Who gets to define the relationship? Attention has gone more to authorship rights than to the effect of various analyst approaches (technique) of various motives. And most recently a compulsory "co-" has been required to chaperone most analytic verbs.

READER: You have the ugliest vocabulary in the business. You go on and on about cross-purposes, the adversarial nature of treatment, the ambiguity of the analyst, the imposition of unwanted freedom (none of which terms do we find in Freud). Your treatment sounds Hobbesian: nasty, brutish and (I should think) short. I can't imagine who would want to go into it in any capacity. And you have the audacity to lay this at Freud's door! Do you have left any saving appreciation of affection, caring, sympathy, or simple humanitarian values?

L.F.: That's quite an indictment. I will mount two kinds of defense for my vocabulary which, by the way, pales beside Freud's many martial metaphors.

Firstly, it should be obvious that any prolonged conversation about personal matters will activate more forces and influences than can ever be canvassed, including many that are common to all therapies, and others that are unique to the individual treatment couple. I have never denied that the major benefits of psychoanalytic therapy could, for all we know, stem from the underlying factors that are common to all psychotherapies described by Jerome Frank (1961). My interest is in the special leverage by which Freud was able to induce the peculiar experience he discovered.

I am not describing the relationship of any actual people, much less sketching the best human relationship we are capable of. Nor am I saying what is seen or felt in any single analyst's office. I am describing just the aspect of the situation that makes psychoanalysis unique. It isn't the most lovable aspect of any psychotherapy, and no purpose is served by making it seem otherwise. To the contrary, it is no kindness to patients to turn away from the truth.

But even if it isn't the most lovable, it is not the hateful Hobbesian scene you imagined. From your list of my "uglies," if I had to choose one term in my defense that was least offensive, the most inclusive, and the most amply illustrated in Freud's text – it would be "ambiguity." The analyst's ambiguity is what allows/forces some measure of freedom for the patient. It is certainly not a warm and fuzzy quality, but it is firmly ensconced in analytic tradition (now often attributed to Sandler in the form of detachment from "role responsiveness").

The analytic atmosphere I have described is not like a battlefield. A measure of ambiguity can be a far more cheerful setting than, for instance, a pseudo-classroom. It allows for more playfulness than a life-and-death confrontation between a seeker and a seer or a dissembler and a judge. I think this is generally appreciated in the profession today as long as it is coded in other terms, such as making a place for humor, tolerance, fallibility, and a generally ironic perspective (Schafer 1970). I use less lovable terms for these atmospheres in order to acknowledge their often unwelcome aspects, since their power is the direct effect of their unwelcome direction. I recommend my bluntness on grounds that living openly and freely with one's own unkindness is kinder than assuming it will be experienced as kindness. And it is much the more therapeutic way of being.

READER: Do you have any simple suggestions for teachers of *Papers on Technique*?

L.F.: I'm glad you put the emphasis on "simple," so that I won't feel I have to summarize my whole book at this point. I would suggest two groups of specific directives to guide students. One group is focused on particular passages, the other on the book as a whole.

Some questions for particular passages:

1. When students reach a familiar recommendation in the text, or one of the famous metaphors, ask "What actual circumstance seems to have prompted this admonition, this slogan, this image or metaphor? Freud sometimes reveals the situation explicitly. If he doesn't, try to infer it, but draw the inference from what he actually wrote in the text."

**236** Freud's own views and the future

2. Then ask: "What is the modern equivalent of that event?"
3. Remind students that Freud was the first beginner, and ask candidates, "Where did you run into that sort of problem when you were (or are) beginning?"
4. Ask: "What practical mind-set did Freud recommend to prevent such errors?"
5. Challenge your students' arbitrary presumptions and preconceptions: "If you have a different understanding of Freud's point than we have discussed, or prefer a different explanation of why Freud thought that way, what textual evidence do you have for your understanding?"
6. When a student offers an unlikely reading, ask: "Are you wondering Why would somebody say such a thing, rather than Why did Freud say it?"
7. Disabuse candidates of easy misunderstandings, and especially the fallacy of inferring imaginary historical causes, instead of bringing to bear historical knowledge, or reasoning from a parallel experience in their own practice.
8. Say, "As a working hypothesis, assume that each analytic trouble that Freud describes is something that burnt him personally. Try to figure out exactly what sort of unwanted 'blow-back' motivated Freud's admonition (his 'Don't's') and say how his remedy protects against it (e.g., his way of suggesting: 'Look at it as though....')"

On a general level –

1. Together with your student, trace the evolution of a given problem through the series of papers. Do not take the solution arrived at in any one of the papers as a final formulation, even if it is stated that way. Instead, watch how our familiar treatment terms are forced to change their meanings to take account of bruises inflicted by experience. These include Resistance, The Unconscious, Transference, Neurosis, Reality.
2. Ask students to point out where Freud saddles us with contradictory instructions. Ask "What should we make of that?"
3. Ask students: "How do these instructions hang together? What is their underlying rationale?"

## REFERENCES

Frank, J. D. (1961). *Persuasion and Healing*. Baltimore, MD: Johns Hopkins Press.

French, T. (1958). *The Integration of Behavior, Vol. 3*. Chicago, IL: University of Chicago Press.

Lipton, S. (1977). An advantage of Freud's technique as shown in his analysis of the Rat Man. *International Journal of Psychoanalysis*, 58: 255–273.

Schafer, R. (1970). The psychoanalytic vision of reality . *International Journal of Psycho-Analysis*, 51: 279–297.

# INDEX

Abend, S. 15, 19–23
abstinence 99, 141–142, 147, 169
adversarial aspect 223, 225
adversarial attitude 168–170
adversarialness 168–169, 173
affection 116, 118, 170, 182, 187, 189
alliance 123–125
ambiguity 60, 100, 151, 166, 177, 180, 186, 203, 223; analyst's 99–100, 225
analytic love 57, 178, 192–193; proper 187
analytic phenomenon 25, 51, 53, 145
anonymity 141–142, 156
attachment, patient's 81, 166
attention: analyst's 57, 166; patient's 44, 59, 78, 90, 98–99, 150
autonomy, patient's 115, 167, 172

Balint, M. 86, 176, 183, 208
Bibring, E. 84, 86

catharsis 15, 42, 50, 83, 99, 112
cognitive style 3, 135
conflict 61, 68, 95, 162
cooperation, patient's 169, 178, 187
countertransference 25, 79, 96, 105, 116, 139, 175–176, 183–184, 186, 188, 191; complementary 183; disruptive 185; positive 182

diagnosis 198–199, 201
discovery, patient's 59, 115, 138
dreams 2, 17, 30–32, 36, 40, 53, 76, 78, 114, 135, 203–204

dynamics of transference 4, 15, 20, 28, 32–37, 39, 44–45, 51, 136, 138, 205–206

ego 8, 15, 65–66, 94–96, 123–128, 132, 137, 220; psychologists 58, 67–68, 139, 150, 171; psychology 68, 96, 139, 171
enactment 9, 13, 77, 79–81, 89, 93–97, 99–108, 115, 117, 139–142, 149, 183, 222, 224

free associations 19, 35, 46, 52, 64, 76, 80, 98–99, 113, 166, 168
Freud, A. 87, 150, 153, 171
Freudian discipline 79, 223
Freudian theory 67, 133, 139, 173
Freudian treatment, weirdness of 208
Freud's adversarialness 169–170
Freud's alterations in Papers on Technique 30
Freud's bellicose treatment images 168
Freud's definition of working through 51, 64
fundamental rule 35, 38–40, 42, 44–46, 61, 100, 164

Gitelson, M. 150, 179, 182
Goffman, E. 80
Gray, P. 102, 132–134, 149–150, 156

Hartmann, H. 58, 67, 94–96, 171, 201
Heimann, P. 179, 182
Hoffman, I.Z. 155–156

**238** Index

human time 205–206
hysteria 21, 23, 29–32, 38–39, 112, 116,
  164–65, 198, 204, 206–207

ideals 53, 77, 89
illusion 81, 97, 100, 111, 113, 115–121,
  149–150, 154, 157, 166, 170, 178,
  207, 210
inclination, natural 25, 38, 46
intentions 35–36, 84–86, 89, 98–99, 101,
  116, 155, 183, 192, 207, 218–219;
  analyst's 84, 89
interest: analyst's 87, 101, 182, 199;
  intense 78
Interpretation of Dreams 2, 30–31, 36
interpretations 61–63, 65–67, 76–79, 83,
  124, 128, 130, 152, 172, 179–180, 182,
  186; analyst's 19, 61, 64–65, 124; ideal
  77–78; target of 87

Jacobs, T. 141, 179, 188, 192

Klauber, J. 85, 156, 188–189

laboratory, the workplace as 171, 173, 219
Lacan, J. 207
Levenson, E. 97, 141
libido theory 14–15, 20–23, 32, 36
Lichtenberg, J. 133–134, 156
Lipton, S. 7–8, 209
Loewald, H. 65–67, 84, 86, 94–95, 179,
  181, 183–184, 186, 193
love: analyst's feeling of 177, 181; appropriate
  expression of 180; erotic 175, 182, 192;
  feelings 176, 191, 193; patient's 182;
  substitute 188; understanding 189–190

manipulation 1, 9, 84, 86, 119, 133, 172,
  199–200, 210
manual, technical 24, 28, 45
memories: discrete 62–63; emerging 38;
  individual 41; meaning of 41;
  resistance-free 38; unconscious 17,
  19, 204
memory-retrieval model 25, 35, 38–39, 43,
  58, 63, 136
metaphors 6, 16, 59, 75, 153, 200
motives 25, 31, 52, 55, 81, 99, 103,
  117–118, 125, 131, 133, 147, 157, 202,
  204; patient's problem-solving 132
Myerson, P.G. 131–132, 179

Nacht, S. 179–180, 182, 188
neuroscience 95–96

neutrality 13, 99, 101, 103, 133, 136,
  141–142, 147
Novick, J. 187
Novick, K. 187

objective reality 139, 147, 150, 152–154,
  158, 168
objective truth 158, 181, 186
object relations theory 116, 154, 208

passivity: analyst's 43; patient's 44
positive transference 93, 107, 128, 150
private experience 51–53, 57, 59, 61,
  63, 65, 67
procedural memory 87, 208, 210
protopsychoanalysis 99, 202, 207
psychoanalytic experience 1, 49, 224–225
psychoanalytic phenomenon 1–3, 9–10, 15,
  17, 19, 21, 49, 51, 53, 148, 150, 152,
  154, 156
psychology, cognitive 95–96

Racker, H. 150, 181–185, 187–188, 193
Rank, O. 21, 23, 31, 83–84
relationship: analyst's 176; analytic 20,
  57, 80, 88, 116, 118, 179–180, 183;
  patient's 176; personal 75, 145;
  see also love
resistance 9–10, 16–20, 24–38, 41–44,
  52–53, 57–61, 63–67, 76, 113–14,
  124–125, 136–138; definition of 36–37;
  new theory of 37, 41; patient's 25, 60;
  redefine 37, 40

Schafer, R. 25, 46, 107, 153, 156, 184–187,
  189–190, 193–195
Segal, H. 179–80
social relationship 85, 106–107, 173
speech 46, 52, 62, 77, 87–89, 104, 191, 199,
  224; analyst's 53–54
Spitz, R. 177, 179, 182
Steingart I. 186–187, 189, 191,
  193–194
Sterba, R.F. 84, 123–134
Stern, D.N. 67, 117, 193
Stone, L. 85, 149–50, 177, 179, 182,
Strachey, J. 52, 60, 65, 84, 123, 126–34,
  137, 198
Studies on Hysteria 21, 23, 29–32, 38–39,
  57, 112, 116, 164, 198

tact, analytic 105, 218–119
theory: appetitive 30, 32; structural 8–9, 15,
  50, 138, 217

therapeutic action 19, 21, 23, 49–52, 66, 81, 94, 127, 220

therapeutic alliance 46, 81, 93, 95, 103, 107, 123–125, 133–134, 138

transference 2, 9–10, 13–16, 18–23, 25, 28–30, 32–39, 44–45, 116–118, 123–125, 136–38, 140, 148–49, 204–6; dynamics of 17–18, 23; and countertransference 116, 188, 191; entanglement 13–14; figure 148, 150, 168; images 98, 152; interpretation 21–23, 116, 132, 159; love 32, 78, 140, 166, 206; neurosis 20–21, 114, 153; passion 36, 39, 131, 188; patient's 13, 79, 199; phenomenon of 32, 205; relationship of 36; resistance 18, 35, 123, 127–128, 130; resistance, interpretation of 123, 127, 130; situation 124–125, 127, 129

virtuality 147–152, 154, 158–159, 206

work and illusion 118; delicate balance of 113, 115, 117, 119

work assignment 100, 103, 106; explicit 98

working analyst's mind-set 223

working at treatment 107

PGMO 07/10/2018